POLITICAL ACTS

Irish Studies

James MacKillop, *Series Editor*

POLITICAL ACTS

WOMEN IN NORTHERN IRISH THEATRE, 1921–2012

FIONA COLEMAN COFFEY

Syracuse University Press

Copyright © 2016 by Syracuse University Press
Syracuse, New York 13244-5290

First Edition 2016
16 17 18 19 20 21   6 5 4 3 2 1

∞ The paper used in this publication meets the minimum requirements of
the American National Standard for Information Sciences—Permanence of
Paper for Printed Library Materials, ANSI Z39.48-1992.

For a listing of books published and distributed by Syracuse University Press,
visit www.SyracuseUniversityPress.syr.edu.

ISBN: 978-0-8156-3490-4 (hardcover)   978-0-8156-3475-1 (paperback)
978-0-8156-5388-2 (e-book)

Library of Congress Cataloging-in-Publication Data
Available from the publisher upon request.

Manufactured in the United States of America

Dedicated to the outspoken women of Northern Irish theatre

Contents

Acknowledgments

I would like to extend deep gratitude to the members of my dissertation committee who responded to the original research for this project and helped shape its expansion to its current book form: Barbara Grossman, Natalya Baldyga, and Monica White Ndounou of Tufts University. Thank you especially to John Harrington, who served on my committee and has also been an invaluable mentor.

A special thanks to Susan Cannon Harris and the readers at Syracuse University Press whose thoughtful comments improved this manuscript immeasurably. Scott Boltwood's generosity in sharing his original research on the Ulster Group Theatre and early playwrights is greatly appreciated. Thank you to Fidelma Ashe for speaking with me at length about her research and to Carysfort Press for permission to revise and publish material that appeared in *Radical Contemporary Theatre Practices by Women in Ireland* (2015) and *The Theatre of Marie Jones* (2015). Deep gratitude to Syracuse University Press and Deborah Manion, who championed this book. Thank you to Abbie Spallen, Tinderbox Theatre Company, Ciaran Bagnall, and Roisin Gallagher for allowing us to use a production photo from *Lally the Scut* for the book cover.

I owe a great debt to the playwrights and practitioners who shared their experiences and perspectives and trusted me with unpublished material: Vittoria Cafolla, Lucy Caldwell, Patricia Downey, Jaki McCarrick, Paula McFetridge, Bernie McGill, Eleanor Methven, Carol Moore, Lynn Parker, Zoe Seaton, and Hanna Slattne. Thank you especially to Stacey Gregg, Rosemary Jenkinson, Abbie Spallen, and Shannon Yee for allowing me to feature their work in this research.

Thank you as well to the women of *Trouble and Strife*: Cara Seymore, Finola Geraghty, and Maeve Murphy.

The American Conference for Irish Studies, the International Association for the Study of Irish Literatures, the University of Notre Dame's Irish Seminar, and the Linen Hall Library were invaluable resources during the formation of this book, for which I am profoundly grateful.

I am grateful for the unconditional personal and professional support from Tufts colleagues Paul Masters, Clayton Drinko, and especially Megan Hammer Stahl and Sean Edgecomb. A special thank you to my brilliant and dedicated friend and colleague Elizabeth Mannion for her critical eye, her sound advice, and her unwavering encouragement. I am in your debt for the many hours you spent helping me improve the manuscript; I am so glad we found each other fifteen years ago at TCD.

Finally, thank you to my husband Niall for giving me the time and support to complete this project, and thank you to the twins, Emma and Adelaide, for doing their best to prevent me from finishing.

Abbreviations

ACNI: Arts Council of Northern Ireland
DUP: Democratic Unionist Party
IRA: Irish Republican Army
NIWC: Northern Ireland Women's Coalition
PSNI: Police Service of Northern Ireland
RUC: Royal Ulster Constabulary
UDA: Ulster Defense Association
UGT: Ulster Group Theatre
ULT: Ulster Literary Theatre
UUP: Ulster Unionist Party
UVF: Ulster Volunteer Force

POLITICAL ACTS

Introduction

Setting the Scene

On June 27, 2012, the Lyric Theatre, Northern Ireland's oldest professional producing house, was at the center of a groundbreaking political event. Although the event had high-profile actors, an eager audience, and was carefully choreographed and staged, it was not a play. Instead, it had higher stakes and more real-life significance than anything that had been staged at the Lyric before. The Queen of England, the most potent symbol of continued British rule over Northern Ireland, and Martin McGuinness, Northern Ireland's Deputy First Minister and former leader of Sinn Féin,[1] shook hands. This historic and highly symbolic act marked a major step in the difficult process toward a lasting peace in Northern Ireland. The fact that it took place at the Lyric emphasizes the highly theatrical and symbolic nature of politics, violence, and the peace process in the North.

The year 2012 was extremely important for the North in general. Along with the queen's visit to celebrate her diamond jubilee (sixty years on the throne), the year also marked the centenary of the *Titanic*, which was designed and built in Belfast. The Northern government used the occasion to launch a marketing campaign meant to combat images of the North as violent, economically unstable, and culturally impoverished. The campaign reintroduced the "new" North as a site of positive historical significance and of renewed diverse culture. The official 2012 slogan promoted by the government and by the Northern Tourism Board read "Your Time, Our Place," suggesting that 2012 was a positive new beginning. The balance between the words "your" and "our" also reflected a dual goal by the government: to have its citizens take personal responsibility for building a positive future while also tempering individual aspirations with collective, cross-community achievement. Furthermore, the phrase "Your Time" suggested that 2012 was the start of a new historical period of confident and optimistic ownership for the North's citizens, while "Our Place" also reflected a fresh push toward seeing the land and space of the North as belonging to everyone rather than as marked by sectarian division.

Since the 1998 Belfast/Good Friday Agreement,[2] which marked the official start of peacetime, the North has engaged in a process of envisioning a brighter and more stable future, redefining and representing its past, and attempting to recast contested space and territory with positive historical associations. With the *Titanic* centenary, Belfast opened a multimillion-dollar *Titanic* museum as well as redesignated and renamed buildings and various areas in the city to reflect the celebrated history of the Belfast shipyards rather than that of the Troubles.[3] Titanic Boulevard, the Titanic Belfast Museum, Titanic Slipways, Titanic Studios (a film production studio), and the Titanic Memorial Garden now comprise a new waterfront section of the city, which is called the Titanic Quarter. This massive waterfront regeneration project includes luxury apartments, an entertainment complex (which houses a cinema, recreation center, and live performance venue), as well as a hotel, shops, and restaurants. Instead of Troubles tourism and visits to political murals, the "peace" walls, and the sites of the most violent sectarian clashes, cultural and tourist activities associated with the *Titanic* have aided in redefining the city.

While the government has worked hard to foster economic and political reforms in the North, significantly, it has also focused on developing and promoting arts and culture to demonstrate the region's social and political renewal. This push to redefine Northern Ireland as a peaceful state was marked by several important cultural events throughout 2012, including the international music concert "Peace One Day Concert" in Derry/Londonderry in June, large-scale art installation projects in the countryside, and several public arts festivals and theatrical events throughout the year. Derry/Londonderry was also selected as the British "City of Culture" for 2013, again bringing attention to the North as a desirable destination for tourism and the arts. The city had over 170 cultural events over the course of a year, with a mix of both Northern Irish and international artists engaged in theatre, dance, visual art, architecture, film, and music. A survey by the Northern Ireland Tourist Board assessing the impact of the year-long celebrations found that audiences from Northern Ireland and the Republic believed that the "City of Culture" designation helped "to create a legacy of an improved image and changed perceptions not just of Derry/Londonderry but [also] the country itself, conveying the message that Northern Ireland is confidently moving on." More-over, 67 percent of those surveyed felt that the year-long festival gave them an increased sense of pride in the North.[4] The government has repeatedly used artistic and cultural events like this one to rebrand the North and inspire greater confidence in the state both at home and abroad.

The year 2013 also marked the four-hundredth anniversary of the founding of Belfast City, which was celebrated with a series of cultural events including a four-day arts festival, historical walking tours, exhibitions and workshops exploring the history of the city, street theatre, concerts, and a vintage car show. That same year, Northern Ireland hosted the G8 summit and the World Police and Fire Games, two complex and high-profile events signaling an evolving global perception of the North as stable and ready to engage on the world stage. All these developments over the past several years indicate a distinct desire by the government to promote the North as a stable and progressive state that welcomes new industry, tourism, and economic development. Most important, these events also reflect a strategic decision to use art and culture as principal mediums through which to reposition the North's past and define its future.

The use of art and culture to redefine a population coming out of a period of great trauma can be seen throughout history. African Americans during the Harlem Renaissance and Indian artists post-Independence used art and culture as a means through which to express their humanity, creativity, and intellect after long periods of dehumanization. Ireland itself experienced the Irish Literary Revival during the late nineteenth and early twentieth centuries, reaching back to Celtic and folk mythology to establish the island as a civilized culture against centuries of British imperialist notions of the Irish as drunk, violent, and subhuman. After thirty years of heightened violence and centuries of conflict, the North is likewise promoting its cultural and artistic contributions as evidence of its progress toward a more peaceful society. In the theatre sector, this cultural awareness has begun in earnest with the emergence of new theatre festivals, the rise of independent theatre companies, and a new generation of playwrights who are interrogating the North's transition to peace.

Theatre, in particular, has played an important yet unrecognized role in the North as a critical and creative voice for civic and social change. Although theatre from the Republic has long been renowned as a vital interpreter of Ireland's cultural and political history, Northern drama has received less recognition for its impact on the state. Without a legacy of internationally recognized playwrights such as Samuel Beckett and J. M. Synge or a strong cultural institution like the Abbey Theatre to help define its history and culture, Northern drama has historically been marginalized from the Irish theatrical canon. A few male playwrights from the North have achieved significant recognition in Irish theatre (Brian Friel, Stewart Parker, Gary Mitchell, Owen McCafferty), but their female colleagues have historically been even more overlooked than their male peers. Few have found success inside the island and even fewer on an international level. Mark Phelan notes that "Northern [women] playwrights have been doubly occluded from the Irish canon, as geography, as well as gender, has placed them 'beyond the pale' of a meta-narrative of Irish theatre historiography that has been profoundly Dublincentric in nature."[5]

Despite being overlooked, Northern drama has played a significant role in documenting women's experiences and showing how their social and political status has changed with the transformation of the state. During the first half of the twentieth century, women playwrights and practitioners such as Alice Milligan and Patricia

O'Connor addressed issues of gender inequality, the confinement of women to the domestic sphere, and the exclusion of women's participation in politics. In the 1980s and 1990s, women playwrights like Anne Devlin and Christina Reid and actresses from the Charabanc, DubbelJoint, and JustUs theatre companies produced stories of the Troubles from a specifically female-centered perspective. Furthermore, playwrights of the twenty-first century, like Abbie Spallen and Stacey Gregg, are writing about the lingering effects of sectarian violence, sexual politics, and restrictive gender norms on the North's social and political development. Women's dramatic writing and performance have often contradicted mainstream narratives of the conflict, creating a rich and daring trove of counternarratives that contest the stories disseminated by the government and media. Through an examination of women's contributions to Northern Irish theatre, a unique history and story of the conflict comes into focus. It emphasizes female perspectives, experiences, and thoughts on the conflict as well as alternate views for envisioning political and social change.

The development of Northern drama is intimately linked to the formation of the state. In the late nineteenth century, Protestants in the north of Ireland had become increasingly concerned about the possibility of Home Rule. They shored up political and financial power in an effort to secure control over the northern counties. The 1920 Government of Ireland Act reflected these concerns, establishing separate Home Rule institutions for the north and south of Ireland with legislation that allowed each to be self-governing while still under the auspices of the United Kingdom. This division was further secured when the six counties toward the north (Antrim, Armagh, Down, Fermanagh, Tyrone, Derry/Londonderry) were officially partitioned in May 1921. However, in the south, the War of Independence (1919–21) and the Anglo-Irish Treaty (1921) led to the establishment of the Irish Free State. Many Irish citizens saw partition as a betrayal of the nationalist cause, and the island erupted into conflict between pro-treaty and anti-treaty parties. Thousands of Irishmen died during the Irish Civil War (June 1922–May 1923) before the pro-treaty supporters of the provisional Irish government were declared victorious, leaving the North officially under British rule. The brutal civil war and the perception that the Free State had abandoned the North left the island deeply divided for generations. The Irish Republican Army, which had first formed in 1919 as a means to end British rule on the island, splintered over the issue of partition with a new branch forming in the North committed to using force to reunite the island.

When partition occurred, the majority of people in the North were Protestants whose families had come over from Scotland and England during the plantation period in the sixteenth and seventeenth centuries. At the time of partition, Protestants had primary control over land, industry, and government in the North. However, with the establishment of the Irish Free State, Northern Protestants felt that the emancipated Catholic majority to the south threatened their status and wealth. In order to shore up power, Protestants rigidly reinforced political and financial control and strengthened ties to Great Britain. The Catholic minority in the North was systemically denied housing and voting rights, creating a two-tiered and unequal system that favored Protestants. Catholics were placed in slum housing, given the least paying and most dangerous jobs, deprived of equal educational and employment opportunities, and denied voting rights and equal representation in the Northern Irish Parliament. After decades of increasing conflict between Catholics and Protestants during the twentieth century, the struggle erupted in violence in the late 1960s.

The Troubles in Northern Ireland refers to the period from roughly 1969 to 1998, which was characterized by violent sectarian conflict between Irish Catholic nationalists and British and Anglo-Irish Protestant unionists. During the conflict, more than 3,600 people were killed,[6] and over 40,000 were seriously injured.[7] By the time the Belfast/Good Friday Agreement was signed in 1998, signaling a new peace, "about one in seven of the adult population, disproportionately Catholic, had been a victim of a violent incident."[8]

Although the conflict typically divides along religious lines, it is not a fight over religious theology. Rather, the conflict is a complex struggle over culture, history, ethnic identity, territory, civil rights, and British rule over the North. Troubles violence has primarily consisted of clashes between the British military and Catholic civilians as well as between paramilitary groups such as the Irish Republican Army (IRA) on the Catholic side and the Ulster Volunteer Force (UVF) and Ulster Defense Association (UDA) on the Protestant side.

Nationalism refers to those who want the Republic and the North to be unified into one country, independent of British rule, and tends to be made up of Catholics, although not exclusively. Unionism refers to those who want Northern Ireland to remain part of the United Kingdom, and is historically, but not exclusively, Protestant. Although the terms "republicanism" and "loyalism" have had different definitions throughout Irish history, within the context of contemporary Northern Ireland, republicanism implies "tacit or actual support to the use of physical force by paramilitary groups" whose aims are "the establishment of a United Ireland."[9] Likewise, loyalism comprises those who are willing to use violence or extremism to maintain the union with the British crown.

The Troubles transitioned into the peace process through the 1994 and 1997 ceasefires, the 1985 Anglo-Irish Agreement, and the 1998 Belfast/Good Friday Agreement. In 1994, the IRA and loyalist paramilitary groups declared a ceasefire, which allowed peace talks to progress. However, demands that the IRA decommission before being allowed to participate in negotiations toward peace caused the ceasefire to be broken in 1996 when the IRA bombed London's docklands (Canary Wharf). In 1997, the IRA renewed its commitment to the ceasefire, but it was broken again in August 1998 when a breakaway faction, the Real IRA (RIRA), which was opposed to the ceasefires and the signing of a peace agreement, committed the Omagh bombing. The explosion killed 29 and injured more than 220 people. Despite the violence, the attack failed to derail the peace process or the enactment of the Belfast/Good Friday Agreement just four months later. In addition to the intermittent ceasefires, the 1985 Anglo-Irish Agreement played an important role in the journey toward peace. The Agreement was significant in that it gave the Republic of Ireland an advisory role in the North, established the precedent that no change of status would occur in the North unless the majority of

citizens consented to join the Republic, and created the foundation
for a devolved, power-sharing government between the Nationalist
and Unionist parties. These initial steps and the cooperation between
the Irish and British governments are credited with laying the essential groundwork for the successful signing of the Belfast/Good Friday
Agreement thirteen years later.

Since the signing of the Agreement, the North has achieved significant advances toward a lasting peace. Belfast has recovered from a
prolonged war and rebuilt itself into a sophisticated metropolis with
high-end shops, luxury apartment buildings, museums, entertainment venues, and trendy restaurants. Derry/Londonderry, Omagh,
and other large towns have benefitted from EU money marked for
peace and reconciliation, which has brought new infrastructure, jobs,
educational opportunities, and conflict-resolution training into the
countryside. A 2010 historic agreement between Sinn Féin and the
Democratic Unionist Party (DUP)[10] has allowed the slow and intermittent transfer of regulation over the judicial and law enforcement
agencies from the British government to the power-sharing executive
of Northern Ireland. Although still present, paramilitary groups are
sparse and have limited influence.

At the same time, the peace process has been arduous and slow.
Despite legal and political changes that have guaranteed more equal
rights and representation between Catholics and Protestants, the North
struggles with how to address its violent past and how to overcome
the still palpably sectarian prejudices that permeate society. Schools
remain highly segregated with less than 7 percent of children receiving nondenominational integrated education.[11] Only about 10 percent
of marriages in the North are between a Catholic and a Protestant.[12]
The vast majority of neighborhoods, especially in Belfast, remain segregated with Catholics and Protestants patronizing different grocery
stores, pubs, and community centers. Suicide rates remain high, poverty and unemployment persist, and the divide between urban and
rural communities remains stratified. Moreover, the Police Service of
Northern Ireland (PSNI) remains dominated by Protestants despite a
mandate from the 1999 Patten Report for the force to recruit equal

numbers of Protestant and Catholic officers. That directive was abandoned in 2011 when the government determined that the "composition of the PSNI [was now] broadly reflective of the community."[13] However, as of 2014, 67 percent of police officers and 77 percent of the PSNI staff identified as Protestant.[14] The recent global economic downturn has also meant greater unemployment, reduced funding for community services and the arts, depressed housing prices, and a reduction in foreign investment.

At the center of these difficult political and economic issues are several questions that the state is struggling to come to terms with: Is the past holding Northern Ireland back and preventing its people from healing? Can a community move beyond its own history? Can the perpetrators be forgiven, pay their debt to society, and move on? Can reconciliation happen on a national level or must it be worked out between individuals? What will the future of the region look like? Will the North ever sever ties with Britain? Will the North ever become part of the Republic? These complex questions and the North's ever-shifting relationship with its difficult past are being explored through economic and political negotiations and, significantly, through the region's cultural and artistic output.

Northern drama has many qualities that distinguish it from its southern counterpart. As early as the turn of the twentieth century, W. B. Reynolds of the Ulster Literary Theatre (ULT) identified a growing difference between Northern and southern drama: "Our art of the drama will be different from the Irish drama which speaks from the stage of the Irish National Theatre in Dublin. . . . At present we can only say that our talent is more satiric than poetic, that will probably remain the broad difference between the Ulster and Leinster schools."[15] Northern drama's dry, satiric, and darkly comedic sensibility, identified early in the state's formation, reflects only one of several distinguishing characteristics that have developed over the past century.

Anthony Roche argues that Northern drama is inclined to be antihierarchical, privileging ensemble stories where multiple voices are heard. Likewise, it "moves in opposition to the well-made play, emphasizing instead discontinuity, fragmentation, and juxtaposition."

Northern drama is also distinguished by unreliable language: words are constantly undermined, questioned, and revealed to be false. It also tends to use a full range of theatrical devices, including "gesture, mime, dance, song, music, symbolism, and stage imagery,"[16] as opposed to the more literary tradition of the Republic, which has historically privileged text and dialogue before visual components of theatre.

Northern drama also leans toward the political, both on civic and personal levels. The Northern practitioners Carol Moore and Eleanor Methven define Northern drama as that which "addresses issues that are particular to the Six Counties: political issues" with a "rugged, robust, and unsentimental view of the world."[17] It is not surprising, then, that the primary archive for theatre research in the North is housed within the Linen Hall Library's political collection, which centers around the history of the sectarian conflict. Because Northern art is often assumed to be politically motivated, it can be difficult for artists to circumvent audience expectations and produce works that are not interpreted through a sectarian lens.

Another distinguishing characteristic is that Northern drama tends to explore the physical, psychological, and emotional effects of violence on individuals and the community at large. This is counterbalanced by an extremely dark humor, which serves as a cathartic relief from that intense and pervasive violence.

Despite these important and distinguishing characteristics, Northern drama has been neglected and often marginalized in both academic scholarship and on the professional stage. The reasons for this are complex and manifold: the dominance of the Dublin-based Abbey Theatre and its significant political history in the formation of an Irish cultural identity, the canonical stature of Brian Friel to the marginalization of other Northern playwrights, the Republic's apathy born from an exhausting past century of unrest in the North, and a history of state censorship and control restricting the forms of drama that were able to flourish in the North. Furthermore, the recent emphasis within Irish studies toward globalization has encouraged scholars to examine critical work through an international lens, focusing on how Irish drama has been received and interpreted abroad and how these influences have affected funding, criticism, and artistic choices at home.[18] Privileging of the global has moved Irish studies away from nationalist and postcolonial discourse, and therefore away from the Troubles and the North in general. This has caused Irish theatre scholarship to center around diasporic theatre and drama that is mobile, reproducible, and readily interpreted by international audiences. As a result, Irish theatre that is rooted in a specific place, space, and time is being overlooked. This book examines drama that is born of very complex historical and political circumstances and that often requires an audience familiar with that particular history. Although the turn in global studies has offered great value and insight to Irish studies scholarship, my research emphasizes the continuing significance of drama that is born of and remains rooted within a very specific and localized context.

In the early years of the Northern Irish state, several women used theatre as a means of political expression and social critique during a time when women were primarily limited to the domestic sphere. Early female practitioners such as Alice Milligan (1866–1953), Patricia O'Connor (1908–1983), and Mary O'Malley (1918–2006) understood the power of theatre to give women public voices on a range of national issues. Many of these female practitioners were politically active, and the lines between their theatrical and political lives often intermingled. This history establishes an early legacy of Northern women using theatre as a political and social tool to cut through the din of masculine political rhetoric and the ongoing conflict in order to allow their voices to be heard.

This legacy came to maturation in the early 1980s when the women-led Charabanc Theatre Company (1983–95) and the playwrights Anne Devlin, Christina Reid, and Marie Jones burst onto the stage, writing and producing some of the most significant Irish theatre of the decade. Charabanc was devoted to exploring Northern Irish history, politics, and sectarianism specifically from women's perspectives. Composed of members from both Protestant and Catholic backgrounds, the company was revolutionary in that it broke the gender barrier as well as sectarian lines to explore issues relevant to all women of the North. Charabanc was a professional theatre company that was community-based in the truest sense of the word, as members of the company interviewed women throughout the North and used their stories to devise plays that directly reflected women's lives. Christina Reid's *Tea in a China Cup*, which premiered at the Lyric Theatre in 1983, refocused the classic Troubles play from a traditionally masculine perspective to a treatment of the conflict as seen through the eyes of a Protestant mother and daughter. In addition, Marie Jones, Anne Devlin, and Jennifer Johnston[19] were committed to giving women a new public voice and to addressing previously taboo subjects such as sexual politics, domestic violence, and gender roles. These women elevated the prestige of Northern Irish drama and also created a small canon of internationally recognized work that promoted women's rights and exposed how confining and restrictive gender roles were in the North.

Although the contributions of these pioneers are important, they are far from being the only or most significant examples of women's theatrical contributions. Irish theatrical scholarship, however, tends to cite Jones, Reid, and Devlin, along with Charabanc, as the only examples of women theatre practitioners from the North. The primary scholarly monographs on Irish theatre history—including Anthony Roche's *Contemporary Irish Drama* (1995), Christopher Murray's *Twentieth-Century Irish Drama* (1997), Christopher Morash's *A History of Irish Theatre, 1601–2000* (2004), and Mary Trotter's *Modern Irish Theatre* (2008)—cite Reid, Devlin, Jones, and Charabanc as the principal examples of women's theatrical participation from the North. In doing so, they overlook earlier contributions and give the erroneous impression that the North has not produced a significant female playwright since the early 1980s. Imelda Foley's *Girls in the Big Picture* (2003) remains the most comprehensive work to date on female practitioners in the North. However, her analysis is also limited to examining Reid, Devlin, and Jones. Though she does devote part of a chapter to Charabanc and DubbelJoint, the companies are analyzed primarily in relation to how they supported Jones's career.

Current scholarship creates a false perception that the North experienced a brief and isolated renaissance of women playwrights in the 1980s only to have their contributions overshadowed by the works of male playwrights such as Friel, Parker, Mitchell, and the Field Day Theatre Company. These men have received enormous critical and scholarly attention, whereas many women playwrights and practitioners have been essentially written out of history and the theatrical canon. This marginalization has only recently begun to be corrected. Tom Maguire's *Making Theatre in Northern Ireland* (2006) and Bill McDonnell's *Theatres of the Troubles* (2009) include much-needed analysis of the women-led JustUs Theatre Company. Melissa Sihra's *Women in Irish Drama* (2007) improves greatly on previous scholarship with several chapters devoted to representations of women in Northern drama. Mark Phelan's chapter, "Beyond the Pale: Neglected Northern Irish Women Playwrights, Alice Milligan, Helen Waddell, and Patricia O'Connor," remains the most comprehensive analysis of early women's contributions.

In addition to the important contributions of these practitioners, contemporary women dramatists like Abbie Spallen, Stacey Gregg, Rosemary Jenkinson, and Shannon Yee have enriched the Northern theatre sector with challenging plays that directly push against mainstream narratives of the peace process. This new generation, political and outspoken, is stimulating new conversations about peace and questioning how much things have really changed in the North, especially for women. The history of politically engaged women practitioners has been lost both in the scholarship and in contemporary Northern playwrights' own understanding of their place and legacy in Irish theatre history. My research seeks to correct this imbalance by recovering and highlighting women's contributions. Because the works of the celebrated playwrights Anne Devlin, Christina Reid, and Marie Jones have already received significant scholarly analysis, this book focuses on neglected and unrecognized contributions by Northern women practitioners in an attempt to begin the process of painting a more comprehensive picture of women's theatrical contributions from the North. Furthermore, the majority of theatre practitioners covered in this book write, produce, and perform in Belfast, which remains the primarily theatrical center in the North. However, there are women practitioners doing strong and vibrant work in Derry/Londonderry, Portstewart, and other regional areas. These women also deserve greater recognition for the contributions they are making to Northern Irish theatre. This book further hopes to serve as a catalyst for greater inquiry and research into the creative work that women are doing all over Northern Ireland.

Defining Irishness has long been a preoccupation of the entire island, North and south, and this debate has arguably been most intense when it comes to defining who is an Irish writer. Oscar Wilde, George Bernard Shaw, and, more recently, Martin McDonagh have all had their national and cultural identities debated. Defining who is a Northern Irish writer can be an equally contentious and difficult matter. There are writers who were born in the North but have spent their lives elsewhere and no longer self-identify as Northern Irish. There are others who have lived outside of the region for the majority of their lives but still consider themselves Northern. There are those who have lived in the borderlands, stuck between the North and the Republic, feeling slightly out of place in each. And there are newly arrived immigrants who have made the North their permanent home. This book employs the definition that the Belfast-based Tinderbox Theatre Company uses in defining Northern Irish playwrights: those who were either born in the North or those who currently live and work in the North.

During the 1980s, the Charabanc women were reluctant to associate words such as "feminist," "political," or "women" to their plays in the fear that it would divide and alienate audiences and ghettoize their theatre into a lesser category. Despite the passing of thirty-five years and significant advances in the peace process, the delay of feminism and the absence of a strong women's movement in the North have arrested the progression of these concerns. Many of today's playwrights are apprehensive about the same exact issues, reluctant to have their work analyzed through a feminist or gendered lens or even included in a study of women practitioners. In addition, many of the women interviewed for this research did not want to be labeled as "feminists" or be defined as addressing gender issues, although their work often spoke to the contrary. Feminism and gender have a complex and highly politicized history in the North, which is discussed in depth in chapter 1. The dominance of sectarian identity politics, a perception of feminism as associated with Irish nationalism, and the persistent onslaught of three decades of violence all contributed to the delay of a strong women's movement. Northern artists as well as critics like Imelda Foley have railed against "the absurdity of equating American feminist politics with those of Northern Ireland in the 1980s."[20] This sentiment remains unchanged in the North, which views its own history as so divergent and unique from that of the United States and Britain that the political impulses and ideas surrounding the feminist movements of the 1960s and 1970s often feel out of place. Because of that complicated history, this research takes pains not to impose theoretical and highly academic notions about gender onto the plays when the women interviewed do not feel it accurately reflects their personal experiences or artistic intentions.

However, despite some playwrights' concerns, consciously or unconsciously, directly or indirectly, the women selected for this study *are* highly engaged in gender politics and gender positioning within the North. This is demonstrated by the themes of their plays as well as through their personal experiences forging careers in what has traditionally been a male-dominated field in Ireland. Where appropriate, my research enters into conversation with theory as a means to enrich but not overwhelm the analysis of the theatrical work.

Using gendered, historical, and sociopolitical lenses as its contextual framework, this book examines how the sectarian conflict and ensuing peace process in Northern Ireland has affected women's social positioning and political voice during the twentieth and early twenty-first centuries and how this ultimately has been expressed by women in the theatre. Part One, "Theatre, Gender, and Politics, 1921–1979," offers a broad overview of the historical, political, and social positioning of women and theatre in Northern Ireland, while establishing the legacy of women's political engagement with theatre during the early formation of the state. The first chapter examines the gendered nature of the conflict, the development of feminism in the North, the effects of sectarian violence on women, and how traditional gender roles have limited women's formal political participation. Consideration of the impact state censorship has played in that theatrical gendering is addressed in chapter 2. Chapter 3 analyzes the work of the suffragette and theatre practitioner Alice Milligan, the playwright Patricia O'Connor, and the founder of the Lyric Players, Mary O'Malley. Each of these women played an important role in establishing an early model for women's civic participation through the theatrical stage.

Part Two, "Troubles and the Stage, 1980–1997," examines the contributions of three women-led theatre companies that were active during the Troubles, beginning in chapter 4 with the literary and artistic contributions of the Charabanc Theatre Company. These artistic leaders were instrumental in creating new jobs and training for women in Northern theatre, in instituting a new audience base and infrastructure for independent theatre in the North, and in establishing a model of bringing artistic work into rural and working-class areas. Chapter 5 examines the highly political and controversial works of DubbelJoint and JustUs. There are analyses of several unpublished plays, including DubbelJoint's *The Government Inspector* (1993) and *A Mother's Heart* (1999), and JustUs's *Binlids* (1997) and *Forced Upon Us* (1999). The chapter investigates the political identities of both companies and the heated public debates inspired by several highly controversial productions. While the Troubles raged and the government called for calm and nonincendiary speech, both companies staged shocking and graphic depictions of violence, injustice, and gender inequality.

Part Three, "The Post-Agreement North, 1998–2012," explores the continued legacy of contemporary women writers who address gender politics, give voice to marginalized groups, challenge constructed images of the North, and suggest that the Troubles continues to radically shape women's sexuality, subjectivity, and professional and personal opportunities. Chapter 6 analyzes Abbie Spallen's *Pumpgirl* (2007) and *Strandline* (2009) with an emphasis on several common themes found in women's writing today: children in peril, bad mothers, proscribed gender roles, sex linked to violence, and the lingering effects of Troubles violence on Northern society. This chapter also looks at the performance histories of the shows and the lack of support that Spallen initially encountered for her dramatic work in the North. Chapter 7 explores the impact of the peace process on working-class Protestants in Belfast through the plays of Stacey Gregg and Rosemary Jenkinson. Gregg's *Lagan* (2011) concentrates on a generation of lost young people who have come of age during peacetime, and the dramatist's larger body of work questions whether the North can escape its history of violence to obtain a productive peace in the present. In *The Bonefire* (2006) and *Basra Boy* (2012), Jenkinson writes primarily young, working-class, Protestant male characters. Her work does not shy away from explicit violence and repeatedly explores the breakdown of the family unit, the disturbing link between sex and violence, and a pervasive pessimism associated with the peace process. Finally, chapter 8 focuses on a queer dramaturgy that has recently emerged in the North. It also reflects the diverse range of immigrant artists who have come to Ireland since the start of the Celtic Tiger, constructing a paradigm for a more inclusive definition of Irish identity. Shannon Yee, an American expat who now resides in Belfast, addresses queer issues in her experimental, multidisciplinary performance work. *Trouble* (2013 and 2015*)*, which combines two taboo topics (homosexuality and the Troubles), and *Reassembled, Slightly Askew* (2012 and 2015), which addresses Yee's personal experience with severe brain trauma, uses immersive, site-specific, and verbatim theatre techniques, bringing a new level of diversity to Northern theatre.

My research ultimately documents the untold history of women's political and civic engagement through theatre, analyzing the complex intersections between performance, politics, and gender in the North. It provides an overview of thematic and structural changes in Northern women's playwriting as the state has transitioned from conflict into the current peace process. And it charts Northern women's contributions to Irish theatre while placing them within the dual contexts of Irish theatre history and the Northern Irish conflict. Recovering

Northern women's significant contributions to Irish theatre history and documenting the importance of their gendered perspectives will, I hope, propagate greater acceptance and visibility of women in Irish theatre and ultimately lead to "a more comprehensive understanding of the realities of conflict and the meaning of security"[21] in the North.

PART ONE

Theatre, Gender, and Politics, 1921–1979

1

Nation, Conflict, and
the Politics of Feminism

For centuries, gender has played a prominent role within Irish politics and culture, and in Ireland's status as a British colony. In Irish colonial discourse, the island was positioned as the pure, innocent, and feminized state, whereas the British Empire was characterized as the violent masculine interloper. Gender has continued to play a prominent role throughout the island during the twentieth and twenty-first centuries, with gender roles being directly linked to national and religious identity. In the south, during the first half of the twentieth century, the Catholic Church and Irish government took great pains to exclude women from political, civic, and government life. Church leaders vigorously derided the suffrage movement, advocated that women be denied any form of political or civic activism, and advised that women work outside of the home only if absolutely necessary for economic survival. These constructions of proper womanhood were further reinforced with the 1937 Irish Constitution, which refers to women as mothers and primarily defines a woman's responsibility to the state as raising children and providing a secure domestic space.[1] The most infamous lines define "the Family as the natural primary and fundamental unit group of Society" and ensure that "mothers shall not be obliged by economic necessity to engage in labour to the neglect of their duties in the home."[2] Motherhood was the most celebrated image of womanhood throughout the early years of the Irish Free State, directly linking it to the stability and success of the newly formed nation.[3]

However, with independence and the nationalist cause no longer the defining struggle of the country, the Republic of Ireland was slowly able to move away from such strictly proscribed views of gender. As the Republic grew stronger during the second half of the twentieth century, redefining itself as an established nation, women were able to make their own needs a priority, embracing the women's liberation movements, enacting antidiscrimination laws, and furthering opportunities in education and employment. The 1970s were watershed years for the development of feminism in the Republic. The early 1970s saw the establishment of the Commission on the Status of Women, the National Women's Council of Ireland, and the Irish Women's Liberation Movement. These groups fought for equal pay, for divorce legislation (which ultimately prevailed when divorce became legal in 1996), for greater representation of women in government, for abortion rights (led by the "Repeal the 8th" campaign), and for contraception rights (first achieved in 1980).

In contrast to the Republic, Northern Ireland has remained a contested state with sustained conflict for over ninety years. Nationalist and unionist discourse in the North has continued to demand a strict adherence to proscribed gender roles. Mark Phelan writes: "Although implacably divided on the constitutional issue of partition, the patriarchal nature of Nationalism and Unionism meant they were ideologically in synch on social issues, most notably that women's position was in the home. The political consensus was reinforced by religious orthodoxy as the social teachings of the Protestant and Catholic Churches also converged in promoting 'women's primary duties as home-makers and mothers, focusing their interests and energies on the domestic sphere.'"[4] Whereas femininity was defined by the role of nurturer within the home, church, and local community, masculinity was directly linked to militarism, political self-sacrifice, and defense of the nation.[5]

In direct opposition to a continued proscribed militant masculinity, feminine identity has been positioned as naturally nonviolent and innately peaceful. Fidelma Ashe argues that "there has been a strong tendency in Northern Ireland to view women as having weaker

ethnic identifications than men and therefore as less sectarian and big-
oted. . . . As a consequence, the notion that women rather than men
are more inclined to seek peace and reconciliation has been popular in
Northern Ireland."[6] Women's sexuality has also historically been syn-
onymous with the community's integrity, unfairly linking women's
bodies to the moral status of the state. Ashe builds on these ideas:

> The body politics of Irish nationalism also operates on the terrain of
> women's sexual and erotic autonomy. Like other nationalisms, Irish
> nationalism has traditionally identified women with the integrity and
> purity of the collective culture. . . . As woman becomes the allegory
> of the nation, in this case Mother Ireland, real women's so-called
> "sexual integrity" symbolizes the nation's integrity. As Nagel . . .
> observes, in nationalist societies women's "purity must be impec-
> cable . . . nationalists often have a special interest in the sexuality and
> sexual behaviour of their women". . . . This is reflected, for example,
> in the policing of women's sexuality in Irish nationalist cultures.[7]

Because women's bodies have been symbolically linked to the sectarian conflict, the feminine body has been repressively policed for
decades in the North. Moreover, women in both the Catholic and
Protestant traditions have the added pressure that their individual
gendered identities directly influence their community's political and
territorial claims on the North.

The complex historical connection between nationalism, religion,
community integrity, and gender politics continues today. Although
strides have been made toward expanding more acceptable notions
of gender normativity in the North, traditional gender ideals remain
tightly intertwined with unionism and nationalism. The Republic no
longer requires nationalism to be a primary marker of identity, but the
protracted sectarian battle intensified by the Troubles has reinforced
reductive binary identity markers as central to the continued security
of religious and ethnic identity in the North.

It is well documented that sectarian divisions in Northern Ireland
have killed thousands, created persistent poverty, and delayed economic development. But the conflict has had equally insidious, but

less obviously visible, effects on social, cultural, and political developments, most notably feminism. Adrian Little views the North as frozen
in the past and entrenched in outdated ideologies that are essentially
delaying women's (as well as other minority groups') full liberation:
"While feminists in Northern Ireland are becoming more attuned to
'the politics of difference,' the dominant feature of feminism in the
North to date is a strategic essentialism that resonates more with first-
wave feminism than contemporary feminist debates."[8]

When second-wave feminism was welcomed in the Republic in
the 1970s, the North was at the pinnacle of intense Troubles fighting. There was little room or energy in the national consciousness to
address women's rights. Women were expected to privilege the priorities of the Irish nationalist and unionist fights before those of feminism.
Though there were attempts to unite Protestant and Catholic women
through groups like the Northern Ireland Women's Rights Movement
(founded in 1975), these organizations inevitably failed owing to the
divided issue of nationalism as well as a failure to acknowledge important differences between the Protestant and Catholic experiences.
Feminist organizations also met with strong resistance from the patriarchal powers that controlled women's everyday lives, including the
government, church, and paramilitary groups. "Women's attempts to
lobby on issues that affect their everyday lives," Imelda Foley writes,
"have been branded by their respective paramilitaries as 'Republican
challenges to the state' (loyalist) or as 'collusion with opposing forces'
(republican). The very act of cross-community single-gender initiatives threatens the patriarchal stronghold."[9]

Essentialist identity politics have been the norm in the North for
some time. Since partition, the binary identity of British-Protestant
and Irish-Catholic has been the dominating and fundamental core of
self-identity. Religious and national identification as the predominant
markers for selfhood has created a system in which identity in the
North tends to be essentialist and dividing. This has created the false
perception that all members of the North conform to two groups: the
Irish-Catholic nationalists or the Anglo-Irish and British-Protestant
unionists.

An emphasis on essentialist forms of identity has required that individuals subvert all other parts of their selfhood (such as gender, class, or profession) to the dominant identifying markers of the larger group. This has required minority groups such as the disabled, elderly, or queer to integrate themselves into one of the larger identity groups or risk marginalization. And it has dictated a subjectivity defined by a single (binary) identity rather than a pluralistic one. For women in the North, this means that they have had to subvert their needs as females to those of their ethno-nationalist group in order to avoid marginalization. Rosemary Sales argues that "sectarian divisions are built into the structures and identity of Northern Ireland. Politics has remained polarized around community loyalties, placing severe limitations on the development of class-based or gender-based loyalties."[10] In this way, essentialist identity politics have historically prevented minority groups from making advancements, most notably with women and feminist politics.

In addition, violence associated with the Troubles, a staunchly masculine political atmosphere, and strong community affiliation with the Catholic and Protestant churches have also greatly hindered the development of feminism in the North. Addressing this complexity, Little identifies four additional impediments to the development of feminism in the North. First, restrictive views of gender within the Catholic and Protestant traditions have prevented women from actively participating in formal politics or nation-building. Both churches have promoted politics as a purely masculine space in which the "good" mother and wife does not engage. Little finds it "clear that the centrality of religion as a major source of identity has constrained the opportunities for women to make a major impact in the public sphere (especially as the churches play a prominent role in the secular life of the province)."[11]

The second obstacle is "the closure of spaces for political debates and the prevalence of a narrow definition of what is political."[12] Here, Little essentially argues that politics have become directly associated with masculine national and ethno-religious identity, creating a limiting and narrow definition of political engagement. In other words, politics in the North center around issues of the sectarian conflict rather than encompassing wider social issues such as poverty or education that might unite both communities. A third barrier to the development of feminism is an overarching focus in Northern Irish politics on practical, material, and economic conditions, paired with a tendency to dismiss more theoretical, moral, or ethical debates on how to create an inclusive society for all members. This emphasis on material conditions provides little space to speak about larger social issues (such as the subjugation of women) that cannot be as easily solved by material solutions.

Finally, the fourth obstacle is the association of feminism within the ideological framework of Irish nationalism in particular. Because feminism has historically been linked to Irish nationalism,[13] many unionists perceive the women's movement with distrust and do not feel that it can encompass their own concerns (which are often seen as fundamentally different from nationalist women's). This has created an unequal voice for women in the North, with nationalist and Catholic women arguably having a louder and more active political voice than their unionist and Protestant counterparts. This was especially true during the 1970s and 1980s when roughly two thousand Catholic men were interned and imprisoned, necessitating that Catholic women take up political leadership within their communities. This perception that Irish nationalism and feminism are linked is so profound that second-wave feminism did not develop within the unionist community altogether until the early 1990s.[14]

Even within the more developed feminist movement of the Irish nationalist communities in the 1970s and 1980s, female involvement in politics was still extremely limited and difficult to enact. A major obstacle for nationalist feminists was the inability to campaign for certain rights that would have recognized British authority: "The campaign to extend abortion legalization to Northern Ireland was a case in point. At the time, some Republican feminists felt unable to support a campaign that called for the extension of British legislation in the North. To do so was tantamount to support for the British presence in Ireland."[15] Thus, although abortion rights were extremely important to nationalist feminists, the perception of supporting additional British legislation and intervention in Catholic lives overrode their ability to advocate for rights over their own bodies. Though abortion was legalized throughout the United Kingdom in 1967, church influence prevented these privileges from extending to Northern Ireland, where abortion remains illegal as of this writing. The few cross-community women's groups that have developed in the North, such as the Northern Ireland Women's Rights Movement, often found themselves unable to take positions on certain political subjects or traditional tenants of feminism (including abortion, working outside the home, and the deprivileging of motherhood) in an effort not to alienate members from both nationalist and unionist sides.[16] The inability of the two communities to work together has been a barrier to the wider development of feminism in the North, preventing women from successfully advocating for rights that are extended throughout the rest of the United Kingdom.

Additional impediments came from the argument that feminist politics were inherently at odds with nationalist and unionist goals, and this was often used as an excuse to marginalize women's involvement in politics or public life. Although women were allowed to speak out on behalf of family issues, prison conditions, children, and nonviolence, they typically were excluded from participating in high-level talks that would affect broader political and socioeconomic conditions for the entire North. In addition, the possibility of Catholic and Protestant women uniting directly threatened the legitimacy of the conflict. For women to join forces was not only to ignore essentialist identity politics but also to suggest that the two communities potentially shared interests more pressing than the opposing goals of the nationalist and unionist factions. As a result, women's groups were attacked when they were perceived as privileging gendered issues over sectarian ones. The feminist activists Avila Kilmurray and Monica McWilliams have recounted the often violent opposition: "During the peace talks, in 1997, the Windsor Women's Centre in a Protestant/Loyalist community was attacked and burned following a visit by the Irish president, Mary Robinson. The paramilitary organization claiming credit for the attack threatened the staff in an attempt to prevent them from continuing their progressive cross-community work on women's issues, driving the center's previously open association with the women's coalition underground."[17]

Sectarian divisions have prevented feminism from developing fully in the North, and important differences in culture, religion, experience, and identity between Protestant and Catholic women have also contributed to this failure.[18] Although all women in the North experience subjugation to patriarchy, the *ways* in which they experience it differ. Women are oppressed in the North as women but also specifically as Catholic women and as Protestant women, and as Irish women and as British or Anglo-Irish women. For example, the Irish nationalist feminists' tendency to tie their oppression as women to British colonialism[19] excludes unionist feminists from identifying with that cause. Northern Ireland's status as a not-quite or almost postcolonial nation has added another layer of complexity to the creation of women's subjectivities and thus to their unification.

Kimberlé Crenshaw developed intersectionality theory in the late 1980s to help explain the multiple intersecting forms of oppression that black women in the United States face.[20] Intersectionality theory argues that oppressive economic and material conditions, social factors, institutional prejudices, race, ethnicity, class, sex, and sexuality cannot be untangled from one another and can be best understood as intersecting, supporting, and perpetuating forms of oppression. Only by examining the ecosystem of how these issues overlap and encourage one another can the full extent of oppression be understood and dismantled. In contrast to the essentialized identity politics of Northern Ireland, which requires individuals to view their experiences through a specific and limiting sectarian lens, intersectionality theory requires individuals to examine how their memberships in overlapping identity categories all contribute in a cumulative way toward oppression and marginalization. Crenshaw emphasizes that "identity politics . . . frequently conflates or ignores intragroup differences. In the context of violence against women, this elision of difference in identity politics is problematic, fundamentally because the violence that many women experience is often shaped by other dimensions of their identities, such as race and class. Moreover ignoring differences *within* groups contributes to tensions *among* groups."[21] Because the Northern Irish Women's Rights Movement downplayed important differences between Catholic and Protestant women's experiences of oppression, they failed to engender a collective sense of community or purpose among Northern feminists. Furthermore, the experience of gender oppression alone was not enough to unify the women of the North. A failure to both acknowledge differences between Protestant and Catholic experiences and to connect the interwoven influences of religion, gender, class, ethno-national affiliation, and economic pressures on their subjugation meant that most Northern women did not feel a strong connection to the women's movement, and it ultimately failed to gain traction.

The closed and localized culture of the North together with the stresses of the conflict also prevented women from connecting to globalized feminist movements that had the potential to unite rather than stratify. In particular, the transnational feminist movement, which came to prominence in the 1970s, had the potential to be transformative. Transnational feminism explores how material and economic conditions, race, ethnicity, and gender work together to oppress women across global borders. In particular, this strain of feminism examines the roles of imperialism, colonialism, and nationalism in the subjugation of women worldwide. Whereas global feminists argue that the experience of patriarchy is universal (i.e., there is a common experience of gender oppression across the globe), transnational feminists recognize that oppression is the result of unique historical, material, and economic conditions that are specific to a location and time. Transnational feminism is also inherently political, calling on women to advocate for women's rights and to challenge oppression. This strain of feminism allows enough space within its ideology to accommodate and acknowledge the differences between the Northern Catholic and Protestant experiences while providing unifying goals and calls for political action to potentially advance the interests of all women. Although transnational feminism flourished in America, England, and Scotland during the 1990s, the exhaustive effects of war and a cultural adherence to nationalism and unionism over all other ideologies dampened any possibility of the movement being embraced or championed in the North.

Along with failed opportunities to unify under inclusive feminist movements, sectarian violence played a large role in the subjugation of women. Not only do gender roles tend to be strictly enforced during intense periods of strife and nationalist fervor, but long-term sectarian conflict can also lead to significant increases in violence against women. This violence, in turn, perpetuates a cycle of keeping women in positions of submission within society.[22] Troubles violence had a direct effect on the suppression of women first through its demand of loyalty to ethno-national identity and second through its normalizing and legitimatizing of violence. Monica McWilliams argues that areas experiencing intense and prolonged conflict, like Northern Ireland, tend to devalue domestic violence over sectarian violence. For example, during the Troubles, physical attacks on women because of religion or sectarian loyalties were viewed as much more heinous than violence within the domestic sphere. Sectarian attacks on women were seen as breaking the rules of warfare and assaulting those who were considered outside the sphere of acceptable victims. Domestic violence, in contrast, was often viewed as a private matter, and one that did not affect the community or nation at large. McWilliams writes:

> When a woman is the target of a sectarian murder in Northern Ireland, invariably there is a great sense of outrage. This outrage exposes the gendered nature of public morality in its opposition to the murder of women in political conflict. However, when a woman has been murdered in a "domestic" assault in the "sanctuary" of her own home, there is less of a sense of violation. In Northern Ireland, as elsewhere, there is a kind of continuum that ranges from the least to the most acceptable type of murders that is perhaps best symbolized in the way in which murders not related to the political

situation have been euphemistically referred to by police officers as "ordinary decent murders."[23]

Thus, during periods of sectarian strife, domestic violence, which is associated with the private sphere, is dismissed as less important compared with the violence happening in the public sphere.

Within regions engaged in conflict, domestic violence often becomes difficult for women to report. During the Troubles, the Royal Ulster Constabulary (RUC) was Protestant controlled.[24] For a Catholic woman, calling the police would be tantamount to calling the enemy. Even in situations in which a nationalist woman felt comfortable calling the police, the physical feat of bringing the RUC into a nationalist neighborhood during the Troubles risked a very public demonstration. McWilliams explains: "In Northern Ireland, telling women in nationalist communities to call the police has even less meaning when the police will not respond to calls because of the perceived risk to their security. . . . When the police do respond, they have to be escorted into these communities by the British Army. The arrangement usually entails a convoy of six to eight heavily armoured vehicles full of soldiers and police, all wearing flak jackets and carrying submachine guns."[25] For the Catholic community, in particular, domestic violence was hidden from view, as it distracted from the nationalist fight, threatened to devalue or illegitimate violence as a means to achieve the community's goals, and embarrassed the community by reinforcing colonial stereotypes of Irish Catholics as innately violent.

Ultimately, the history of conflict in Northern Ireland has made women more susceptible to violence within the private sphere and also left them without many resources to prevent or report the violence. The strong link between militarism and masculinity has prolonged a violent atmosphere in the North, subjugating women through sustained and normalized violence on their bodies.

Despite the obstacles outlined above, Northern women were able to accomplish some significant political advances during the Troubles. Because of the North's inclusion within the United Kingdom, the women's liberation movement in Britain brought several important antidiscrimination laws to the North, including the Equal Pay Act (1970) and the Sex Discrimination Act (1976). The Equal Opportunities Commission was also created in 1976, and a series of women's health and rape crisis centers were founded in subsequent years. The early 1980s saw the founding of prominent neighborhood women's centers that gave support and community to local women. Advocacy groups that lobbied for women's rights were also established in the 1980s and 1990s. The nationalist group Clar na mBan (Women's Agenda for Peace) was founded in 1994 because women's voices were not being included in the peace talks. The group presented a series of important reforms to the government-sponsored Forum for Peace and Reconciliation, highlighting demilitarization, economic equality, and protective rights for children, lesbians, and the disabled. The Northern Ireland Women's Coalition (NIWC) (1996–2006) ran on a nonpartisan platform in the elections leading up to the peace talks. Emphasizing gender over sectarian identity or politics, it obtained two seats at the Members of Northern Ireland Forum, becoming the only female voices in the negotiation of the Belfast/Good Friday Agreement. Women have also been the leaders of grassroots activism and community politics for decades, having significant influence over local legislation and domestic affairs. This was especially true of Catholic women who became politicized in the late 1960s fighting for civil rights, and then again in the 1970s and 1980s during internment and the hunger strikes.

However, feminists like Linda Edgerton have argued that much of the political action that Northern women have taken has been untransformative, remaining within the boundaries of conservative gender norms. For example, Catholic women's initial political impulses stemmed from the jailing of sons, brothers, fathers, and husbands, making motherhood and marriage the motivations for political intervention:

> Linda Edgerton has suggested that women's activism against the repressive policies of the state was motivated by the same gender ideology that maintained motherhood as the primary responsibility

of women in Northern Ireland. While this ideology furnished the motivation for political action, she argued, such involvement did not challenge the hierarchical system of gender that constrains the space and social possibilities of women. Thus, for Edgerton, women's political resistance during these years was—from a feminist perspective—fundamentally untransformative because women were locked in a system of *de facto* transgression of gender roles while ideologically reproducing them. . . . Thus political deployment of motherhood by nationalist women in Northern Ireland is understood by Edgerton as a form of gender false consciousness that maintains a system of gender inequality.[26]

For many feminists, the limited political awakening within the Catholic community as stemming from mistreatment of men (rather than women) was disappointing in its scope and ultimately misdirected in its goals.

The failure of women to make a strong political impact is further evidenced by the limited influence they have had in formal politicking at the state level. Although a few women held local political offices during the Troubles, they tended to be isolated examples and failed to have a significant impact on long-term issues of peace. A good example is Bernadette Devlin, who was an exceptionally high-profile political activist and is rightfully lauded as playing a central role in the advancement of the Northern Irish civil rights movement. She was the youngest MP to be elected to Parliament and, for many years, was an internationally recognized and respected figure who advocated for civil rights for the working classes. However, after the events of Bloody Sunday[27] (which ushered in a new period of IRA recruitment and paramilitary domination of the North) and the devastating effects of two hunger strikes in 1980 and 1981, Devlin's status waned as Sinn Féin and hypermasculine paramilitary violence hijacked the political dialogue. The primary goal of the civil rights movement in the late 1960s was to secure better conditions for the working classes. Devlin had hoped to achieve a socialist state that would take care of both the Protestant and Catholic working-class communities. However, as violence erupted, these goals were overtaken by a new priority led by Sinn Féin and the IRA: unification with the Republic. Thus, the Troubles, which began during a broad civil rights movement, soon morphed into a larger ideological battle over British rule. Devlin's socialist politics and previously significant influence in the North was completely overrun by a new decade that was marked by a strident and militant masculine violence. Her dismissal from the dominant political discourse was further shown when Devlin was shut out of peace talks during the 1990s.

Another significant example can be seen in the Peace People, which was created in the late 1970s and run by Betty Williams, Mairead Corrigan Maguire, and Ciaran McKeown. The organization was a strong cross-community grassroots political movement that advocated for peace through education. Williams and Maguire organized many large-scale peace marches that united the Protestant and Catholic communities in a common cause, and they were awarded the Nobel Peace Prize in 1976. However, as the Troubles became dominated by sectarian violence, several of their marches were attacked and disrupted by paramilitary groups. By 1980, the organization, which had been lauded by the international community, withered under the pressures of an increasingly intolerant, violent, and militant political atmosphere, and their influence in the North diminished significantly.[28]

Furthermore, in 1996, Monica McWilliams and Pearl Sager created the NIWC in protest against female exclusion from the peace talks that would eventually lead to the Belfast/Good Friday Agreement. The NIWC made important strides, with several women elected to the Northern Ireland Forum and the Northern Ireland Assembly in 1996, 1998, and 2001. The organization was a significant step in the progress toward women's rights in the North, "manag[ing] to do something that had eluded the women's movement in Northern Ireland for many years: unite and organize around an identity as women."[29] However, an overt and entrenched sexism minimized the organization's impact. During the May 1996 elections, when the NIWC ran for and gained several seats, Peter Robinson of the Democratic Unionist Party infamously commented, "Women should leave politics and leadership alone." When McWilliams ran for elected office, she "was subjected to graffiti outside her office, instructing her to 'get back to the kitchen,' as well as more misogynous, objectionable drawings, including penises painted on posters near her home."[30] Furthermore, the strides that the NIWC made during the initial peace talks had limited effect: "While the NIWC won wording about ensuring greater representation for women in decision making in Northern Ireland, it was the British government that signed up to implement that statement of intent, and in the years following the agreement the influence of the British government waned once the devolved government was in place in Northern Ireland. Local politicians could, in turn, argue that they were not committed to any action in this regard."[31] By 2005, all the representatives of NIWC had lost their seats and the party officially disbanded in 2006. Although there have been strong, prominent women involved in the political processes in the North, their influence has often been undermined by a lingering prejudice that women should not be involved in high-level politics.

Just as women's participation in politics was limited during the Troubles, women are again being sidelined from direct and essential political engagement in the transition to peace. As Linda Connolly writes,

> Feminism, as both a set of political ideologies and mobilising social movement, is generally not considered as an integral element in resolving or upholding the conflict, in the dominant political discourse. In particular, prominent academic representations of the Peace Process tend to depict feminism as something consensual which (some) women "do" in isolation from the pivotal political processes at work—not as a transformational consciousness and heterogeneous movement which diffuses and mobilises across society, to some effect. "Doctrinal" interpretations of the Peace Process simplify feminist politics and occlude diversity and conflict both within and between different groups of women.[32]

Connolly maintains that feminism is typically not viewed in the North as a transformative ideology that can help improve relations across sectarian divisions for both men and women. Instead, it is regarded as a movement that addresses only individualized "women's issues." Simona Sharoni agrees: "The narrow definition of 'women's issues' has been used to justify women's exclusion from domains that men have sought to maintain as their own primary positions of social and political power."[33] This was demonstrated during the peace talks in the late 1990s when the NIWC "challenged a draftsperson as to why women were not mentioned in a central section of the agreement that dealt with human rights and the outworkings of the Troubles. The women's coalition was told that the conflict was between nationalism and unionism—what had that to do specifically with women?"[34] This historical dominance of a masculine militancy over the cultural and political landscape of the North has marginalized women and hindered the success of reconciliation during the peace process.[35]

Despite the limiting roles that women have often been allowed to play in the North, many have found creative ways to insert their voices into the public dialogue and to present alternate views for envisioning political and social change. In the theatre, there is a strong history of politically and socially active women who have harnessed the dramatic stage to cut through worn-out political rhetoric. Through the medium of drama, these women have injected their voices into a national dialogue and presented alternative ways of both viewing the past and envisioning a positive future.

In the years leading up to and directly after partition, Alice Milligan toured her nationalist *tableaux vivants* all over the island, becoming a central figure in the Irish Literary Revival and directly advocating for women's rights through her participation in the suffragette movement. During the 1940s and 1950s, Patricia O'Connor's plays for the Ulster Group Theatre advocated for women's independence and criticized the state on issues such as the broken educational system and antiquated land ownership traditions. O'Connor's work featured strong, independent female characters who often were single and employed outside of the home and who championed options for women outside of the roles of wife and mother. Mary O'Malley had a profound impact on the cultural and theatrical life of Belfast. During the 1950s and 1960s, she founded the Lyric Players Theatre along with *Threshold* (a literary and cultural magazine), an Irish craft shop, and a drama and music school that focused on training young people in the arts. The breadth and impact of her artistic contributions to the Northern Irish arts scene were enormous, transforming Belfast from an "arid cultural desert"[36] to a city with several burgeoning independent theatre companies.

During the 1980s and 1990s, the women-led theatre companies of Charabanc, DubbelJoint, and JustUs dramatized the development of the sectarian conflict in an attempt to show how historical and political conditions perpetuated violence and divisions. In their plays, women's strength and bonding were positioned as antidotes to the militarized masculinity of the conflict, and their plays argued that Northerners were capable of achieving the political and personal changes necessary to break the cycle of violence. These companies provided new jobs and training for women in the theatre, created a new audience base, and established a model of bringing artistic work into rural and working-class areas. In doing so, they, along with playwrights like Anne Devlin and Christina Reid, secured a new respect for women on the Irish stage.

Early twenty-first-century female playwrights continue a rich legacy of politically engaged and socially conscious playwriting that challenges normative views of the peace process. These plays often express frustration over the slow pace of change and cynicism that the state and Northern culture can transform for the better. In addition, as the North adapts economically, socially, and ethnically, these plays identify new problems such as growing class divisions, increasing drug and alcohol abuse, racism, poverty, lack of jobs and education, and the subtle pressure for women to resume traditional gender norms.

In opposition to essentialist identity categories, the plays examined in my research actively explore the intersecting and perpetuating ways that economic, religious, cultural, and material conditions affect the way that women are oppressed in the North, embracing the tenants of intersectionality theory, which argue that gender oppression alone cannot fully explain the complex and intertwining factors that work together to marginalize and subjugate women.

Presenting female characters as funny, sexual, powerful, and sometimes violent, Northern women playwrights have repeatedly shattered the trope of the devoted wife and the peace-loving mother. In doing so, these dramatists have created nuanced and realistic portraits of womanhood, imbued female characters with a powerful political voice on the public stage, and allowed audiences to see honest and realistic depictions of Northern women and their lives. Whereas female political activists have historically struggled to have a direct and lasting influence on Northern politics, women theatre practitioners have defied expectations by crossing sectarian and gender barriers and allowing women to enter into the political dialogue in creative ways. By looking at women's voices in Northern theatre over the past century, a compelling narrative develops that challenges mainstream views of the conflict and rails against an enduring gender inequality that has continued to restrict women's political and social positioning even into the present-day peace process.

2

Theatre and State Censorship

Northern drama has always had a fundamentally different relationship to its people and government than theatre within the Republic. Starting at the turn of the twentieth century, drama from the Republic was an important part of Irish culture and identity. It became indelibly linked to the fight for Irish Independence when W. B. Yeats, J. M. Synge, Lady Augusta Gregory, and others used drama as a powerful political tool of Irish nationalism. The historical importance of the Abbey, the elite standing of playwrights such as Sean O'Casey and Samuel Beckett, and the international success of Frank McGuinness, Conor McPherson, Martin McDonagh, Garry Hynes, and the Druid Theatre Company have earned the Republic an international reputation as a literary and artistic epicenter. Drama is a prestigious part of Irish society and is generally recognized as playing an important role in nationalism and in establishing a unified Irish cultural identity.

The North does not have this same deep historical relationship to theatre. Instead, Northern Ireland is typically known for its history as an industrial center for the linen and shipbuilding industries and for sectarian conflict. The strong connection between theatre and Irish nationalism in the south threatened many unionists in the North who historically have looked on drama with suspicion. Writing for the Ulster Literary Theatre magazine *Ulad* during the late nineteenth century, W. B. Reynolds remarked: "In Dublin, the project for a national theatre was bound to find many supporters . . . here we guard ourselves against new ideas as against a plague. The theatre is not recognized but merely tolerated and the idea that the stage may

39

afford a medium for the expression of national sentiment, as vital and as sincere as a great poem or a great picture, would be regarded by thousands as little short of blasphemy."[1] A century later, the Northern actress Eleanor Methven echoed these sentiments:

> In the Republic, writers were in the vanguard of a social and political movement, Yeats and O'Casey, so interest in theatre is a hangover from when writers were recognized as national heroes rather than just people living at the edges of socialism or whatever. It's a very different state here. How could you possibly have here a playwright who was a hero? Whose hero? Belfast has an industrial base, and it's been a Protestant base, and it's therefore been the state base. If you own the state, the last thing you want is theatre, which has been (and should be) both a tool of challenge and subversion. It's only very recently that there's been a kind of indigenous theatre. . . . It's a very, very different atmosphere here.[2]

Additional impediments to the status of theatre in the North include Protestant dismissal of art as primarily the domain of Catholics as well as practical concerns regarding the safety of theatregoers during the Troubles. Many theatres and entertainment venues were subjected to bomb threats, and venturing out at night was often a dangerous proposition. Furthermore, a history of state censorship and control over drama in the North has shaped citizens' relationship with theatre in ways that are fundamentally different from that of the Republic.

Although the early twentieth century afforded playwrights the opportunity to interrogate the increasing conflict and political tension in the North, this was quickly replaced with government intervention along with a pervasive societal pressure to avoid addressing contentious political matters. An early example of drama that was initially able to directly engage the political status of the state is St. John Ervine's pre-partition play *Mixed Marriage* (1911). It centers around two young labor activists, the Protestant Hugh and the Catholic Michael, who support factory workers in a strike for better working conditions. Hugh intends to marry a Catholic woman (Nora), but his father (John) opposes the match. When John reneges on his promise to rally the workers, the strike collapses into rioting, increasing sectarian tensions. Hugh's family becomes trapped inside their home as violence and unrest grow outside. Nora is ultimately shot and killed while fleeing the house. The play positions the domestic space as threatened by external sectarian violence, and it also employs the Romeo and Juliet trope; both themes would figure prominently in later classic Troubles plays. Other early dramas addressed sectarian tensions and life in the Belfast shipyards, such as Thomas Carnduff's *Machinery* (1933), Nora MacAdam's *Birth of a Giant* (1940), Joseph Tomelty's *The End House* (1944), and John Coulter's *The Drums Are Out* (1948); however, all were staged at the Abbey, reflecting both the limited venues for theatrical productions in Belfast and Northern discomfort with the themes of the plays.[3] The Belfast Repertory Theatre, which was in existence from 1929 until the late 1930s, is notable for staging the Belfast shipyard plays of Thomas Carnduff as well as plays that addressed sectarian tension, such as Hugh Quinn's *A Quiet Twelfth* (1937). The Ulster Literary Theatre (1902–40) also staged challenging plays that reflected the long history of sectarian strife in the North, including William Paul's *Sweeping the Country* (1912), Gerald Macnamara's *No Surrender* (1928), and William Liddell's *A Majority of One* (1934). However, the political subject matter of these earlier plays became stifled as the atmosphere during the 1940s and 1950s was increasingly characterized by state censorship over the arts.

A primary goal of the post-partition Northern government was to legitimize the North as separate from the Irish Free State and to reinforce its connection to the United Kingdom. Starting around the 1940s, theatre in the North was regulated by the Protestant-run government, which supported and advocated art that reflected a pro-unionist and pro-British ideology. In aid of this goal, the late 1940s and early 1950s saw the start of a national theatre initiative coinciding with Ulster Regionalism, a cultural movement that promoted and reinforced Protestant control in the North.

This was, in essence, a state-sponsored arts movement meant to legitimize partition and advocate a unionist ideology. Lionel Pilkington argues:

> Stormont's unprecedented enthusiasm for developing a state or
> regional theatre in Northern Ireland may also be explained in terms
> of the unionist government's incorporation of elements of the post-
> war cultural ideology of the British state. Middle-class culture, and
> especially the theatre, was regarded as an important means by which
> a regional identity might be fostered with the minimum of political
> dissent. . . . The attractiveness of a state theatre and of a canon of
> "Ulster" drama for a regionalist cultural policy was that it mani-
> fested Northern Ireland's political normality.[4]

Because theatre was state led and its primary goal was, as Pilkington
asserts, to normalize and legitimize Protestant rule over the newly
partitioned state, theatrical productions in the North during the
1940s and 1950s rarely addressed the sectarian conflict or represented
everyday Northern Irish life on stage. Instead, the state encouraged
the production of British classics as a way to reinforce the link between
the United Kingdom and the North and to assert unionist authority.

State control over the arts only increased as the nationalist community protested over civil rights violations during the 1950s and 1960s.
An example of this was the government's mandate that the British
national anthem, "God Save the Queen," be played before the start of
performances. The indignity of having to sit through the anthem and
the British subject matter of the plays alienated Catholic audiences.
Any art that engaged with sectarian politics or questioned the authority of the government was condemned and often censored. Whereas
British and American theatre of the 1960s and 1970s was feminist,
socialist, alternative, and experimental, the North had a staunchly
conservative and inward-turning culture that produced a very limited
range of Anglo-Irish and British dramas. This conservative repertoire
was aided by audience taste that leaned toward comedies, musicals,
thrillers, and commercial theatre, driving independent companies
like Belfast's Little Theatre (1932–37) and the Ulster Group Theatre
(1940–59) to abandon more literary and artistic aspirations for commercial offerings that aided their financial stability.[5] With the closure
of several performance halls, Roy Connolly reports that "by 1962,

there was no longer a venue for serious theatre in Northern Ireland."[6] To exacerbate the problem, the start of the Troubles in the late 1960s discouraged audiences from attending the theatre at night, and several performance venues were subjected to repeated bombs threats.[7] Most of the Belfast theatre companies shut down by 1971, leaving the Lyric Players the primary producing theatre company.

As a result, Belfast theatre in the 1960s and 1970s was primarily British imports. Touring productions from London were seen in Belfast, and English actors were shipped over to perform British classics, whose plots and characters reflected neither the class issues nor the sectarian problems that the city was experiencing on a daily basis. The Belfast playwright Marie Jones recounted of her girlhood and youth: "What little theatre there was in Belfast was all classics, drawing-room comedies and Yeats. People like me just didn't exist in plays."[8] A lack of funding for indigenous drama exacerbated the situation. In 1964, the Council for the Encouragement of Music and Arts (which allocated a small portion of its budget to theatre) rescinded a funding commitment to the Belfast-based Arts Theatre "after overspending on tours by a Scottish theatre company, a Spanish dance troupe and the Western Theatre Ballet."[9] This widespread notion that British and continental theatre was more prestigious and of higher quality than its Northern counterpart inhibited the funding and development of an indigenous theatre tradition for decades.

During this same period, as part of a larger attempt to curb the proliferation of public unrest in the North, the government repressed media coverage of civil rights protests and sectarian violence as well as any art that engaged with these issues. "Whereas by 1967," Pilkington observes, "the modernization of Ireland in the late 1950s and 1960s had culminated in an unprecedented liberalization of Ireland's literary and film censorship laws, the early 1970s [in the North] witnessed the reintroduction of an array of draconian censorship legislation to deal with the effects of the conflict in Northern Ireland."[10] In the decades leading up to this reinforcement of censorship, a few significant theatre practitioners had made early attempts to free Northern theatre from state regulation. The foundation for Belfast's largest professional producing house, the Lyric Theatre, was started in 1951 when Mary and Pearce O'Malley founded the amateur Lyric Players Group. The Lyric Players was established in part as an antidote to the commercial theatre that dominated Belfast by providing a high-quality literary theatre that emphasized the poetry and lyricism of the written word. The O'Malleys were greatly influenced by the socialist and nationalist New Theatre Group in Dublin and aimed to create an independent theatre in the North free from government or sectarian agendas. The Lyric Players' mission sought "a pluralist, nondiscriminatory state in which nationalist self-expression could freely exist."[11] The largely apolitical substance of its productions allowed the theatre to operate for years without much government intervention. In 1968, the Lyric Players became professional, marking its later rise as the most important full-time professional producing house in the North.

Along with the development of a theatre group devoted to non-government-controlled art, several plays began to address the sectarian conflict head-on. In 1960, the Ulster Group Theatre's board of directors refused to produce Sam Thompson's *Over the Bridge* because it exposed how class divisions and sectarian prejudices were rampant in the shipyards. The artistic director James Ellis resigned from the theatre and successfully mounted a production independently, which was seen by more than forty-six thousand audience members in its first six weeks.[12] The next major play to address the sectarian conflict was John Boyd's *The Flats* (1971), which is considered to be the first play to engage directly with the Troubles. It follows a single day in the life of the Catholic working-class Donnellan family as they attempt to live and survive amid the conflict. The play charts the increasing violence between the loyalist Shankill Defense Association and the nationalist Citizen's Defense Committee. It is also notable for exploring how violence and politics increasingly encroach on the domestic space as the conflict begins to dominate the Donnellans' family life.[13]

Scholars consider *The Flats* to be the start of the classic Troubles play, which is characterized by its use of reductive plots that ultimately fail to address the larger sociopolitical issues surrounding the conflict. A typical (now rehashed) storyline often involved a Protestant boy who falls in love with a Catholic girl, and violence ensues. Christopher Morash describes Troubles drama as typically set in an interior, domestic space (often a kitchen) and revolving around the tragedy suffered by a family as the result of sectarian violence. Typically, an off-stage riot takes the life of an innocent family member, often a young woman. Morash sums up the standard formula of early Troubles plays as "one family, one day, one death." The primary conflict in these plays "is between the onstage world of the family, and the unseen off-stage world, a realm of mindless violence where death can come from an anonymous mob or a hidden sniper." Morash goes on to argue that the classic Troubles play presents the family as apolitical innocents and portrays sectarian violence as "mindless and unmotivated."[14] Thus Troubles violence was shown in early plays to be a senseless and incomprehensible phenomenon rather than the product of decades of increasing tension and conflict between Catholics and Protestants. By severing the connection between sectarian violence and its historical and economic roots, early Troubles plays failed to effectively engage the political situation in the North. Field Day was founded in 1980 in part to correct this disturbing disconnect between economic and historic realities and their representations on stage. Likewise, Charabanc and DubbelJoint spent significant time dramatizing the history of the conflict in order to demonstrate the connection between Troubles violence and real material circumstances.

Slowly, the 1970s brought an increase in plays that began to directly address the sectarian conflict and the developing violence of the Troubles. The Lyric produced multiple Troubles plays during this period, including John Haire's *Between the Two Shadows* (1972/73 season), Patrick Galvin's *Nightfall to Belfast* (1973/74 season), and Stewart Parker's *Catchpenny Twist* (1977).[15] In 1975, John Arden and the Northern Irish actress and playwright Margaretta D'Arcy performed *The Non-Stop Connolly Show*.[16] The play, with a cast of over thirty actors, dramatized the life of the Irish socialist leader John Connolly and took twenty-four hours to perform. Despite new representations of the Troubles, the conflict, and Catholic life on stage, these plays invariably revolved around *male* experiences of the conflict and rarely showed women outside of the supporting roles of wife and mother. As Mary Trotter writes, early Troubles plays "made the domestic space an apolitical sphere, with women as victims but not participants in the ideological struggle surrounding them."[17]

The 1970s, however, also brought an important new mandate from the Arts Council of Northern Ireland (ACNI), which would play an instrumental role in allowing women to emerge as artistic leaders during the 1980s. Up until the mid-1970s, the Arts Council (endowed by the British government) had rarely supported local theatre, adhering to the philosophy that the more "sophisticated" and "cultured" arts coming from England and the Continent could better enrich and cultivate the North.[18] However, the importance of the independent and community theatre movements in England during the 1960s and 1970s led ACNI to adopt funding strategies similar to those being enacted in Britain. This led to a new investment in independent and community theatre in the North. Previously, only commercial and established theatres like the Lyric had received significant funding from the government. This new funding scheme, which targeted community groups, allowed the playwright Martin Lynch to found the extremely influential Turf Lodge Fellowship Community Theatre in Belfast in 1976. Other groups such as the Playzone Community Theatre (1977–79) were also started with this funding.[19] Playzone, which was committed to social change, brought theatre into deprived areas, performed in schools, retirement homes, and community centers, and employed many women actors and writers. Although in existence for only two years, it was an important reflection of a radical change in funding structures for the arts and provided new job opportunities for women in the theatre. Both Turf Lodge and Playzone would ultimately serve as inspirations for the Charabanc Theatre Company,[20] and particularly for Marie Jones, who was an original member of Playzone.

The impact of the growing community arts sector in the late 1970s encouraged the ACNI to begin funding independent regional companies in the 1980s. These theatres, which were often outgrowths of the amateur and community theatre sector, allowed some professional companies to develop outside of Belfast. One of the most significant examples of this funded growth was the Field Day Theatre Company, founded by Brian Friel and the actor Stephen Rae. Field Day produced several new plays that are now central to the Irish canon, including Friel's *Translations* (1980), Thomas Kilroy's *Double Cross* (1986), and Stewart Parker's *Pentecost* (1987). As other independent companies like Playzone, the New Writers Theatre, Belfast Actors Co-op, and Stage '80 became more established,[21] they created greater opportunities and platforms for new playwriting and acting, and the ACNI responded by funding more theatre training and workshops. In 1988, five independent theatre companies appeared, all founded by graduates of Queens University and the University of Ulster: Big Telly, Tinderbox, Replay, The Great Pretenders, and Point Fields.[22] In part because playwriting had historically been a male-dominated profession throughout the island (North and south), few women had viewed it as a potential career. However, with the proliferation of community and independent theatres, stronger funding schemes, and the movement of theatre from Belfast into regional areas, more women were encouraged to participate in professional drama and to view theatre as a potential career.

Despite significant advances in the community and independent arts sectors along with the slow but persistent development of an indigenous drama, there remained only three professional centers for theatre in Belfast during the 1980s: the Grand Opera House, the Belfast Civic Arts Centre, and the Lyric. All three were controlled by male boards and still primarily staged British classics and imported productions from London and the Continent. Things were especially bad for Northern actresses when Leon Rubin took over as artistic director of the Lyric (1981–83). Under his leadership, the theatre rarely employed Northern actresses; instead, Rubin imported English actresses to say three or four lines in an entire show. This discrimination against Northern actors, particularly women, stemmed from bigotry within British theatre that Northern actors were not as professional or as highly trained as their English counterparts. It also derived from prejudice against having working-class Northern bodies and accents on stage, which were considered too rough to appear in elite British classics. In 1973, the playwright John Boyd remarked:

> So we in Ireland—the country of Yeats and Shaw, O'Casey and Synge, the Abbey Theatre in Dublin and the Lyric in Belfast—have little to congratulate ourselves on. Few theatres; a dearth of first class directors; unemployed actors in Dublin; a scarcity of actors in Belfast; middle class audience (in the main) that relish the ready laugh, the unthinking, "unfeeling" immediate response; managements unwilling to experiment, being too timid (a timidity born perhaps from poverty and the fear it engenders): these are some of our handicaps.[23]

Limited theatre work, government censorship, narrow representations of women, inadequate depictions of working-class life, and few plays from a women's perspective were the norm within Northern theatre throughout the 1950s, 1960s, and 1970s. It was into this vacuum that Christina Reid, Anne Devlin, Marie Jones, and Jennifer Johnston defiantly pushed themselves, creating complex and realistic representations of the challenges that women in the North endured on a daily basis. Refocusing the standard Troubles play told from a masculine perspective, these playwrights reset the conflict as experienced through the eyes of women. Their plays addressed the complex interplay between gender roles, politics, sexuality, domestic violence, marriage, motherhood, feminism, and sectarian divisions. Christina Reid's *Tea in a China Cup* (1983) followed three generations of Protestant women as they negotiated female identity and domestic space within the violent clashes of the annual July 12 parades.[24] Anne Devlin's *Ourselves Alone* (1985) followed three sisters from a prominent IRA family as they dealt with jailed husbands, political obligations to a patriarch, romance, and dreams for a better life. Jennifer Johnston wrote a series of monologues addressing the Troubles: *Twinkletoes* (1993) explores the inner life of a top IRA prisoner's wife who struggles between her commitment to her jailed husband and her desire to live a full and free life, whereas *Christine* (1989) follows a wife whose husband is killed by the IRA, leaving her childless and alienated from her community.

In these new plays, women were no longer positioned in supporting roles. Instead, these "dutiful wives" and "patient, peace-loving mothers" became the protagonists. Moreover, these tired tropes of womanhood were subverted as female characters were portrayed as complex, fully rounded women who felt constant pressure to both fulfill and rebel against gender norms in the North.

Whenever scholarship addresses women's playwriting in the North, it almost exclusively points to the 1980s as the one period of great theatrical output for women. People inevitably reference Reid, Devlin, and Jones as examples of this phenomenon. However, women's contributions to the development of an indigenous Northern theatre began during the early twentieth century with Alice Milligan's feminist and nationalist drama and continued into the mid-twentieth century with the plays of Patricia O'Connor and the artistic direction of Mary O'Malley. This untold story of early Northern women's political engagement through the theatre establishes a strong early legacy of women using theatre as a tool for political and social change.

3

Raising the Curtain

Alice Milligan, Patricia O'Connor, and Mary O'Malley

The post-partition period leading up to the mid-twentieth century was a time of great transition for the North. Pressure to legitimize the new state and shore up Protestant power weighed heavily on the local government and British Parliament. Incendiary topics like sectarianism, segregation, and unemployment dominated public debates. Unionist political power was reinforced through gerrymandering, and a Protestant-controlled media and government worked to diminish Catholic voices and influence. During this early period, there were only a handful of local theatre companies based in Belfast. Most theatre productions were shipped in from Britain and the Continent. The commercial imports from Europe were primarily comedies, musicals, and European classics, and the locally produced work generally avoided politically charged topics or criticisms of the state. Within this conservative and politically charged environment, early women theatre practitioners found success as actresses, directors, producers, and (less frequently) as playwrights, helping to grow and diversify the North's limited range of dramatic offerings.

Nita Hardie was a producer, director, actress, and founding member of the Ulster Group Theatre (UGT). Though the UGT (1940–59) also performed Irish and international classics, it became primarily known for premiering new indigenous playwriting. The theatre had a close-knit group of well-known actors and actresses who served in a repertory capacity and became known for their naturalistic acting style and ensemble performances. The company supported the theatrical careers of several prominent women during the first half of the twentieth century and became an important center for women's voices and bodies on stage. Hardie directed six productions in UGT's first year and acted in nine within the company's first two years.[1] She proved herself as a principal member of UGT and was a significant leader in Northern Irish theatre during the 1930s and 1940s. The celebrated actress Elizabeth Begley (1907–1993) appeared in ninety-two productions for UGT between 1940 and 1960, having one of the longest relationships with the company.[2] She was considered the leading lady of Northern Irish theatre and commanded central billing in all the productions in which she appeared. Significantly, Begley also directed and starred in *In Donegall Square* for the UGT in 1953. The play (adapted from *Nine till Six* by Aimee and Philip Stewart, 1930) consisted of an all-female cast and took place in a Belfast gown shop. It explored the world of women's working lives, class dynamics, relationships between employers and the employed, and the social positioning of working women.

Anna McClure Warnock wrote and performed radio dramas and short comedic plays that she coined "Ulsterlettes" for community theatre festivals as well as for the UGT. Her play *Dinsmore's Cash* was staged by the UGT in 1948, and several of her short plays and skits were published by the Educational Company in Belfast: *The Wee Stones and New Ulster Playlets* (1946), *The Way of the Woman and Other Ulster Sketches* (1950), *Ulster Playlets/Ulsterettes* (1950), and *More Ulster Playlets* (1950). In 1940, *The Northern Wig and Belfast Post* featured an article highlighting Warnock's work as a significant contribution to the burgeoning Northern Irish theatre scene, noting that her writing "is of a quality that definitely augurs more notable achievements in the future," describing it as full of "rich, racy humor, and coloured by an evidently intimate knowledge of the Ulster character."[3]

Several more actresses made names for themselves within the early Northern theatre scene. The performer Beatrice Duffell was a founding member of the UGT. Margaret D'Arcy was part of the UGT's ensemble cast and rivaled Elizabeth Begley as one of the best actresses in the North. In addition, Doreen Hepburn, Barbara Adair,

and Catherine Gibson appeared regularly in UGT productions. Hilda
Taggart remained the leading speech and drama teacher in the North
for more than forty years. Several other women also cofounded some
of Belfast's first local theatre companies. Dorothy Wilmotin and her
husband, Hubert, founded the Belfast Arts Theatre in the 1940s. It
played a variety of American and British classics and was the first amateur theatre in Belfast to become professional. It eventually morphed
into Interplay in the 1970s, specializing in touring productions to
schools.[4] Doris Richmond, her husband L. Griffith-Knight, and Nicholas O'Donnell Grimshaw founded the Little Theatre (1932–37).[5] The
company specialized in large casts and produced Christa Winsloe's
Children in Uniform with an all-female cast of twenty-nine actresses.[6]

In addition to many actresses playing important roles in the development and formation of an indigenous Northern theatre, several
practitioners strategically used art and culture to insert women's voices
and bodies into the public sphere and to advocate for women's rights.
In particular, Alice Milligan (1866–1953), Patricia O'Connor (1905–
1983), and Mary O'Malley (1918–2004) are significant for their political and cultural impact on the state. In the years leading up to and
directly following partition, Milligan used the stage to advocate for
social change and women's rights, performing nationalist and feminist
theatre. During the 1940s and 1950s, O'Connor was the single most
produced female playwright in the North. Her work advocated for
social and educational reforms, and for women's autonomy over their
marital options and careers. Finally, the 1950s, 1960s, and 1970s were
dominated by the powerhouse producer and director Mary O'Malley
of the influential Lyric Players Theatre. Reflecting the ideals of the
Irish Literary Revival, O'Malley believed strongly in the power of art
and culture to transform society and to engender a uniting sense of
Irish ethnic identity. In the North, where formal politics is a form
of entrenched warfare, Milligan, O'Connor, and O'Malley strategically used drama to advocate for social change and critique the state.
These women were civically active through various forms of participation such as holding public office, publishing political writings, and
being active members of political and cultural organizations. Each

ultimately turned to the theatre as the most productive and direct way
to have her voice heard amidst the din of political rancor, and their
work establishes a strong early legacy of Northern women harnessing
the theatre as a political tool to envision social and civic change.

Recently the scholarship of Catherine Morris, Mark Phelan, and
Scott Boltwood has started to recover the lost history of early women
theatre practitioners in the North. In particular, Morris's work on
Alice Milligan has brought to light the significant contributions of the
prominent playwright, actress, and choreographer. Milligan was an
important political figure in the late nineteenth and early twentieth-
century Irish Literary Revival in the North. In the southern Revival,
nationalists used Irish history, culture, and art as a way to promote a
cohesive Irish ethnic identity and to combat the effects of British colonialism. Correspondingly, the Northern Revival was "marked by the
search for a counter-narrative to that of the emergent Ulster-centric
unionism."[7] Tension between Catholics and Protestants was at a high
leading up to partition in 1921, and the Northern Revival was an
attempt to insert a nationalist narrative into an increasingly polarized
and repressive unionist culture. As a Northern Protestant, Milligan
was unusual in her championing of the nationalist and suffragette
agendas. Her activism was expressed in part through a multitude of
prominent political and cultural memberships. She was a founder of
the Ulster Anti-Partition Council and a member of the Irish Academy
of Letters. Her commitment to women's liberation was demonstrated
through her outspoken support of the suffragette movement as well as
through her leadership in several politically engaged women's groups:
as a founder of the Irish Women's Association (1894) and as a member
of the Irish Women's Centenary Union (1897).

Milligan was prolific and diverse in her civic activism: she wrote
political pamphlets, gave activist lectures, founded two literary journals, wrote plays, and produced nationalist theatre in the form of *tableaux*.[8] In her articles, which were published in local, national, and
international newspapers and journals, Milligan addressed a wide range
of pertinent political and social issues such as "land wars, evictions,
the 1641 massacres, the seventeenth-century plantations, emotional

dispossession, the denial of language and native cultural identity, state executions, imprisonment, escapes and rebellions, war and Partition."[9] She also used local newspapers to publish her short plays, as this was an inexpensive and efficient way to encourage community theatre groups to produce her nationalist work.[10] It also allowed non-theatregoing patrons to read her dramatic work, ensuring greater dissemination of her ideas. Overall, Milligan was published in more than sixty newspapers and journals, making her one of the most influential and prolific voices in the Irish Literary Revival.[11]

Shan Van Vocht, which Milligan founded in 1896 with Ethna Carbery, was a nationalist literary journal. It published a range of political writings in an effort to encourage women's civic participation. Mark Phelan recounts: "Through their journal, they sought to engage more women in politics and, indeed, many *Shan Van Vocht* editorials appeal for solidarity in the face of bitter political division and call for 'the women of Ireland' to come forth so unity could be facilitated."[12] Supporting this feminist interpretation, Catherine Morris describes the journal as "giving space to the marginalized voices of women, of people who expressed new opinions, of those who were not represented in the official narratives of the state."[13] Milligan used her varied cultural and artistic projects to spark conversation regarding issues of women's liberation: "From 1891, every organisation she founded and every cultural event she organised caused a stir of controversy from many quarters. She exposed the gender discrimination she often encountered (even from committees that she had been democratically elected to serve on) in the international cultural journal [*Shan Van Vocht*] that she founded."[14]

Milligan's early feminist advocacy was matched by her passion for nationalism. In addition to the political pamphlets, novella, and articles, eleven of her nationalist plays were produced by the Ulster Literary Theatre, the Irish Literary Theatre, and the Gaelic League. Several of her plays were translated into Irish, and her productions often directly addressed important historical and political events,[15] including the 1798 uprising by the United Irishmen.[16] Perhaps her greatest contribution to Irish drama was through her nationalist *tableaux vivants*, which she wrote, acted, and choreographed. These plays often displayed scenes from Irish mythology, drawing parallels between ancient Irish history, folklore, and current politics. Given the variety of mediums and political memberships through which to express her opinions, it is significant that Milligan spent a substantial amount of her energy writing, producing, and touring nationalist theatre. She firmly believed that theatre should be harnessed to advocate for direct political change, and she "argued in 1893 that Irish art should exist 'not in some quiet paradise apart' but within the 'noisy field of political warfare.'"[17]

Milligan used her *tableaux vivants* strategically, as a platform for women's empowerment. She partnered with several feminist organizations, including Maud Gonne's Inghinidhe na hÉireann (Daughters of Ireland) and the Irish Women's Association, to perform feminist *tableaux* that depicted Ireland as a shackled, constrained woman. This familiar representation of the island fettered by British colonialism was "textured with a contemporary feminist depiction of the undemocratic treatment of Irish women in society."[18] Milligan's early advocacy on behalf of women was recognized by her female contemporaries. Catherine Morris reports that the "importance of Milligan's attempts to find a voice for women throughout the Revival was acknowledged in 1919 by poet Susan Mitchell. . . . Arguing that Alice Milligan exemplified the struggle of Irish women, Mitchell portrayed her as a dynamic force that helped shaped new political and cultural conceptions of the Irish nation."[19]

Starting in the 1890s, Milligan's *tableaux vivants* toured extensively throughout Ireland, arguably making her the most prolific and successful theatre producer on the island before the start of the Abbey Theatre. *Tableaux vivants* reflect a style of performance in which actors freeze, forming a visually stunning and symbolic stage picture while a narrator explains the plot (often underscored by music). The form was extremely popular in Europe and the United States between 1830 and 1920 and was often used as a form of political protest. The visually impressive scenes, emotional music, and strong narrative voice leant strength, gravitas, and emotion to political causes and also rallied audiences to the larger fight. In her *tableaux*, Milligan used stories from "melodrama, the nationalist presses, songs, stories, contemporary political protests, legends or social life."[20] She staged her productions in schools, community halls, fields, and on the streets; the surrounding communities often helped with costumes, props, and audience seating. Milligan used native Irish actors and community members on stage, and her *tableaux* were often narrated in both English and Gaelic. She occasionally invited well-known politicians or community leaders to enter the *tableaux* and make nationalist speeches as part of the theatrical experience, thus creating a direct connection between the active, ongoing debate regarding nationalism and the theatrical representation of it. Morris argues that Milligan "devised a theatre movement in which people themselves embodied the pictures that they projected back into their own communities."[21] By using local citizens and politicians in her plays, the community personified the dramatic images that they staged, becoming politically active through theatrical participation. *Tableaux* already had strong political resonance in Ireland, as it was a "theatrical form that had developed out of state censorship of spoken language in drama."[22] Morris explains:

> At issue in the debates about native language and national theatre in the Revival period was the question of who had the right to speak for the Irish nation and how that nation could be spoken for. For Milligan, the Gaelic League wasn't just about reinstating the Irish language: it was about creating the cultural conditions that would give that language meaning. In this anti-colonial context of protest and solidarity, tableaux were a symbol of the body awaiting speech. At the turn of the century these living picture shows were crucial for the huge numbers of people who didn't have Irish but who wanted to participate in the formation of 'national' theatre.[23]

Thus Milligan's *tableaux*, which offered visual representation and dual narration in Irish and English, provided both Catholic and Protestant audience members without Irish-language skills the opportunity to connect to a more inclusive sense of Irish identity.[24] Milligan was particularly focused on convincing Northern Protestants that the Irish Revival was an inclusive cultural movement and that Protestants could have a positive future within nationalism.[25]

Like the founders of the Abbey Theatre, Milligan was deeply committed to creating a national theatre initiative. However, instead of a single building based in Dublin, she envisioned a large-scale cultural enterprise involving island-wide literary and political organizations helping to produce and tour shows celebrating Irish identity. Milligan hoped to bring theatre across the island, especially into rural communities and areas without dedicated theatre houses. She eschewed elaborate scenery and costumes, preferring makeshift sets constructed by locals. These sets were cheaper, toured more easily, and also reflected the material conditions and labor of the communities in which they performed. She even proposed a traveling collection of play scripts, props, scenery, and costumes that community theatre groups throughout the island could employ. This commitment to bringing theatre into communities without access to the arts would also become a strong focus for women-led theatre groups in the 1980s and 1990s, and Milligan's agit-prop performance style and rough minimalist aesthetic would also be replicated by many women practitioners in the years to come. Furthermore, Milligan's goal of connecting the community to its shared political history through the theatre would become a hallmark of the Charabanc, Dubbel-Joint, and JustUs theatre companies almost a century later. For Milligan, "staging the nation at the most local level was . . . the greatest step towards forging a community that could create an independent nation state."[26] This sentiment would be echoed in the work of the women theatre practitioners who were her beneficiaries throughout the twentieth century.

Milligan's influence on the Irish Cultural Revival, on Irish nationalism, and on drama was significant. Mark Phelan argues that her work deeply affected Yeats, influencing his own style and aesthetic,[27] and Eugene McNulty names her as "*the* key figure in northern cultural nationalism throughout the 1890s."[28] McNulty further argues that she "profoundly inspired those involved in setting up a nationalist theatre for Ulster" and "established many of the imaginative frames of reference within which the Ulster Literary Theatre would later operate."[29] As an ardent cultural revivalist, Milligan understood how theatre could be used as a political tool to cut through the increasingly deafening rhetoric between unionism and nationalism in the years leading up to partition. Moreover, she is an important early figure in establishing a history of politically engaged Northern women using art and culture as a means through which to express political and social change.

Despite several women in leadership roles as directors and producers during the early years of the Northern state, few female playwrights had their work produced on the professional Northern stage in the first fifty years after partition. Although women wrote for the community theatre scene and local drama clubs, few female dramatists had more than a single play staged in professional theatres. Though Helen Waddell (*The Spoilt Buddha*, Ulster Literary Theatre, 1915), Janet McNeil (*Signs and Wonders*, UGT, 1951), Elsna Hebe (*The Season's Greetings*, UGT, 1957), and Joan Sadler (*The Mustard Seed*, UGT, 1957) all had shows produced with leading theatre companies, few had a second play staged. An important exception was Patricia O'Connor, who wrote extensively for the Ulster Group Theatre. O'Connor's work is distinct for being one of the few female voices on the early Northern Irish stage, for its clear feminist impulses, and for the politically engaged nature of its subject matter.

O'Connor (1905–1983) was born in County Donegal, Republic of Ireland, but moved to the east coast of Northern Ireland, where she was principal teacher at the Viscount Bangor Primary School in Killough, County Down.[30] She became involved in the Ulster Group Theatre shortly after its founding in 1940. The UGT produced at least seven of O'Connor's plays, many of which critiqued the government as well as women's sociopolitical standing in the North.

In 1959, the UGT directors issued a statement saying that it was their policy to keep "political and religious controversies off [the] stage."[31] However, Scott Boltwood has challenged this claim, arguing that many of the company's productions addressed political controversies in both understated and direct ways, especially in plays by O'Connor.[32] In fact, O'Connor's writing proved to be a perfect fit for the theatre, since her drama critically addressed contemporary social problems without a sectarian agenda. Her plays explored issues that affected all Northern citizens: state education standards and overcrowding in schools, marital options for women, emigration, religious hypocrisy, and more. Between 1942 and 1959, the UGT staged *Highly Efficient* (1942), *Voice out of Rama* (1944), *Select Vestry* (1945), *Master Adams* (1949), *The Farmer Wants a Wife* (1955), *Who Saw Her Die?* (1955/56), and *The Sparrow's Fall* (1959). As a schoolteacher and passionate education activist, several of O'Connor's plays starred teachers (as both heroic and flawed individuals) and addressed the damage that outdated and conservative educational standards were causing on the Northern school system. *Canvassing Disqualifies* (1948), *The Sparrow's Fall*, *Voice out of Rama*, and *Highly Efficient* all feature female schoolteachers, whereas *Master Adams* centers around a male schoolmaster.

Highly Efficient (1942) was O'Connor's most successful play for the UGT.[33] It is considered to be the first play to explore the Northern educational system and is notable for being highly critical of state educational standards and policies during a time when censorship over arts and culture was strong. It is also significant in being one of the first post-partition plays to critique the state. The UGT actor John Keyes argues that *"Highly Efficient* was, perhaps, the first Belfast play which used the theatre as a forum for the discussion of public issues. The old Irish drama had dealt with conflict within the family and community usually arising out of land or money. Now politics had become a legitimate concern for the theatre. In Northern Ireland alarm bells sounded."[34]

Highly Efficient features a young and idealistic new teacher, Margaret Henderson, who is the sole instructor at an overcrowded Protestant school in a small village. She is the first Catholic teacher at the school and must pass the state inspection standards for new instructors before she receives her teaching diploma. The plot centers on Margaret's struggle to reconcile her own personal beliefs about education with the strict statewide standards set by the school inspectors. Margaret enthusiastically offers extra tutoring support to fifteen-year-old Mary. Margaret hopes the young student can pass the post-office exam and get a job in civil service rather than becoming a maid like her mother. Despite her parents' misgivings at allowing their daughter to pursue a professional career, Mary passes the exam and receives a job at the post office. However, she is later found to have helped a friend cheat on a scholarship application and is fired, rejoining a life of servitude in the small parochial town. Margaret's desire to expand Mary's options in life is questioned by the townspeople as naïve, misled, and elitist. Teachers, parents, and school board members argue over opposing views on the educational system, teaching standards, school conditions, and the responsibility of education to create upward mobility for the poor and working classes.

The play is set in the fictional town of Ballydim, the name suggesting the parochial and often dim-witted residents who make up the population. Margaret Henderson, as the play's heroine, rails against the poor state educational standards she is expected to follow. Her bright-eyed enthusiasm and naïveté is juxtaposed with two other strong female characters: Mrs. Davidson (Mary's mother) and Miss Burke (a more experienced teacher from the town's Catholic school). Mrs. Davidson is described as "broad, tidy and Presbyterian." This is in stark contrast to Margaret, who is "nice-looking, but inclined to be untidy and frail-looking."[35] Unlike Margaret, who is a single professional woman, Mrs. Davidson performs the traditional roles of wife and mother. She also has a very conservative view of the life she wants for her daughter. As members of the working class, Mr. and Mrs. Davidson are extremely aware of their place in the social order and expect their daughter to accept her limited position in the world by taking the same job as a maid that Mrs. Davidson had when she was young. She tells her daughter, "The Manse's the best place in the village for a Presbyterian girl—good food and the very best o'training" (8). She sees Mary's attempts to rise above the "natural" social order as "flying in the face o'Providence" (10), and she remarks that her husband is "dead set against folk as are aye trying to be a wee thing better nor their own ones" (11). Mrs. Davidson's conservative views about her daughter's future are primarily influenced by her husband, and she often parrots back his misgivings. However, after hearing Margaret's arguments on the social mobility that education can provide, Mrs. Davidson's views start to shift and she eventually supports her daughter's efforts at obtaining the post-office job. Although Mrs. Davidson chose a traditional path for her life, she begins to envision the freedom and opportunity that a civil job would afford her daughter and, by association, the larger family. This implicit feminist argument is reinforced in the play through the championing of teachers to enact change within society. Mark Phelan considers *Highly Efficient* "all the more interesting when one considers it in the context of the Irish theatre canon, constructed as it is from the extraordinary efflorescence of plays that self-consciously address the state of the nation, whilst ignoring the state of the State. *Highly Efficient* is perhaps the first play to critique the failure of a key structure of the new Northern state, and it is all the more significant that her attack is anti-patriarchal, not anti-partitionist in nature."[36] This feminist slant is consistent throughout O'Connor's work. She repeatedly identifies patriarchy and conservative social norms reinforced by state institutions and laws as the primary source of subjugation for Northern women, Catholic and Protestant.

In contrast to Margaret's bright-eyed enthusiasm, Miss Burke is described as having a "sharp" face and "a brisk, decisive way of speaking. She is not unpleasant, she is not pretty, and she narrowly misses being smart. She looks exactly like a wide-awake teacher of thirty-three" (19). Miss Burke serves as a mentor and guide to Margaret, showing the naïve young teacher how to temper her own educational views with the standards she will have to meet in order to receive her diploma. Miss Burke, who is considered an old maid at the age of thirty-three, does not possess Margaret's enthusiasm for teaching. She does it in order to support herself and because it is a respectable profession for a single woman. She has long since reconciled her own passions with the realities of working within a state-run institution. This practical cynicism is contrasted with the idealism of Margaret, who eagerly proclaims that teaching is "the most important work in the whole world. If I weren't sure of that I couldn't bear it" (14).

Throughout the play, Miss Burke helps Margaret reign in her enthusiasm and liberal teaching methods in order to effect change within the confines of the state system. Burke advises Margaret to "put all your high falutin' theories out of your head until you get your hands on that diploma. . . . That you don't believe in corporal punishment, and you do believe that children should be happy in school, and teachers should be paragons of gentle patience, and inspectors should be models of courteous justice. Forget it. Every probationer who comes out thinks the whole system's rotten—the rest of us *know* it is" (25). The two teachers debate the often contradictory and uncoordinated reports from the state inspectors who visit the school every few months. The male inspectors are often woefully undereducated and have never taught in a school, making them uniquely unqualified to pass judgment or enforce teaching standards on the female teachers. The misogyny of some reports is revealed as certain inspectors criticize not only classroom organization and teaching style but also the dress and voice of the female teachers. Miss Burke knows the inspection is just an artificial measure that does not truly reflect the quality of the school or teaching. She advises Margaret: "You won't be allowed to be yourself, you won't be allowed to be honest, you'll have to accept the views of every inspector who turns up" (28). Indeed, the underfunded, overcrowded school system in the North is in such crisis that perfunctory school inspections cannot begin to fix systemic problems. Miss Burke exclaims: "Trying to get a diploma in one of these one-horse schools is preposterous. An inexperienced girl can't teach over thirty children at eight different stages, the inspector knows that" (26).

The decade leading up to the play's first production had seen a series of failed reforms in the Northern educational system. Between 1936 and 1937, a new controversial system of teacher evaluation was introduced with financial penalties for those who performed poorly. In addition, 1941 saw more than thirty thousand school children from Belfast and the immediate environs evacuated to the countryside owing to bomb threats during World War II. This caused overcrowding in rural schools, placing teachers under increasing pressure and in difficult teaching environments. Many schools, such as the one O'Connor writes about, had a single instructor charged with teaching dozens of students from a wide range of ages. Through *Highly Efficient*, O'Connor propelled her own voice into an ongoing national debate on school models and educational reform.

O'Connor's central argument in the play is articulated during a debate between Margaret and the school board. Margaret has asked the board for money to provide new desks and ink pots and to lessen overcrowding. A member of the board councils Margaret that her singular focus on improving the lives of her students is misguided: "Teachers take themselves far too seriously, and no one else does. Don't think about the school—at three o'clock put it clean out of your mind. Ballydim is just a backward country place. The school isn't an Eton or Harrow. Most of the boys will be labourers and most of the girls will go into service" (73). Appalled, Margaret angrily replies: "Are you trying to tell me that public elementary education is an attitude of mind inflicted on the poor with the backing of the law. . . . And the only escape is to be able to afford to pay the fees demanded by Eton or Methody or Blackrock College? Are we training three-quarters of our children to be servants for the other quarter?" (73). Margaret's progressive belief in the ability of education to lift families out of poverty and provide social mobility is juxtaposed by the village townspeople who see schooling as a way to provide children with basic reading and writing skills before releasing them to their inevitable futures as farm hands and maids. This conflict about the value, goals, and purpose of education in the North becomes the central debate of the play. Mary's father views education as distracting children from their predetermined roles in life and criticizes it for creating a society of overeducated professionals who lack real-world skills. While "*wav[ing] both arms, indicating all the maps and anything else of an educational purpose in sight*," he furiously tells Margaret: "'Tis the ruination of the country. What's it done for me? . . . There's no a dacent hard-working fellow left in the country. . . . They're all gentry these days—thon's what education's done for us" (84). This senti-ment is echoed by the Presbyterian clergyman Mr. McFee, who gently advises Margaret: "I feel your motive was entirely altruistic. . . . You decided entirely on your own authority and from your own youthful inexperience that Mary would be happier and better off in a position and sphere of life for which she . . . was . . . er . . . *not intended*. You used your influence over Mary . . . to instill into her mind an ambi-tion, *a foolish* ambition, to which her parents were opposed. . . . You may have unfitted this pupil of yourself for the type of . . . er, employ-ment to which she would have naturally turned" (89–90). Whereas the town residents see their options in life as inevitably restricted to a predetermined socioeconomic hierarchy, Margaret understands edu-cation to be transformative. However, Mary's inability to maintain her position at the post office within such a short period of time and her proclivity toward dishonest acts throughout the play does suggest that Margaret's enthusiasm for her student's intellect perhaps clouded her judgment.[37] Although O'Connor clearly champions Margaret's liberal views on education, she is also careful to show how inexperience and naïve optimism have the potential to mislead and cause problems.

Attacks on women's professional lives are also examined through-out the play. The townspeople ridicule Margaret's singular focus on teaching and not devoting enough time to pursuing marriage. The town attempts to marry Margaret to a local farmer (John), assuming that a life as a wife and mother would be her natural and correct aspira-tion. When Margaret rebuffs John's advances, the town is appalled. In an important scene toward the end of the play, John condescendingly warns Margaret that she will be undesirable to men if she becomes "one of those people who can talk of nothing but school examinations and inspectors" (76). However, O'Connor cleverly undermines this chau-vinist admonishment by having Margaret ignore John. While John is chiding her, Margaret discovers that she has succeeded in earning her teaching diploma, transforming the focus of the scene from women's domestic responsibilities to their professional aspirations. John sput-ters in frustration, "They're not worth it, girl—but you're not even *listening* to me!" (76). Despite Margaret's initial naïveté, O'Connor ultimately celebrates career ambitions over those within the domestic sphere. The play ends with the school inspector returning and telling Margaret that she has improved greatly, and she may get a grade of "highly efficient": the top designation a teacher can receive. Thus Margaret has ultimately shed her naïve enthusiasm and learned to work within the system, fulfilling state requirements while also employing her own pedagogical style and prioritizing what she believes is important in education. Significantly, the plays ends with Margaret shunning societal expectations that she retire to a life of motherhood and instead has her renew her commitment to her chosen profession.

In her Foreword to the published version of the play, O'Connor positions *Highly Efficient* as an educational manifesto, "written by a teacher, about teachers for teachers." She also acknowledged the importance of the UGT's willingness "to produce a play concerned solely with the subject of Public Elementary Education" (3), reinforcing Boltwood's argument that the UGT proactively produced plays to engage with current events and important national debates. Several years after the initial production of *Highly Efficient*, the Education Act of 1947 was passed, increasing access to free education for all Northern students and raising the legal leaving age to fifteen years. In response, the UGT revived the production, again emphasizing both the company and O'Connor's commitment to have the play in direct dialogue with current debates on educational reform.

O'Connor clearly frames *Highly Efficient* as a political statement about state educational standards and obstructive parochial views on education. In the Foreword, she comments on recent newspaper articles about school reform and she also addresses public criticism toward the play, using the opportunity to reiterate her central thesis:

> Parents have rebuked me for showing Mrs. Davidson as a typical parent. A number of people have objected to Mr. McFee as a typical Presbyterian clergyman . . . and I figured that Mr. Andrews was not generally accepted as a typical Inspector. Almost everyone agreed that neither Miss Henderson nor Miss Burke were typical teachers. I agree with all of this. None of these people were typical. Personally

> I do not believe in the existence of typical people. A bad educational
> system has tried to create them. Let us hope that the Good System
> that has been promised for us "To-morrow" will abandon the effort
> as impossible and undesirable. (3–4)

Throughout the play, Margaret (Miss Henderson) rails against an
uninspired curriculum designed to reinforce an ordinary, unimagina-
tive middle-class life. People in Ballydim cannot conceive of a different
life for their children and instead perpetuate the same limiting options
and worldviews. O'Connor believed in the ability and responsibility
of education to improve social mobility and job opportunities for the
poor and working classes and to expand people's understanding of the
world and their role in it.

In addition to the Foreword, O'Connor's political writings on
women's limited career options and the failure of the state to prop-
erly train teachers further frame *Highly Efficient* as a direct political
attack on the state educational system. In a 1944 essay she wrote for
the Belfast literary magazine *Lagan*, O'Connor criticized how restricting young women's career opportunities to teaching tended to produce extremely unqualified and uninspired instructors. Giving the
title of the essay, "Choosing Teaching as a Career," an acerbic tinge,
O'Connor writes: "Like most other teachers I did not choose teaching as a career. I was conscripted. . . . If the use of the word *choice* is
to indicate a reasoned selection, few people have the opportunity of
choosing to be teachers. Some children are manufactured into teachers, who in their turn help to manufacture more children into more
teachers. The result is that a too large portion of teachers are unhappy,
unsatisfactory or bored, in a profession that does not suit them and
which they do not suit." Referring to the other young women in her
school who were, by default, funneled into a teacher-training program,
she writes: "I doubt if any one of these forty-odd girls had considered
what she wanted to do. No one seemed to have considered the suitabil-
ity or otherwise of turning us into teachers." She also rails against the
narrow and conservative training of teachers that privileges facts over
critical or creative thinking. Young teachers' "brains are replete with

the thoughts and opinions of others but they are too tired and have insufficient time to think for themselves."[38] The essay goes on to recommend that young teachers take several years between finishing their training and beginning to teach to explore different types of careers in order to gain greater knowledge and experience in the world.

The play ran for five weeks to full audiences. Despite the clearly political impulses at work, critics focused primarily on the comedic elements of *Highly Efficient*,[39] suggesting an unwillingness to acknowledge or examine the play's criticisms of state educational standards. The *Belfast News Letter* acknowledged that "the light-hearted approach" contained "evidence of a critical mind at work," and praised "the acidulous but good natured criticism of school inspectors and the Ministry of Education."[40] The *Irish News* reported that O'Connor "presents the case of an over-enthusiastic young teacher whose efforts, according to her own methods, only result in disillusion. Cynicism, wit, and humour abound . . . brilliant dialogue make[s] this play one of the best seen at the Group for a long time."[41] The *Belfast News Letter* agreed, reporting that "unusually large audiences" were enjoying "this laughable production."[42] Critics seemed to gloss over the play's criticisms, not knowing how to react or interpret the play's argument. Audiences, however, which were filled with schoolteachers, rallied around the political message of the play. John Keyes, an actor with the UGT, recalls: "The educational establishment reacted with horror to the suggestion that the present system was less than perfect. Audiences were augmented by parties of teachers excited by the play and by school inspectors who were not. Joseph Tomelty was accosted by an irate inspector demanding a ticket. None was available. . . . Disgruntled, the inspector slunk off. Two young teachers approached the actor with shining eyes. 'Oh Mr. Tomelty,' one said 'could we buy you a drink? That man is the bane of our lives.'"[43]

O'Connor's canon of dramatic work not only addresses education reform but also marriage, land inheritance, religion, economic issues, and, always, the patriarchy of the Northern state. Her plays star smart, conscientious, empowered women who attempt to change systemic flaws within their community. *Select Vestry* (1945) explores the power of wealth and big business to improperly influence politics and religious power. Anne Semple is the wife of David Semple, a Church of Ireland clergyman. When a wealthy businessman pledges money to support David's dream to start a home for unwanted boys, David allows the allure of money to affect his role as clergyman. He gives the businessman an unearned chair on the vestry committee and an unfair advantage in town elections. Throughout the play, Anne remains the moral voice of reason, challenging her husband to question whether his desire to help poor children truly justifies or outweighs the inappropriate use of his power within the church and town.

In *The Farmer Wants a Wife* (1955), a young country girl, Margaret, refuses to wait for her beau (John) to return from Australia, where he intends to make his fortune. Margaret's aunt Emma waited for twenty years for a local farmer, Frank, to inherit his family land before he could afford to marry her. Margaret refuses to waste her life waiting for a man, angrily telling Frank, "The women of your generation were silly. . . . I'm not going to wait twenty years for John."[44] Along with this clear feminist argument, the play addresses property lineage traditions that force young men to emigrate and limit women's ability to marry. John's two uncles never married, since they waited for the previous generation to pass away before they were able to inherit the family property.

Although John pleads with Margaret to wait for him, she refuses to be trapped by outdated traditions:

JOHN: I'll make good. I'll come back for you. You'll wait for me.

. . .

It won't be long. I promise you.

MARGARET: (*blazing suddenly*) *You* promise! What's that worth now? There's more to marriage than keeping a promise you made twenty years ago! I am a Wylie! We have no money to keep . . . but we keep our word!

. . .

JOHN: I'm going to Australia so that you and I won't be caught in the same old trap as Uncle Frank and old Uncle Davy.

MARGARET: I'm being caught in no trap, old or new.

JOHN: . . . Uncle Frank didn't marry your Aunt Emma. And there's no point in their marrying now.

MARGARET: (*raging*) Fine! You aren't marrying me . . . and in twenty years time there won't be any point in our marrying.[45]

John's allusion to Emma's infertility making her unsuitable for marriage outrages Margaret, who views her aunt as a victim of an old-fashioned patriarchal custom. Margaret refuses to bow to societal expectation that she should sacrifice her youth and her life in the service of a man. Throughout the play, her intelligence and passionate outrage are contrasted against the men's protestations that she conform to societal traditions. However, Margaret's arguments ultimately convince the men to change their ways. The play ends with Frank bequeathing the farm to his nephew so John can afford to marry Margaret instead of emigrating. Frank realizes that an obsession with land and money prevents Ireland's young people from building lives on the island. With Frank's early gift of his farm to John, he breaks the cycle of emigration and disenfranchisement for the youth of Ireland.

In *Highly Efficient*, *The Farmer Wants a Wife*, and other plays, O'Connor's dramatic work has a clear feminist agenda, repeatedly attacking the patriarchy of the Northern state. The female protagonists of her plays challenge gender politics, assert their independence outside of the domestic sphere, and rail against social injustice. Her championing of women is also reflected in her edited collection *Four New One-Act Plays* (1948), which features three plays by female playwrights, including her own *Canvassing Disqualifies* (1948). Her sole novel, *Mary Doherty* (1938), was also radical for its time by directly addressing sectarian divisions and abortion. Mark Phelan notes: "O'Connor's work thus creates a coherent feminist position and perspective which contests the structural inequalities in Northern society. The transgressive plurality and transformative possibilities presented by her female characters challenge the normative cultural representations of women in Nationalist and Unionist discourse and dismantle the religious-politico forces which frame their reductive constructions of 'woman.'"[46] Furthermore, O'Connor's conscious effort to make her work relevant to both the Catholic and Protestant communities make her a unique voice within an increasingly polarized political atmosphere. Writing in the embittered aftermath of partition and during the increasingly sectarian decades leading up to the outbreak of the Troubles, she used the theatre to argue for the improved standing of all Northern citizens. Phelan argues: "In the male dominated, socially repressive, religious, ultra-conservative and censorious Northern state (itself a mirror of the Free State), O'Connor's plays critically interrogate the patriarchal hegemony of the 'Imperial Providence' through her investigation of non-constitutional issues."[47] O'Connor's commitment to nonsectarian representations of gender, which positioned the subjugation of women as a reflection of state patriarchy (instead of unionist or nationalist discourse), made her a unique voice and champion of women's professional opportunity and social positioning within the early Northern Irish state.

Whereas O'Connor was the most significant female playwright of the early Northern period, Mary O'Malley had the greatest and longest-lasting impact on the wider development of theatre and culture. O'Malley was born and raised in Cork and moved to Belfast after marrying her husband Pearse, a psychiatrist. In 1951, the O'Malleys founded the Lyric Players Theatre. Like Milligan and O'Connor, O'Malley believed in theatre's ability to transform culture and politics. As a passionate nationalist, she expressed her political identity through performance, cultural nationalism, civic activism, and political office. Her political and cultural memberships included the Irish Society for Intellectual Freedom, the Women's Social and Progressive League, the White Stage Painters Group, and the Irish Film Society.[48] She also was a member of the Irish Labour Party's Central Branch (the leftwing, socialist, nationalist branch of the party) and was a supporter of the Republican leader Eamon de Valera. In her 1990 memoir, O'Malley writes: "I had come to the North and moved in like a bull-dog to tackle a situation which I felt could be changed. . . . I wanted to see a solution to the problems in my lifetime, and that was the reason I involved myself in politics in 1951. Maybe I was naïve but I truly hoped to influence change."[49]

Her understanding of how theatre could engage with politics was developed during her time in Dublin with the New Theatre Group (NTG). Before moving to Belfast, O'Malley had been an actor and stage manager with the NTG during the 1930s. The NTG "cited its objective as the use of theatre 'as a means of socialist propaganda' and, in an effort to attract the proletariat to performances, offered cut price tickets to trade unionists, free admission to the unemployed, and incited all to join in singing labour songs in the intervals of plays."[50] This initial experience in a highly political and socialist theatre group deeply influenced O'Malley's politics and also demonstrated how political beliefs could be expressed through art and culture. It is unsurprising then that she founded the Lyric Players in 1951 while simultaneously running for office, viewing both these actions as unified with her political aspirations and interrelated in their goals.

In 1952, she was elected as an Irish Labour Party member to the Smithfield ward of the city. The Irish Labour Party was anti-partition and anti-disestablishment, and the Northern branch was seen as one of the more radical and subversive political parties. The party sought to attack and dismantle unionist political power and members were notorious for refusing to attend government functions or ceremonies, eschewing the traditional clothing of government officials, and declining to stand during the British National Anthem.[51] In her role as party member, O'Malley concentrated on welfare issues: primarily slum housing in poor neighborhoods. However, her work with the outspoken Irish Labour Party branded her as a radical nationalist. She quickly became uncomfortable with the North's harsh and destructive brand of sectarian politics.[52] Disillusioned with political office as a means of productive change, she resigned from the party in 1955: "This brief incursion into politics had taught me a lot. I had been full of hope in the beginning. . . . If we did our job well, we couldn't but improve the situation. I hadn't reckoned on the monolith. . . . Local Government had considerable power. It controlled

Education, Health, City Planning and above all Housing. Even if the legislature passed ameliorating laws, their implementation could be delayed . . . or the laws could be swept under the carpet. 'One man, one vote,' was yet a pipe dream. . . . I stepped into the wings to do my bit in another way."[53]

Withdrawing from formal politicking, she turned to her newly established theatre company to re-channel her creative and political views into a medium that could better express her cultural and political aspirations: "I thought of the New Theatre Group and felt perhaps in this medium, one can make an impact, and plant a discreet message now and then. I got caught up with the idea and the Lyric was born."[54] Having seen how unproductive and often brutal political office was in the North, O'Malley believed that social justice and nationalism could be better expressed through art and culture. Using artistic mediums to promote political and cultural views was a strategy often used by early nationalists in the North (such as Milligan), especially during periods in which unionism dominated the political structure, leaving little room for nationalist voices. O'Malley continued this legacy with the Lyric. "From the outset," Roy Connolly argues, "the Lyric thus provided a forum where the O'Malleys might foster an alternative to local political and cultural traditions . . . prior to the late 1960s this was a commonplace strategy for nationalists. In this period, nationalist identity tended to be expressed through abstention from the unionist regime and engagement with alternative cultural practices, not through confrontation."[55] The Lyric Players seemed to embody this strategy wholeheartedly by forming a company made up of both Protestants and Catholics, (initially) maintaining a nonsectarian reputation, and performing a range of shows that avoided overt political statements and instead encouraged pride in Irish culture. Connolly argues that the Lyric's project was "to foster a nonsectarian revolution through rejection of existing cultural practices."[56] Bernard Adams has likened the Lyric Players to a "cultural peace process," arguing that O'Malley saw the arts as a means through which to work out some of the most difficult challenges and divisions that the North faced: O'Malley "looked to the literary heritage of the island as a whole and

strove mightily to use drama to promote debate and historical understanding in a community that found the simplicities of sectarianism
so seductive."[57]

From 1951 to 1968, the theatre operated privately out of the
O'Malley's home. Intimate audiences of about twenty-five invited
guests sat (first in the O'Malley's drawing room and later in a pur-
pose-made studio space) and watched one-acts, classics, as well as
newer plays by Irish, British, American, and European playwrights.
The theatre, which was initially invitation-only, helped to create a
regular group of literary and artistic intellectuals who came together
to experience O'Malley's theatre and to debate culture and politics,
creating a literary salon of sorts. Deeply influenced by the drama of
Yeats, O'Malley envisioned her theatre as a rejuvenation of the Irish
Literary Revival of the early twentieth century. She was attracted to
Yeats's poetic style of dramatic writing and highly stylized, symbolist
aesthetic, which she sought to replicate:

> When we founded the Lyric Players group in 1951, we had already
> very definite views on theatre, and we have consistently worked on
> the basis of these ideals. The restriction to poetic drama was quite
> deliberate. Interpreted widely, however, it did allow us to include
> all the world classics (if we so desired) and any good contemporary
> play could be included on the basis of poetic content in the inter-
> nal structure. . . . The poetic play also had a special place for the
> artist and craftsman and permitted experiment in colour, lighting,
> stagecraft. . . . The total achievement exists only when the theatre is
> alive with dramatic action and audience response and a harmonious
> blending of the several arts is present.[58]

With their emphasis on text, language, and "poetic drama," the
Lyric actors were celebrated for their diction, projection, articula-
tion, and clarity by critics and audiences alike.[59] O'Malley described
the theatre's minimalist symbolist aesthetic (influenced by Yeats):
"Scenery and costumes were simple and nonrealistic and each play
is designed to a narrow color scheme . . . expressive of its particular
atmosphere."[60] The Lyric staged Yeats's plays frequently and tried to

honor his artistic tradition, which was "a theatre of collaboration, in which all the arts—poetry, music, painting, sculpture, mask-making and the interpretative arts of dance, speech, mime, and acting—are in harmony, no one art dominating the others."[61] O'Malley made a point of performing at least one Yeats play per season (though many seasons during the 1960s included seven or more Yeats plays), and the Lyric Players earned a reputation on the island as the foremost interpreters of the playwright's dramatic work.

Although her productions generally avoided overt political statements, O'Malley's political aspirations were implicit in that she viewed the Lyric Players as an opportunity to celebrate and promote Irish art and culture. During the 1950s and 1960s, O'Malley opened a series of schools, shops, and galleries promoting Irish art and culture. She established an arts space called the New Gallery, which produced poetry events, lectures, and exhibitions of Irish photography, painting, and sculpture. In 1962, she also started a small store, Irish Handcrafts, which sold Irish-made products in the same building as the gallery space. In 1957, she founded the quarterly magazine *Threshold*, which published political, literary, and cultural commentary. She also saw the education of young people within the arts as vital to the quality and longevity of cultural life in the North. She started the Drama School in 1957 "to stimulate creative imagination and aesthetic appreciation, to provide a cultural recreational medium, and to cater to the serious student of acting and production."[62] The school offered classes in speech, movement, and acting to children and young adults twice a week. Like the Lyric Players, the school had a diverse student body with children from all over Belfast.[63] A youth theatre company grew out of the drama school in 1959, performing shows in Belfast. The Lyric actor and teacher Sam McCready later expanded the Drama School to include the Lyric Drama Studio: a pre-professional training institute for actors, which remains part of the Lyric Theatre today. Additionally, the Lyric established a music school (the Belfast Academy of Music) in 1962. The Drama School eventually joined the music school, morphing into the Belfast Academy of Music and Drama before the Belfast Academy of Music became independent in

1966. O'Malley's early commitment to producing such a wide array of creative offerings demonstrates her strong belief in the ability of art and culture to not only express but also improve civic life.

In addition to infusing Belfast with high-quality cultural and artistic offerings, the Lyric Players generated rare cross-border interest. Roy Connolly reports that friends, writers, intellectuals, and theatre practitioners based in Dublin traveled to the North to see O'Malley's unique production aesthetic and to see the foremost interpreters of Yeats perform his dramatic work: "Many of her friends came to see her plays, some contributing to productions. The Lyric specialized in plays that other groups felt ill-equipped to tackle and, in doing so, acquired a reputation more than commensurate with the modest resources at its disposal. . . . This cross-border traffic in artistic energy brought new influences to bear on the theatre's expressive vocabulary."[64]

A board of trustees was established in 1960 to oversee the financial stability and artistic integrity of the theatre. With its increasingly prominent role in Northern culture and the start of the Troubles in the late 1960s, the board wanted the company to maintain a politically neutral reputation. The actor Sam McCready remembers that the company was "comprised [of] people of different religions and political viewpoints and there was never disharmony,"[65] and Bernard Adams argues that O'Malley "wanted the Lyric to be politically neutral but totally inclusive."[66] The initial reputation of the theatre as an inclusive cross-community space committed to quality art rather than a specific sectarian viewpoint started to create tension between O'Malley and the new board. O'Malley was dedicated to producing inclusive, nonsectarian creative work and chafed at encroachments on her theatre by unionist politics.

A particularly damaging issue was the requirement to play the British national anthem before performances. For O'Malley, the Lyric "was there to serve the two traditions in the North." Playing the British national anthem changed this dynamic dramatically and also deeply "affect[ed] artistic independence and vision."[67] On principle, O'Malley refused to stand for the anthem and eventually resigned from the board in 1968 in protest against playing the song before

Lyric productions.[68] In doing so, however, her political beliefs became conflated with those of the theatre, threatening its neutrality and making it difficult for her to obtain public arts funding. McCready explains: "Her unwillingness to stand for the British National Anthem was a flagrant demonstration of the Nationalist politics; she wanted to get rid of the border and coerce the Protestant majority into a United Ireland governed by the Catholic Church. Such ambitions could not be overlooked in a Unionist-controlled state and made her plans to establish a new theatre in Belfast all the more difficult in the years ahead. She knew this but refused to alter her stance."[69]

As the Lyric became an increasingly important player in Northern theatre and the board gained greater control over its future direction, O'Malley had to reconcile her personal political beliefs with those of the trustees and the overall mission of the theatre. The board wanted to maintain a policy of avoiding plays that directly dealt with issues of partition, sectarianism, or nationalism and unionism in an attempt to remain politically neutral. However, this desire for neutrality was often undermined by O'Malley's widely known nationalist reputation and her proclivity for producing plays by Irish nationalist writers such as Yeats. Roy Connolly remarks:

> The Lyric's celebration of Irish culture without reciprocal recognition of unionist traditions inculcated the sense that there was something covert about the theatre, and recollection of O'Malley's activities with the Irish Labour Party reinforced this sense. There was thus tension between her and certain members of the establishment, most unfortunately, between her and the President of C.E.M.A. (until 1963), Ritchie McKee, who, allegedly, turned down the Lyric's first application for funding with the words: "Why should we support the Lyric or Mary O'Malley who is a subversive element in the community."[70]

In 1969, the Lyric's fund-raising committee addressed the issue of how the lingering taint of nationalism was hampering its fundraising efforts: "the Lyric is still politically suspect in some business circles and its attitude to the Constitution, etc., must be clarified if the good-will of the business world is to be won." The committee demanded that each trustee sign a letter declaring the theatre's political neutrality. The proposed letter stated: "The Lyric Players Theatre is a charitable Trust. Its constitution is non-political and non-sectarian. Its management and its policy are free from political bias or influence of any kind."[71] Pressure to sign the letter caused several trustees to quit in protest, further fracturing the leadership of the Lyric and threatening its financial longevity. O'Malley's deep and abiding belief in the power of art and culture to champion a brand of inclusive nationalism in the North was directly at odds with the increasingly tense political climate during the late 1960s as the North entered the first bloody years of the Troubles.

A year after her resignation over playing the British national anthem, O'Malley returned to direct and produce additional plays for the company. However, tension between O'Malley and the board grew during the 1970s as the Lyric's reputation became increasingly suspect. Despite most seasons packed with productions that did not directly engage politics, the Lyric did stage several plays with nationalist leanings, including Lady Gregory's *The Rising of the Moon* in 1961 and 1962, James Plunkett's *The Risen People* during the 1962/63 season, several productions of Sean O'Casey's *The Plough and the Stars* and *Juno and the Paycock* throughout the 1960s, and various Yeats plays each season.[72] O'Malley's well-known political views in conjunction with several nationalist-leaning productions caused a permanent rift between herself and the board, which was tasked with maintaining the stability of the Lyric within an increasingly hostile political climate:

> There then followed a whispering campaign about the Lyric's sympathies, with speculation that the Lyric was "politically suspect" and "antigovernment". . . . After these early skirmishes, the Lyric sought to allay concerns about its alleged sectarians, by promoting a politically impartial profile. Thereafter it continually asserted its political neutrality, painting itself as "idealist" and encouraging the

perception that the Lyric represented the spectrum of different religious and political colours in Belfast and that for many years people had worked there harmoniously.[73]

O'Malley's strong political beliefs and commitment to Irish cultural nationalism had been the initial impulses behind creating the Lyric. It is ironic, then, that these foundational beliefs became the primary source of tension as the board tried to neutralize the Lyric by maintaining a mission of political impartiality. Although it became increasingly painful for O'Malley, this impartiality may have allowed the Lyric to continue operating throughout the Troubles and to remain the only professionally subsidized theatre in Northern Ireland that survived the violent outbreak of the conflict. Owing to increasing tensions during the late 1960s, most theatres shuttered their doors, including the Grove, The Group Theatre, and the Arts Theatre, which all shut down in 1971.

Despite her tension with the board, O'Malley continued to usher the theatre through several tumultuous years of a harsh political climate and the start of the Troubles. She advocated for the Lyric, secured Arts Council support, and spearheaded a fund-raising campaign to build a permanent space. After an intense fund-raising effort, the company moved to its permanent home in south Belfast in 1968. O'Malley remained as artistic adviser until 1976 and directed productions until 1978; she retired from active involvement in 1980. Her leadership and vision steadied the Lyric during the Troubles and allowed the theatre to become the North's oldest subsidized year-round producing theatre as of this writing.

Throughout her tenure, O'Malley's political aspirations remained motivated by nationalism, and the Lyric ultimately did little to support other women playwrights or practitioners. In 1954, *Seadna* by Joy Rudd and *The Falcons in the Snare* by Elizabeth Boyle were the first two plays by female dramatists that the theatre produced. These were followed in 1956 by Rudd's *The Children of Lir*, and in 1958 by Mary Manning's *The Voice of Shem* and Dorothy Watters's *The Wolf in the Woods*. Over the next several years, only a few more women playwrights were produced.[74] *The Heart's a Wonder* by the O'Farrell sisters in 1958 and 1971,[75] *The Rising of the Moon* by Lady Gregory in 1961 and 1963, *Smock Alley* by Mairín Charlton in 1967 and 1969, *The Gathering* by Edna O'Brien in 1977, and *Once a Catholic* by Mary O'Malley in 1979 remained the few and infrequent female voices to grace the Lyric stage. During the 1980s, the Lyric produced the powerful works of Christina Reid and Marie Jones, but rarely branched out from these two playwrights.

Furthermore, between 1951 and 1968 only 4 out of 180 plays were by Northern writers, which is less than 3 percent of total productions.[76] The theatre continued this practice in the 1960s and 1970s, rejecting works from local writers such as Stewart Parker, Robin Glendinning, and Graham Reid.[77] Roy Connolly notes: "The Lyric conspicuously ignored other Ulster writers, choosing perversely to champion the work of a succession of dramatists from the Republic and plays that had been successful or won awards there. . . . The avoidance of local cultural values was central to the theatre's ideology as the theatre was focused on persuading people to appreciate a particular programme."[78] With O'Malley's primary emphasis on lyrical and poetic drama and the celebration of Irish culture, the theatre concentrated on giving audiences an elevated cultural and artistic experience rather than reflect native writing or stories. It was not until the early 1980s that the Lyric would start embracing local writing, which "radically altered the theatre's profile and sense of purpose."[79]

Bernard Adams described the cultural landscape of Northern Ireland during the 1940s as "arid" and a "desert," arguing that the Lyric Players Theatre had a transformative impact on the theatrical and artistic life of Belfast and the North.[80] Sam McCready also asserts that the Lyric's influence was much greater than simply establishing a high-quality professional theatre company in the North. Its varied artistic contributions transformed Belfast and were the start of a cultural movement that would elevate the North: "A drama school, a literary magazine, exhibitions and improved facilities at the theatre: expansion on all fronts was the order of the day. To the observant, the Lyric was beginning to take on the semblance of a literary and dramatic movement and indeed, at its best, that's what it was. Too often the general public thinks only of the Lyric as a theatre but to understand that theatre fully, especially its policy, it is necessary to see the theatre as being part of a burgeoning arts movement."[81]

Indeed, the Lyric's diverse cultural offerings established an infrastructure that would allow for the continued training and development of future artists and cultural critics. Within an atmosphere of increasing polarization, political warfare, and sectarian violence, the Lyric emerged as evidence that culture, art, and creative imagination could remain alive during the darkest times. Mary O'Malley's deep commitment to her theatre and her belief in the power of art to change and improve lives had a singular and transformative impact on the North.

Within the increasingly polarized atmosphere of sectarian politics, Alice Milligan, Patricia O'Connor, Mary O'Malley, and others used theatre as a way to voice their aspirations and visions for a better Northern Ireland. Despite these early accomplishments, however, women's opportunities in theatre remained severely limited throughout the mid-twentieth century. Patricia O'Connor would be the only female playwright to have her plays repeatedly produced and supported by a major theatre until the 1980s. Without many women playwrights, roles for actresses remained sparse and uninspired throughout the early years of the state. It would not be until the 1970s brought new arts-funding initiatives that encouraged the development of amateur and community theatre companies that women would slowly emerge as leaders in Northern drama. These initiatives would give rise to the celebrated voices of Christina Reid, Anne Devlin, Jennifer Johnston, Marie Jones, and establish the foundation of several prominent women-led theatre companies during the 1980s and 1990s.

PART TWO

Troubles and the Stage, 1980–1997

4

Community Engagement
The Charabanc Theatre Company

The Charabanc Theatre Company[1] was created in direct response to a lack of acting jobs and strong roles for women. Despite earlier advances for women and the increase in community and independent theatres during the 1970s, there remained few writing and acting opportunities for women. Theatres continued overwhelmingly to produce male playwrights, who in turn wrote plays with male leads, discouraging women from pursuing theatrical aspirations. Charabanc was started in 1983 by the actresses Marie Jones, Maureen Macauley, Eleanor Methven, Carol (Scanlan) Moore, and Brenda Winter, with initial help from Martin Lynch. In addition to the male-led Field Day Theatre Company, Charabanc was one of the most significant Irish theatre companies of the 1980s. It helped to establish an independent theatre sector for the first time in the North, and it secured an international reputation for Northern Ireland as the progenitor of significant and high-quality theatre. In its twelve years of existence (1983–95), the company performed eighteen new works and four existing plays. It became one of the most widely toured theatre groups on the island, performing in both the North and south of Ireland, at a time when cross-border touring was rare. International touring also included Russia, Germany, Canada, London, the United States, and performances at Glasglow's Mayfest, the Edinburgh Festival, and the Brighton Festival at Cardiff, Wales.

Although the impulse to start the company arose from practical concerns, Charabanc was also greatly influenced by the women's and

83

socialist movements stirring in Britain during the 1960s and 1970s. Reflecting on the sociopolitical conditions that led to the emergence of the troupe, Eleanor Methven recalls "the 60s, 70s [as] highly politicized decades. . . . Catholic or Protestant, it didn't matter, you were influenced by Britain obviously, and we were influenced by British feminism and British socialism. Those two things had an extraordinary grip. . . . We were just tired of being someone's wife, someone's mother. Why couldn't we be the somebody? We were influenced by [the women's movement] coming from Britain—it was just in the ether."[2] In addition, several of the Charabanc actresses worked and traveled in the United Kingdom before founding the company and brought these feminist and socialist influences to the work. Methven, for example, acted in Scotland during the early 1980s, where she worked with WildCat, a socialist musical theatre company. Its productions centered on working-class life in Britain, and it used an agitprop performance style, both of which would be employed in Charabanc's own work. In addition, the socialist theatre festival Mayfest in Glasglow, where Charabanc performed several times, was a significant influence. The company was thus created from a place of political impulse by a group of women who wanted to upend the status quo. In reaction against British and male-dominated theatre, they set out to write "through working-class women's eyes because those are the voices that weren't heard. [Women] don't write the history books, so that became the two things that framed Charabanc: a feminist impulse and a socialist impulse."[3]

Another important influence on the formation of the company was the professional children's theatre group Playzone, which was part of the first wave of independent theatres created during the 1970s. Marie Jones had been an actress for Playzone, and the company provided a model for what Charabanc strove to be: a community-based theatre dedicated to social change that toured working-class areas. Brenda Winter explains: "Playzone prefigured and influenced Charabanc by its position and politics as 'a theatre of social engagement—committed to bringing about change in specific communities.'"[4] Thus feminist, socialist, and community-based ideologies were the company's foundation, and this dedication to promoting a working-class and female experience of the North became the primary contributions of the group to Northern Irish theatre.

Another extremely important aspect of Charabanc's identity was that the women came from both Protestant and Catholic backgrounds, creating a unique model for an integrated, nonsectarian theatre group.[5] Given the history of plays and performance venues associated with Protestant or government rule, Charabanc was decidedly cross-community and purposefully performed in loyalist and republican neighborhoods as well as more neutral performance spaces. This integration came naturally to Charabanc's members, who were used to performing professionally with actors from both religious backgrounds. Methven reflected: "We were all in theatre before we were in Charabanc, and when you work in theatre it's a nonsectarian profession. Theatre's a place where you don't have to belong to a tribe. Or rather, you belong to a tribe in theatre anyway, so you can actually cut loose from your childhood tribe."[6] Deriving strength from this identity as theatre practitioners meant that the women of Charabanc put their professional identities before their religious or ethnic identities. Their status as an integrated group allowed them the legitimacy and access to perform in both Catholic and Protestant neighborhoods and to include stories from both communities in their repertoires.

One of the most significant examples of this cross-community acceptance was the group's ability to interview Catholic women from the nationalist Divis flats for their play *Somewhere Over the Balcony* (1978). For this production, staunchly nationalist and republican women shared intimate and previously untold stories about the hardships of their lives with three Protestant actresses and then allowed those same Protestant women to portray Catholic voices, bodies, and stories on stage. This was an incredibly significant demonstration of connecting to one another first and foremost as women rather than through their sectarian identities. Methven has said that one of the most important techniques that Charabanc used in its work was to create compassion and empathy for those identified as the adversary.[7] Charabanc often presented female characters who were funny, smart, and hard-working, and showed their common humanity before their sectarian identity.

Charabanc conducted interviews with women in their neighborhoods and did historical research in libraries and newspaper archives. The group, which often met at night or on weekends, improvised and sketched out scenes, which Marie Jones would revise into a formal script. The characters tended to be a compilation of many different women who had been interviewed, and the actresses intermixed verbatim dialogue from political speeches or news reports with the dialogues they created based on real women's stories.

Because the Arts Council would not initially support a group of unproven actresses, the women first financed their productions through a government unemployment scheme that gave them funding to hire actors who were out of work. The group had initially wanted to hire men for the male roles; however, they were unable to find enough out-of-work male actors who would qualify for their specific funding scheme. As Eleanor Methven reflected, "it was a very feminist thing that started us off. The guys were all employed, and we weren't. So that's a statement in itself."[8] The company's director, Pam Brighton, suggested that the women play the male roles as well. This started Charabanc's hallmark tradition of actresses playing both male and female roles in the company.[9] The audiences loved the humor of women portraying husbands, sons, and bosses, and it also was the first time on the Northern stage that the long tradition of male-constructed portrayals of women was subverted. This decision, initially born out of practical and economic necessity, led to the development of what Charabanc has called the *female gaze*: portraying the world (and men) through the eyes and experiences of women. When they played male roles, the actresses indicated the change primarily through voice, body language, and an occasional prop. The actresses were often still costumed in skirts or dresses and just substituted a hat or coat to show the audience they were now portraying a male character. The obvious and visible layering of the male on top of the female body made it clear that this was a man as seen through the eyes (and body) of a woman. If the male characters were never as fully formed as the female characters, as some critics have contended, it was because the plays reflected the role that men played in real women's lives. In a 1987 interview, Marie Jones defended their portrayals of men: "We took these women's perceptions of men and used that in our play. When they talked about their lives, the men really weren't mentioned very much except things like, 'He really wasn't home very much, and he got drunk, and he gave me a hayden [a hit] every now and again.' But the men didn't figure very much in their lives; they were just there to bring the money home. That was how they saw it, so that's how we portrayed the men."[10]

Just as the company was known for its cross-community and cross-gender casting, the production aesthetic of the company became another distinctive and well-recognized feature of the group. Sets were extremely minimal, typically comprised of platforms, crates, and scaffolding, which allowed the company to tour cheaply and easily. Costumes were equally streamlined: shirts, dresses, blouses, and aprons with the addition of hats, coats, and other props that would identify a change in character. Their minimalist aesthetic was influenced by practical and artistic concerns. Their constant lack of funding and the need to tour the plays made their production values necessarily sparse. However, their aesthetic was also born out of a desire to make theatre accessible and unintimidating to the communities that came to see their productions. For the working-class audiences of the North, theatre was considered the purview of an educated elite who could afford to attend performances and who could also travel to the theatre at night in safety. Charabanc made theatre accessible financially and physically by traveling to community neighborhoods and performing in safe spaces where families could go without fear of violence.

Charabanc's minimalistic style also incorporated Brechtian elements and a Living Newspaper aesthetic. In the Brechtian tradition, the actresses changed costumes and roles on stage and broke the fourth wall to speak directly to the audience. In a nod to the American Depression-era Living Newspaper, they often used verbatim dialogue from political speeches and direct address to explain important historical information about the time period or highlight relevant facts or statistics. The form and structure of Charabanc's work was influenced heavily by the director Pam Brighton, who had worked with several socialist and feminist theatre companies in Britain. Brighton's direction exposed the company to the traditions of groups like Monstrous Women's Regiment and 7:84, both important feminist agitprop theatre companies that were active in Britain during the 1970s. Brighton encouraged the use of antirealistic devices, and the women embraced this direction because these techniques naturally aided in their storytelling and contributed artistically to their anti-elitist, bare-bones aesthetic. The staging and structure of their plays were anti-illusionistic, and the women's acting style was naturalistic.

Charabanc's plays were so significant and influential, in part, because they staged the historical development of the class and ethnic conflict in the North in order to chart how the past influenced the sectarian conditions of the present. The Charabanc women wanted to disprove the widely held opinion that the North was locked in an inescapable cycle of violence. Much of Charabanc's work emphasized the cyclical and generational nature of the conflict, hoping that if individuals could recognize these historical patterns they would be empowered to change them. The company's first production, *Lay Up Your Ends* (1983), looked at how sectarian divisions and poor work conditions in the early twentieth-century linen mill industry repressed women from both communities. *Gold in the Streets* (1986) charted the history of emigration to England during three different time periods: 1912, 1950, and 1985. Each period showed the same sectarian prejudices driving people from the North, with little changing in over seventy years. As reflected in these plays, much of Charabanc's work engages a fundamental question: "Must we as a culture continue to behave this way?"[11] In each of their plays, Charabanc also emphasized the role of economic conditions in the repression of Northern women. In *Lay Up Your Ends*, women worked long hours under poor work conditions for desperately low wages. In *Gold in the Streets*, women were motivated to leave the North owing to an inability to financially support their families. In this play, London is the land of economic fortune where they will find gold in the streets. Similarly, *The Girls in the Big Picture* (1986) followed a group of women in the country-side whose lives are stunted economically, socially, and romantically by poverty and by limited options in their rural community.

In addition to staging historical dramas, Charabanc did not shy away from addressing controversial political issues in the present. Their 1985 play, *Now You're Talking*, centered around a group of Catholics and Protestants at a peace and reconciliation center and showed them talking (and fighting) through some of the most difficult issues of the Troubles. Charabanc was careful to represent both sides of the conflict in the play and also to show a realistic range of moderate and extreme viewpoints. The segregated nature of neighborhoods during the 1980s meant that these types of conversations did not typically occur, and this imagined dialogue, staged by Charabanc in a complex, honest, and fair manner, could be the audience's only opportunity to witness a conversation with the other side that was not entirely partisan.

The complex interplay of all these influences meant that Charabanc's dramatic writing was markedly different from standard Northern drama. Whereas the plots of many Troubles plays centered around sectarian violence, Charabanc approached the conflict from a non-paramilitaristic or violent perspective. Although the company did not shy away from the *effects* of violence on individuals and the North as a whole, their productions never centered on violence or sensationalized it on stage. Instead, they used the private politics of selfhood and womanhood in the North to enter into a broader dialogue about the conflict. As Jones commented in 1994, "Our stuff very much reflected what was happening to the working people of Belfast and how politics affected their lives. It was politics with a small 'p' in that it dealt with how social issues affected 'small' powerless people."[12] Although second-wave feminism failed to achieve a stronghold in the North, its famous slogan, "the personal is political," certainly encapsulates Charabanc's ideology. While the company's plays directly addressed the political and economic conditions that led to the sectarian conflict, the Charabanc women tempered their historical and political analysis through their intense attention on the personal cost of war and its effects on women's subjectivity.

Charabanc's commitment to the personal politics of female identity and gender norms can be seen clearly through its first production. After premiering with great success in Belfast, *Lay Up Your Ends* toured community and leisure centers throughout the North, running from May 15 to October 22, 1983, and ultimately was seen by more than 13,500 people.[13]

Lay Up Your Ends (1983) is set in Belfast during the historic 1911 linen mill strikes when Catholic and Protestant women protested against low pay and atrocious working conditions. In the nineteenth and early twentieth centuries, the working classes were packed into crowded, filthy housing near the polluting factories. Mill women often worked in knee-high water for twelve to fourteen hours each day. This, combined with poor nutrition and unsanitary conditions at home, created the conditions for high infant mortality, consumption, and typhoid fever. The play charts the political awakening of the mill women as they fight for basic working rights. When the mill manager, Jim Doran, cuts the women's hours (and thus their salaries) and institutes new stringent rules that the women cannot talk, sing, or stop to fix their hair during working hours, this causes an uproar. The women are further outraged when the mill owner, Mr. Bingham, fires Mary for disobeying the new rules, leading a small group of women to strike. Their decision to protest ultimately inspires two thousand women all over Belfast to walk away from their mill jobs. The women's strike for better working conditions quickly transforms into an impulse to unionize in order to improve conditions for all women in the mills. The play follows a small group of these mill workers as they negotiate the fallout from striking and the resulting financial hardships to and social ostracism of their families.

As in all Charabanc plays, the characters in *Lay Up Your Ends* represent a diverse range of experiences and backgrounds. A bright young girl, Florrie, comes from the Northern countryside with her four siblings in tow. She works at the mill in order to make enough money so that her brothers and sisters may eat. Another mill worker, Lizzie, is trapped in a cycle of poverty because she has too many children to raise. She has stopped sleeping with her husband because her health has been badly compromised by work and multiple pregnancies. Her doctor has warned her not to have any more children; however, her husband beats her when she refuses to sleep with him. Belle, the most politically aware of the women, leads the walkout. She tells her fellow millworkers, "No one man shud have all that money when the ones that made it for him haven't even got what wud put a meal's mate on the table." Belle's determination to have her voice heard and to participate in the political process serves as a catalyst for the others to fight for their basic rights. As Belle sees it, they are in such desperate straights, they have nothing to lose: "ye can't take nothin' away from nothing."[14]

The play, which is far from a sentimental and heroic tale of courage, does not paint the women as strong, unwavering leaders in the fight for women's rights. Instead, it takes a hard look at the financial and personal tolls on these women, who worry that they will be permanently fired for striking. The protest has other high stakes: the women rent their homes from the mill owner and are afraid he will evict their families. One striking woman can no longer pay for her sick child's medication and must go door-to-door and beg for money from her neighbors. Far from depicting a uniformly heroic image of the striking workers, the play also demonstrates how many of the women cave under the pressure of their husbands and the factory owners and go back to the mills. This is characteristic of Charabanc's work, which never shies away from hard, truthful, or unsentimental depictions of life.

The play also illustrates the internal debates between the women who are conflicted as to whether they should follow the trade unionist leader Mary Galway's advice to return to work or the socialist and nationalist leader, James Connolly, who urges the women to remain on strike until their demands are met. This dilemma is discussed on both a political level, through the women's heated verbal debates, as well as on a personal level, through the storyline of Lizzie, a Protestant whose husband, Charles, has a good job down at the docks. Charles believes that it is inappropriate for women to demonstrate publicly and that politics are unnatural for women. He tells his wife,

"Surely til God, y'don't believe that a crowd of weemin is gonna do anything, do ye?" He goes on to argue that the women should follow the more modest (and, in his eyes, dignified) model of Mary Galway because "she's not runnin' around the streets singin' and carryin' on and makin' an eegit of herself" (77). Because Connolly advocates Home Rule, Charles does not want Lizzie to be seen joining Connolly's support for the women's strikes. Charles believes this would cause other Protestants to think their family supports Home Rule. The play thus illustrates how women have historically been required to subvert their individual needs as women to those of the larger ethnonational group. Charles also manipulates Lizzie's responsibility to her family as a woman, pressuring her to return to work: "Ye can't deprive your wee childer of a bit in their mouths. I can't be expected til carry on supportin' them on my wages alone. Sacrifices will haft til be made if ya don't. . . . Many another man wud not take this business so light" (78–79). Lizzie agrees to return to work, and after she leaves the stage, Charles turns to the audience and says, "See weemin? Ye don't bate them wi' that. [*He makes a fist.*] Ye bate them wi' that! [*He points to his head.*]" (79).

The play argues that men's manipulation of women is a powerful force from which it is difficult for the women to break free, politically and personally. Throughout the play, various men weigh in on the women's strike:

> BISCUIT: Strikin' is for men. See weemin', see my Sadie, she's gonna get that. (*He smacks his fist into the palm of his hand again.*)
> ALFIE: Ya don't talk to weemin', Charlie. A good hidin's the only medicine my Ethna knows. See weemin, they shouldn't be allowed out on strike.
> BISCUIT: Out on strike! They shouln't be allowed outta the house!
> (88)

These male roles were played by women in makeshift costumes. Thus, while acknowledging the power of men in women's lives, the men's words were also undermined and often derided as they were spoken on stage by female voices.

Ultimately, the play is a hard and unsentimental look at the personal cost that these women endured to publicly protest the conditions that were keeping them repressed and locked in cycles of poverty. The play does not shy away from the women's internal disagreements or from how deeply the strike affected their personal relationships, emotions, and financial circumstances. The play also condemns the out-of-touch, wealthy Protestant women who ignored the plight of their working-class sisters. The play paints the mill owner's wife as a hypocrite for dismissing the workers' pleas and not seeing how their fight for basic rights affects her as a woman as well.

Although *Lay Up Your Ends* concludes with the women returning to the mills after the strike collapses, the play ultimately does not position the protest as a failure. The women enter the mills defiantly singing, they stop their work and comb their hair, they chat and laugh, taking back some of the privileges they had lost without asking permission. The play argues that the shared strength the women gained from uniting in opposition to unfair working conditions was a success in its own right. Thus women's bonding and their power as a collective voice are positioned as possible antidotes to male authority and control, encouraging working-class Protestant and Catholic women in the audiences to join their voices together in order to enact real change. It was significant that Charabanc's first production reenacted a historical period in which working-class women from both traditions came together to fight for their common rights as workers and as women. This cooperative cross-community action reflected the very project that Charabanc itself was endeavoring to create: bringing Protestant and Catholic women together to advocate for their rights as working-class women and to provide a creative space for their public and private, personal and political, ethnic and gender identities.

The attention to women's lives in Charabanc's work is even more significant given what Enrica Cerquoni calls "the forgotten world of women in post-hunger-strike Northern Ireland."[15] After the 1981 hunger strikes (during which ten men died), the Catholic community was consumed by the dramatic and very public bodily sacrifice of their husbands, brothers, and sons.[16] The years after the hunger strikes led to an increase in IRA recruitment and paramilitary violence, enveloping the North in a hypermasculine political atmosphere. Charabanc started performing in 1983, directly in the aftermath of the hunger strikes and during a time when the space for women's voices was more restricted than ever.

Although Charabanc was not initially founded with the specific goal to create a feminist or even an all-women's theatre troupe, the company's feminism was implicit in the subjects of its plays, in its mission statement, in its initial impulse to create more and better jobs for actresses, and in its desire to show the sectarian conflict from a female perspective. However, the company was careful to reject feminism as an elitist, upper-class ideology that did not encompass their identities or the project of their company. Eleanor Methven explains that they did not foreground their feminism because "we were dealing with working-class women, and the term tended to alienate them."[17]

In the North, feminism has been often viewed as an antimale or, alternatively, purely nationalist ideology. Additionally, in a society that has imposed essentialist, binary identity markers on all its members (Catholic versus Protestant, Irish versus English, North versus south), the company was wary of embracing yet another label. In a 1987 interview, Eleanor Methven acknowledged that "it would be stupid to say we're not 'feminist,' but every time someone says 'feminist,' I want them to define it for me. It has a bad ring to it. If we said we were feminist or socialist or any 'ist'—it would completely alienate those people back in the community centers in Northern Ireland. It would alienate them completely. So what's the point of saying it?"[18] Reinforcing these fears, some audiences ignored the company's denials and aligned its work with a strident antimale ideology. Despite the fact that Charabanc's project was overtly and insistently about promoting women's rights, experiences, and voices, the word "feminist" was clearly not going to be a productive label for the company, and it fought against the media branding the group as such. Other female playwrights during this same period struggled to distance themselves from labels that would color their work as sectarian. In a 1982 interview, Christina Reid commented that she "would be appalled at any sort of label—I mistrust labels, whether they be social, religious or sexual. I think labels diminish good art. I don't make political statements, I present words and images that are open to interpretation."[19]

In a society dominated by essentialist identity politics and binary labels, it is understandable that artists would distance themselves from anything that would box them into a preconceived category. Critics like Imelda Foley have agreed with the company's historical repudiation of the term "feminist," writing in 2003: "While some journalists have practically begged for approval of the ready and common assumption that Charabanc is a feminist company, a binary replacement of male with female does not in itself constitute a feminist ideology. . . . Charabanc cannot be accused of *not* being what they never *meant* to be."[20] This rejection of feminism as a legitimate lens through which to view Charabanc's work appears to be a reflection of continued Northern discomfort with issues of gender. It also reflects a narrow definition of feminism. Foley goes on to quote Helen Lojek that "the issue is power, not gender, and the play [*Lay Up Your Ends*] presents no idealized female world in which things are better when women are in charge."[21] Foley's interpretation of Lojek's comment reduces the complex and multifaceted ideas that encompass different strains of feminist thought to that of so-called radical feminism, which argues for a reordering of society with women in power at the top of the hierarchy. Relegating all feminist ideas to such a narrow definition denies more sophisticated ways of looking at how gender dynamics and gender identity influence society. However, the delay of the women's movement, the complex political history of the North, and a narrow definition of feminism have continued to result in Northerners rejecting feminism as an ideology that has little historical or political relevance in the North. Despite this continued discomfort, gender is indeed at the very heart of each Charabanc play and at the core of the company's work and mission. Lojek herself considers Charabanc to be a feminist theatre company despite its initial inability to embrace the term.[22]

This conflicted relationship between the clear feminist and socialist arguments of its repertoire and the group's rejection of such labels has created a very complicated gap between what Charabanc claimed it was doing and what its performances actually conveyed. Just as Charabanc rejected the label "feminist," it also denied writing specifically from a "woman's perspective." In an interview with Carol Martin in 1987, the actresses denied the significance of their status as women in their writing. Marie Jones told Martin, "We never actually think [writing from a female perspective] is desperately important—it happens because we are women. We never think we better do this from a feminine point of view. It's just there because we are women." Carol Scanlan added, "It's an unconscious thing; it just comes out."[23] Pushing back against ghettoization into the marginalized category of "women's writing," Methven argued: "You either make it or you don't, regardless if you're a woman or not. We can't deny the fact that we are women and because we're women we write from a woman's point of view. But it's not meant to be agitprop. It's more like human rights than women's rights. We'd fight for a male cause if we saw something that was bad that was being done to males."[24] These comments demonstrate a concern about being placed in a special category that prevents their work from being compared with or added to the canon of elite male playwrights. In the same interview, Methven went on to say: "More women are now writing plays, but, compared to the number of men, it's minimal. And people seem to think we're inundated with women's plays. But they only notice them because they're written by a woman. It's like people are constantly asking us, 'Tell us you're a feminist theatre company.' Yet if there's a theatre company entirely composed of men, which is quite normal, nobody thinks—not even women—about the fact that they're only seeing men on stage or just one woman. It doesn't occur to them. Suddenly there's something odd about having all women on stage." Jones added: "We've been fighting for three-and-a-half years to say we're a working-class theatre company. That's all we are. People will not accept that. Maybe they're looking for an angle for the press or something. We never really say we're a Belfast women's theatre company."[25] When Jones insisted they were a working-class theatre group, the company was embracing a nonsectarian term that might unite disparate groups within Northern Ireland who shared many of the same daily economic struggles and goals. Thus Charabanc saw "working class" as a term that could unite, whereas attaching words such as "feminist" (i.e., nationalist and anti-male), "political" (i.e., sectarian), or "women" (i.e., lesser) threatened to divide and alienate their very audience. Instead, in creating female characters that both nationalist and unionist women could relate to, Charabanc's plays attempted to create empathy for and identification with the opposing group, and it fiercely repudiated any labels that could potentially threaten this project.

Similarly, Charabanc refused to define the company as being politically motivated, in the fear that audiences would interpret its work as sectarian. Instead, the women argued that their plays concentrated on the issues of selfhood, identity, and individual experience rather than sectarian politics. Despite the valid reasons for rejecting an identity as political theatre, it cannot be denied that the company continually explored politically sensitive topics. In 1993, Maria DiCenzo wrote:

> Charabanc does not promote itself as a "political theatre" group, but a glance at the programs for these black comedies places them squarely in the political arena. The programs often include documentary material, statistics, and polemical writings. The plays were also intended to serve a political function; along with promising audiences a night's entertainment, Methven claimed that they were interested in getting Catholics and Protestants to listen to one another and in breaking down some of the myths of barriers that are reinforced in a context where the politics become ever more polarized.[26]

Helen Lojek agrees with this assessment, arguing that "Charabanc's founders may not always have conceived of themselves as political, but their repeated statement that one motivation in forming the company was fatigue at always being cast 'as somebody's wife or mother or sister' is a political statement however unselfconscious its political nature."[27] It was only after Charabanc disbanded in 1995 that the actresses felt comfortable acknowledging the company's political nature. In 2001, Carol Moore invoked the political theatre scholar Michael Etherton when she defined Charabanc's work as plays "that describe Irish politics, but . . . are not plays which commit their audiences to any political meaning for them."[28] This emphasis on addressing political issues without forcing any specific political ideology on the audience reflected the company's desire to create drama that engaged the political debates of the day without alienating or dividing their audience. Eleanor Methven also confirmed the political nature of Charabanc's work in 2001 when she defined all Northern theatre as drama that "addresses the issues that are particular to the Six Counties: political issues."[29] Methven argued that in contrast to theatre from the Republic, all Northern drama, including Charabanc's, is inherently political.

Thus, in a region marked by strange contradictions, Charabanc was unable to claim ownership over many of the aims of the company for fear of polarizing the base it was trying to reach. Charabanc also feared having its intentions misrepresented by the media, which tended to attach a sectarian agenda to all forms of politics. As a result, the Charabanc women, who wrote, created, and performed clearly feminist, socialist, and political drama, spent a lot of time denying that status in an attempt to create a neutral space in which to perform. Despite their denials during the height of their fame, many of Charabanc's members are now able to speak freely about the company's true intensions and embrace feminism as associated with the company. Eleanor Methven defines feminism as "having a female gaze on society,"[30] which was one of the most recognized and celebrated hallmarks of Charabanc's style.

From its initial production, Charabanc was widely embraced by the theatre communities in both the North and south. In a review of *Lay Up Your Ends*, Belfast's *Fortnight Magazine* wrote that the women were embarking on a larger project that would add vital importance to the Northern theatre sector: "And the world of theatre here is invigorated by the energy, reach, and scale of the project; by the wider competence and new skills gained by local members of the theatre community who form the company; by the new audiences for theatre who are touched by such work; and by the commitment to accessible but serious forms of theatre. This, finally, is the sort of work we must be proud of and quick to encourage."[31] The sentiment that the North must embrace Charabanc's work was felt throughout the critical and

artistic community. There was an immediate sense of pride that innovative creative expression was coming out of Northern Ireland, especially during the Troubles. The cross-community nature of the theatre
group also made it easier for critics to validate the company's success,
since the group was promoting understanding and dialogue rather
than sectarian division.[32] *The Irish News* wrote that *Lay Up Your Ends*
struck "a perfect balance between frequently bawdy comedy and raw
social comment, to deliver one of the most powerful works to come
out of Belfast for some time."[33] Rosalind Carne of *The Stage Guardian* wrote that the company "marked the beginning of an alternative
theatre movement in a place which has relied for a long time on the
inspiration of outsiders," noting as well that British theatre had sadly
lost much of the "humour and exuberance" that characterized Charabanc's work.[34]

Some critics, however, did not understand how to critique the collaborative nature of the company's devised work. One critic from *The
London Times* acerbically declared his confusion when he described
Girls in the Big Picture as "devised by the company and written by
Marie Jones (whatever that precisely means)."[35] In addition, their
rough and minimalist production style performed in makeshift halls
and community centers compelled a few critics to dismiss the wom-
en's work as amateur community theatre. In reality, Charabanc's performances in nontraditional theatre spaces allowed it access to larger
audiences than the formal performance venues of Belfast could hold,
giving the company wider exposure than most other professional theatre companies.

Charabanc's influence throughout the island created a new
vibrancy and respect for Northern theatre, and it also demonstrated
that independent theatre could flourish in Belfast. In the years after
Charabanc's success, a series of independent theatres and women-
led companies formed. In 1987, Big Telly was established by Kate
Batts, Jill Holmes, and Zoe Seaton. Founded in 1988, Tinderbox
has become one of the leading independent theatres in the North
today.[36] Replay, a touring theatre-in-education company for children and young adults, was also started in 1988 by Brenda Winter of

Charabanc. Kabosh, the North's only site-specific theatre company, was established in 1994. All of these enterprises "owe a debt to Charabanc. The persistence, energy and diversity of theatre companies like Charabanc . . . bear witness to the popularity of alternative forms of theatre, particularly for audiences who are excluded from or exclude themselves from mainstream or 'high art' theatre."[37] Moreover, Carol Moore thinks one of Charabanc's greatest contributions was helping to found the independent arts sector in the North: "There is no doubt that the emergence of other independent theatre companies became a reality because we demonstrated that it was possible to create your own work, company, and power base with nothing but creative ideas and energy."[38] In addition to helping establish an independent sector, Charabanc, along with the success of playwrights like Anne Devlin and Christina Reid, showed that women were creating some of the most innovative theatre on the island, encouraging a new generation of women to view theatre as a potential career. Each of the previously mentioned companies—Big Telly, Tinderbox, Replay, and Kabosh—are currently led and managed by women. Thus a strong independent sector and the women who are now reenergizing Northern drama are the successors of Charabanc's increasing visibility and achievements during the 1980s and early 1990s.

Furthermore, Charabanc was both a training ground and a launching pad for the career for Marie Jones, one of the island's most critically acclaimed and financially successful playwrights. Jones began her career as an actress and took over the primary writing responsibilities for Charabanc. The company was important in that it gave Jones the space and opportunity to write plays that were immediately produced and widely toured (instead of having to struggle and submit her work independently to Irish theatres). The initial success she found with the company led her to write plays independently and have them performed internationally (including on Broadway and the West End). *A Night in November* (1994) and *Stones in His Pockets* (2000) went on to be among her most critically and financially successful works. Being a founding member of Charabanc afforded her the experience to found DubbelJoint in 1991, which also had a significant impact on Irish theatre.

Perhaps, though, one of the company's greatest contributions was paradoxically the least visible and most often dismissed by critics. Most scholars view Charabanc's decline as beginning in 1990 after Jones and Brighton left to start DubbelJoint. At that time, Charabanc switched its focus from producing original devised works to thinking strategically about the larger infrastructure for the arts in the North. This period of supposed decline (when the company was producing fewer and less critically successful works) was also a period of great contribution to the larger strength and health of the theatre sector. Rather than producing new plays, the reduced company, led by Eleanor Methven and Carol Moore, devoted time and funds to create playwriting workshops, advocate for new funding initiatives, and establish the International Workshop Theatre Festival, which brought in foreign theatre professionals to work with Belfast practitioners. In addition, they founded and ran the Small Scale Theatre Managers Association (SSTMA), a lobbying group for the growing independent sector. SSTMA was the first of its kind in the North and was, arguably, the forerunner of today's Northern Ireland Theatre Association, which currently advocates for theatres and provides training and support opportunities. Charabanc's later contributions—workshops, theatre festivals, and increased funding and advocacy—were less tangible or easily measurable achievements that did not directly benefit the company itself, leading many critics to dismiss its contributions during the 1990s.

Despite its significant impact on the development of independent and women's theatrical participation in the North, Charabanc's contributions are underacknowledged. One explanation is that Charabanc's plays were not published until 2006. Currently, only six have been published in limited editions.[39] This lack of previous publication may also be why Charabanc's work has not been studied or produced more extensively. Steve Wilmer cites the lack of presses interested in publishing feminist theatrical writing as a major reason for the dearth of women's dramatic writing in Ireland.[40] This situation is steadily improving, but female dramatists remain underpublished. In addition, many of Charabanc's plays can be difficult to understand for an audience unfamiliar with the history of the Troubles. The plays' specificity in terms of time and place potentially make them challenging to a wider audience. Few productions have been staged of Charabanc's plays since the company disbanded. Oregon State University did a production of *Lay Up Your Ends* in April 1997, directed by Charlotte Headrick,[41] and Martin Lynch produced a short revival of the same play at the Grand Opera House in Belfast in 2009. Significantly, in this production, Marie Jones reprised the role of Belle, the strike leader, which she originally played in 1983. This arguably allowed greater success in capturing the essence of the original production than if the play had been performed without a single member of the original cast.

The company ultimately disbanded in 1995. The *Irish Times* literally bemoaned its fate and questioned what group would be able to fill the gap: "Howl, howl, howl. Could there possibly be more depressing news for the Irish theatre lover than that Charabanc Theatre Company has disbanded?"[42] As Charabanc's reputation grew in the 1980s, it became a cultural and perhaps national symbol of a strong, positive, and artistically accomplished North. As the company toured across the island and the world, Northern media and audiences became invested in the symbol of Charabanc as a working-class theatre company that devised original work about Northern life.

As the North embraced its accomplishments, however, Charabanc's actresses arguably lost ownership or control over the company, which had become an important public voice and storyteller of the working-class experience during the Troubles. When the company shifted its priorities in the early 1990s, producing classic plays like Pierre Corneille's *The Illusion* (1993) and Frederico Garcia Lorca's *The House of Bernarda Alba* (1993), the backlash was swift and brutal. Critics condemned the company for losing its original mission and producing unoriginal and undistinguished work. When Charabanc tried to grow and vary its offerings, the North and Republic rejected these changes. While this was frustrating for the company and contributed to its demise in 1995, it can also perversely be seen as evidence of just how influential its plays had become in the North and how important the company was to the working classes who viewed it as an expression of their experiences and lives.

Although the company struggled constantly to maintain financial solvency and was described in 1986 as "chronically short of funds" and "often work[ing] out of pure desperation,"[43] Charabanc was one of the most influential Irish theatre companies of the 1980s. It revolutionized the subject matter and performance style of Northern drama and played a significant role in creating opportunities for women and independent theatre. Its cross-community, cross-border touring model as well as its commitment to bringing theatre to areas that rarely had access to the arts served as a model for new theatre companies throughout the island. The company supported and grew vital infrastructure during the 1990s, which led to the healthy and sustainable development of the independent theatre sector today. Perhaps most significantly, Charabanc's productions played a fundamental role in reframing traditional ways of looking at and engaging with the Troubles. The plays illuminated the historical and economic circumstances that led to the sectarian conflict, stressed the commonalities between women's experiences in the Catholic and Protestant communities, retold the Troubles from a women's perspective, and reflected the lived realities of the working-class communities of the North. Carol Moore summed up the company's contributions best when she wrote: "Charabanc reflected the lives of people back to them, gave them a voice, and illustrated that their stories were culturally valuable. It also reflected and/or challenged their political worlds and entertained them in troubled times."[44]

5

Political Drama and Controversy

DubbelJoint and the JustUs Community Theatre Company

The DubbelJoint Theatre Company was founded in 1991 by Marie Jones, Pam Brighton, and the actor and director Mark Lambert after Jones left Charabanc to pursue writing on her own.[1] DubbelJoint was initially conceived as a cross-border touring project, and the name reflected this melding of the main theatrical centers in the North and south: DUBlin BELfast Joint.

Collaborative theatre projects between Northern and southern companies and cross-border touring was (and continues to be) a rare occurrence on the island. Even in the early 1900s (before partition), the Irish Literary Theatre toured extensively across the south as well as Scotland and England, but failed to travel north. Mark Phelan argues this was due to the south's "imaginative failure to envisage the North in the nation."[2] The Abbey Theatre's minimal Northern representation on stage also speaks to the national theatre's historical exclusion of the North in representations of the Irish nation. Cross-border projects were also more difficult with the onset of the Troubles in the late 1960s, when the North experienced increasing political isolation from the south. Financial obstacles have also hindered island-wide touring. The Arts Council of Northern Ireland has a smaller budget

Sections of this chapter were published as "Marie Jones and the Dubbel-Joint Theatre Company: Performance, Practice, and Controversy," in *The Theatre of Marie Jones*, ed. Tom Maguire and Eugene McNulty (Dublin: Carysfort Press, 2015), 107–21.

than the Arts Council of Ireland, and it has proven difficult for both organizations to find funding that can be used for collaborations or for cross-border touring. In addition, theatre practitioners from the North are constrained by UK equity laws, whereas practitioners from the Republic abide by Irish equity rules. Starting in the late 1990s, both arts councils established a joint fund for cross-border touring (Touring and Dissemination of Work Scheme); however, it did not significantly increase collaboration or exchange, in part owing to limited funding.[3]

Despite these obstacles, during the 1980s, the Field Day Theatre Company and Charabanc broke ground by widely touring productions across the island. With these models of success, Jones, Brighton, and Lambert believed that theatre could connect and find common ground between the two states. "Its aim," as the DubbelJoint board member Eileen Pollack explained, "is to express the absence of boundaries in theatre."[4]

In addition to its cross-border model, the company dedicated itself to producing plays that reflected the real lives of ordinary people, with the desire to expose the dignity and honor of everyday struggles. Pollack described the company as "devoted to producing plays that reflect the worth of everyday lives. Theatre shouldn't necessarily be some kind of escapist activity; people should be able to see appreciations of their own lives on stage, too."[5] In contrast to the Abbey Theatre in Dublin or the Lyric Theatre in Belfast, DubbelJoint prided itself on producing theatre that was accessible and relatable to those beyond a narrow cultural elite. In a 2003 play program, DubbelJoint described itself as having "a strong commitment to community venues, particularly in areas that suffer from social, economic, and cultural disadvantage and to local writing, and through these, strives to democratise theatre and make it accessible to all."[6] With this mission, DubbelJoint's tenure was defined by cross-border touring of politically engaged work, performing in areas without access to theatre, and support of community and women's theatre groups.

Whereas Charabanc had encountered resistance as it tried to grow and diversify its offerings, DubbelJoint was a new enterprise with an unproven record and no critical or audience expectations against which to chafe. This freedom allowed the company to initially experiment with a range of productions, mounting both original plays written by Jones as well as adaptations of classics. The company was immediately successful. Audiences embraced a wide range of challenging original plays, commercial holiday hits, and European classics. One of the company's first productions was *Hang All the Harpers* (1991), written by Jones and Shane Connaughton. The play examined the role of Irish music in the formation of national identity. In contrast, the next year the company premiered a commercial hit, Jones's musical comedy *Christmas Eve Can Kill You* (1992), at the Old Museum Arts Centre. This proved to be a commercial success for both DubbelJoint and, later, the Lyric Theatre. One year later, the company switched focus again, producing Terry Eagleton's *The White, the Gold and the Gangrene* (1993), about the 1916 Easter Rising, and performed Jones's much-lauded adaptation of Nikolai Gogol's *The Government Inspector* (1993). Audience acceptance of such diverse offerings along with the transfer of a DubbelJoint production to the Lyric signals how quickly the company established itself in the community.

Jones's highly successful adaptation of *The Government Inspector* established the company's reputation for high-quality theatre. The play premiered in August 1993 at Féile an Phobail, beginning DubbelJoint's tradition of premiering new work at the west Belfast summer festival. Jones reset the play in the late-nineteenth-century Northern countryside where a small town of corrupt unionists mistake a young English lothario for the government inspector sent by the English crown. A decade earlier, Field Day had also succeeded in adapting classic plays to the North. In 1985, it produced Tom Paulin's *The Riot Act* (an adaptation of Sophocles' *Antigone* that recast Creon as a unionist politician and Antigone as a republican martyr) and Derek Mahon's *High Time* (based on Molière's *School for Husbands*, reset in 1984 Derry). The company also performed several translations of Chekov classics, resetting them in an Irish dialect, such as Friel's *Three Sisters* (1981) and Frank McGuinness's *Uncle Vanya* (1995). These productions served as models for how foreign classic work could illuminate the social and political life of Northern Ireland. By resetting *The Government Inspector* in the pre-partition North, DubbelJoint demonstrated a similar goal to that of Field Day: to disrupt old narratives about the conflict and show parallels between the North and other societies.

Jones's *Government Inspector* is set in a small northern town during the late nineteenth century. The play captures the hysteria of corrupt local politicians who fear their power will be diminished if Ireland is divided. The critic Peter Cromer described the production as "a new play about the prejudices revealed by the threat of partition."[7] Unionists are concerned that their land and farms will end up on the wrong side of partition, making them a unionist minority in what will become the Irish Free State rather than a powerful majority in a unionist-controlled North. When they hear that the English queen is sending an inspector to town, the unionists become panicked because they have been illegally evicting Catholic tenants from their land and deporting them to America. The Protestants have been using the newly abandoned land to raise cattle, which they have been exporting to Europe without paying tax to the British crown. Afraid the inspector will report their tax fraud, the play revolves around the town's bribing and cajoling the spurious inspector into keeping their secret.

Although reset in Ireland, Jones stayed loyal to the original plot; she did, however, make a significant change to the ending, which infused a subtle feminist slant to the play, reflecting her heritage with Charabanc. The mayor's wife and daughter both try to seduce the inspector, but they are not the flighty, foolish females of Gogol's original. In fact, the daughter is the first to see through the impostor's affectations: she realizes that he is recycling the poems of Yeats and Merriman and claiming them as his own. The wife and daughter reveal at the end of the play that they both knew the lothario was a fake all along, and they blackmail the con artist into returning all the bribes the town had given him, thus saving the day. Jones positions the daughter and wife as intelligent and educated women who do not fall prey to the same phony charms and seduction that the male officials are taken in by, "making the female characters the only honest voices amongst a horde of ineffectual, cowardly and bullying hypocrites."[8] Despite the mother and daughter's intelligent wit, however, the town does not learn its lesson. When the real inspector arrives the next day, the unionists, not wanting to be duped again, treat the man as another impostor. They tie him to a chair, harass him, and proceed to humorously confess their sins of tax evasion and eviction of the Catholics, guaranteeing their own downfall.

The production was highly satirical, and Brighton's direction included heavy physical comedy. Brighton used a melodramatic acting style that included double takes, freezes, stage *tableaux*, stage tricks, and grotesque exaggeration reminiscent of slapstick. Irish and English critics overwhelmingly agreed that Jones had successfully written a highly provocative and politically astute satire of partition, British-Irish stereotypes, cultural misunderstandings, and unionist corruption while making it accessible and enjoyable through a fast-paced physical production that used humor to critique society's ills.

In addition to exploring unionist corruption in a comedic way, the play satirized stereotypes of the Irish long established within English imperialist culture. In one scene, the false inspector becomes convinced that the Irish are cannibals, believing that Jonathan Swift's *A Modest Proposal* (1729) has been written into law. Throughout the play, the locals serve the inspector and his servant their best beef, which results in panicked hysteria as the British con men believe that they have been served human flesh. The play also uses unapologetically bawdy humor. The Anglophile unionists in town are enthralled with anything British, and since the inspector comes from London, this gives him an air of glamour and sexual allure for the women of the village, who attempt to seduce him and his assistant at every turn. In one of the funniest scenes in the play, the mayor's wife has orgasms just listening to the impostor recite poetry.

While the play is rife with comical observations about Irish life, it also does not shy away from revealing a dark unionist history that systematically abused Catholics: massive numbers of Catholics in the town are hanging themselves because they have been evicted or can no longer afford to pay the rent. The town officials grumble about the number of corpses that are piling up, since the Catholics cannot afford to bury their families. Thus the primary plotline (the humorous, lavish entertainment of the inspector) is counterpointed by constant reminders of death, poverty, and suicide caused by the greedy corruption and systematic abuse of the Catholic population by the unionists. This riotous humor in juxtaposition with serious political and social commentary would become a hallmark of Jones's work, and the plays she wrote for DubbelJoint build on this model.

After its premiere at Féile an Phobail, the play toured throughout the island in early 1994, playing in Derry/Londonderry, Newtownabbey, Hollywood, Armagh, Sligo, and Galway. In addition, it played at the Grand Opera House, then Belfast's largest commercial receiving house, demonstrating the production's wide appeal. Glowing reviews and ticket sales allowed the play to transfer to the Tricycle Theatre in London later that year.

With tours of *The Inspector General* in the North, the Republic, and England a great success, DubbelJoint established its reputation as a new theatrical force. For the next few years, the company produced several successful plays. *A Night in November*, one of Jones's best-known works, premiered at Féile an Phobail in August 1994 and toured through the fall. The Provisional IRA had declared a three-day cease-fire that July and, as the play premiered, there was mounting expectation that a second ceasefire would be declared. That ceasefire was confirmed just as the play went out on tour, adding further political resonance to the production. The monologue play is delivered by the character of Kenneth McCallister, who recounts his evolution from intolerant Ulsterman to compassionate Irish citizen, embracing the multiplicity of his identities as "a free man . . . a Protestant man . . . an Irishman."[9] The catalyst for the transformation was the real-life events of November 17, 1993 when sectarian clashes broke out during a World Cup football qualifying match between the Northern Ireland and Republic of Ireland teams. The play toured the island and was later produced in London and New York. Crucially, it sustains the same border-crossing trope that the company sought to fulfill in its own touring. Two years later, Jones wrote the first version of what would become the international hit *Stones in His Pockets* (1996). The play, which Jones reworked in 1999, ran in the West End from 2000 to 2003 and on Broadway for 198 performances in 2001. The comedic two-hander follows a series of movie extras on the west coast of Ireland, where an American film crew is making a movie. The comedic play is marked by tragedy when a young local man drowns himself in the ocean owing to poverty and lack of opportunities in the rural West. The play illustrates that the idealistic and romantic rural Ireland depicted by Hollywood often does not represent the destitution and isolation that can characterize real life in the West.[10]

Whereas Jones remained committed to the Charabanc model that crossed sectarian boundaries in what was represented and the audiences to which they toured, Brighton began to direct a series of increasingly nationalist plays in the mid-to-late 1990s. In 1996, DubbelJoint helped several women from west Belfast form the nationalist JustUs Community Theatre Company. Together, the two companies staged several highly controversial productions that resulted in outraged public calls for DubbelJoint's Arts Council funding to be rescinded. Controversy surrounding the company's political sympathies was exacerbated when DubbelJoint produced the four-person monologue play *A Mother's Heart* (1999), by Pearse Elliott. This original work explored the emotional and psychological journey of four women whose children had been killed during the Troubles.

The idea for *A Mother's Heart* was based on a real-life UDA murder in Belfast in 1994. Sean Monaghan, a young father of twins, was abducted by members of a violent loyalist gang and held in a house in the loyalist-controlled Shankill area of Belfast. Monaghan escaped but was recaptured by neighbors and given back to his abductors, who tortured him and dumped his body on the street. The community's complicity in the killing was especially chilling and reverberated throughout the North. *A Mother's Heart* is significant in that it was the first post-Agreement play to come out of the North that specifically addressed how people come to terms with the violence of the past. It is also significant in that it marked a clear return to examining

the conflict specifically through women's experiences, which Jones
and Brighton had done during their time with Charabanc.

A Mother's Heart took grieving and angry women out from
behind the private curtain of mourning and presented them in a very
public manner, dramatizing and exposing their grief on stage. The
actress Brenda Murphy, who played one of the mothers, said, "It is
the first play during my lifetime, during the war, that has addressed
the issues that women have kept hidden, and this play allows them to
become public."[11] The playwright, Pearse Elliot, recognized it as "a
real first. I don't think there has ever been a play like it, that articu-
lates women's rage and humanity, done by women who have lived
through it and have something to say."[12] Painful moments in women's
lives had previously been performed on stage, but Charabanc usually
employed humor and satire as the means through which to express
women's fears and hurt. In contrast, *A Mother's Heart* was a serious,
painful, and unflinching portrait of four women consumed with grief
and anger, and it was also the first play to center around women's
experiences of losing a child through sectarian violence.

The play generated such controversy that DubbelJoint again risked
losing its Arts Council funding. The dispute was created mainly
through casting decisions. Three of the four actresses—Brenda Murphy, Bridie McMahon, and Rosena Brown—were ex-republican prisoners. Brown was especially notorious because, in 1992, she had lured
a prison officer with the promise of sex into a trap where the IRA
executed him. The event earned her the nickname "the IRA's Mata
Hari," after the Dutch exotic dancer and courtesan executed by the
French after being accused of spying for the Germans during World
War I. Brown had been sentenced to twenty years in prison in 1993
but was released only a few years later under the Belfast/Good Friday Agreement. Public outrage, which was already high over her early
release, was exacerbated when she agreed to appear on the public stage
acting the role of a *loyalist* mother grieving over her dead child. Much
of the public felt that it was outrageous and offensive for a former IRA
operative to embody the story and grief of a Protestant mother on the
public stage. The character Brown played was based on the mother of

the UVF member Brian Robinson, who was shot dead by the British military in 1989 only minutes after murdering a Catholic. All the killings in the play mirrored other actual victims, such as a woman who was beaten to death in a Belfast band hall, Monaghan's abduction by a loyalist death squad, and an IRA volunteer executed by the British military after he killed a policeman. None of the victims in the play died at the hands of the IRA, which added to the public criticism. Furthermore, all the Protestant characters were played by Catholic and nationalist women, which was seen by many as offensive.

Brown had been an actress before her imprisonment and had performed briefly with Charabanc. The controversy over her performance exposed how delicate the early post-Agreement period was and how uneasy the public felt over the early release of prisoners, which had been an integral element to the signing of the Agreement. Jim Rodger, the Ulster Unionist Party (UUP) councilor for Belfast, reflected community outrage: "This is absolutely disgusting. For Rosena Brown to play this role when the real victims of terrorism are having to come to terms with the early release of prisoners shows she has no conscience."[13]

Criticism of the play tended to reflect sectarian affiliation, and there were multiple press claims that Rosena Brown was "living it up" by performing on stage right after being released from prison. Many critics found the play to be unbalanced and highly polemical, threatening DubbelJoint's initial reputation for producing complex and evenhanded work. Jane Coyle wrote: "Now that DubbelJoint's vision has become more closely aligned with a republican agenda, the days when it produced fine and politically astute work like *The Government Inspector* and *A Night in November* are fading into fond and distant memory."[14] Whereas Jones's *The Government Inspector* had strong criticism of unionist corruption and abuse of Catholics, the satirical take, the historical distance, and the resetting within a classic drama gave audiences enough critical distance to appreciate the message of the play without taking offense. However, when DubbelJoint productions took a critical look at more recent historical events, unionist audiences viewed the plays as accusatory, histrionic, and biased.

Elliot's play, which was supposed to be about the universal experience of losing a child, was transformed by public debate into a biased sectarian polemic. The *Mother's Heart* controversy did much to damage DubbelJoint's reputation in the North, and calls for the cessation of funding to the company followed soon after.

Funding has always been a highly political issue because there is always intense community scrutiny about whether public money is being funneled to support sectarian causes. Unionist critics of *A Mother's Heart* attacked DubbelJoint by calling for an end to its government funding. The unionist politician Jim Rogers declared he would "be asking for an investigation into how this play was given funding by us. The people of Belfast will be horrified when they find out where their money is going."[15] In 1999, DubbelJoint received £62,500 from the Arts Council of Northern Ireland as its yearly funding; £20,000 of this was used for *A Mother's Heart*, along with an additional £6,500 from the Belfast City Council for the production.[16] When applying for this public funding, DubbelJoint had agreed that it would hold workshops in nationalist and unionist areas in conjunction with the production and that it would cast Protestants in some roles. However, this was not done, and it raised the question of whether the company had violated its funding agreement. These attacks on its funding sources were potentially damaging because DubbelJoint had previously had its funding questioned when it coproduced *Binlids* with JustUs only a few years earlier. To make matters worse, the company coproduced another highly controversial JustUs production, *Forced Upon Us*, the same year as *A Mother's Heart*. The combination of three highly provocative and arguably nationalist productions called into question whether DubbelJoint was a sectarian theatre company and whether public money should be funding a seemingly nationalist-leaning group.

Whereas unionist politicians called for the withdrawal of DubbelJoint's public funding, nationalist newspapers highlighted Rosena Brown's difficult experience in prison and her brave involvement in the no-wash protests, during which republican prisoners refused to leave their cells to bath or use the bathroom.[17] Nationalist critics also fixated on Brown's isolation after being released from prison, and the fact that she had first declined the role because she was aware that the Protestant community would perceive her involvement as insensitive. Brown herself stated that she eventually accepted the role as a therapeutic way to rejoin society after years in prison.[18] The Belfast/Good Friday Agreement called not only for the release of political prisoners but also for their reintegration into society, and this became the nationalist justification for her appearance in the play.

Critical and audience reception continued to be split down sectarian lines. Negative reviews reported that the quality of acting was terrible and that many people left during intermission, whereas positive reviews claimed the play received standing ovations. Unionists argued that although the plays purported to be balanced by showing both Catholic and Protestant women's experiences of losing a loved one, it was highly biased and sympathetic to nationalism. They further argued that the play insinuated that the two Protestant women were bad mothers for failing to protect their sons from Troubles violence, whereas the Catholic mothers were positioned as appropriately loving and protective.

Interestingly, the most consistent criticism from Catholic and Protestant reviewers alike came in the form of discomfort with the anger and rage expressed by the mothers on stage. Audiences had expected the play to be about healing and forgiveness, and women in Irish society have historically been positioned as the arbiters of peace and reconciliation. However, the women in *A Mother's Heart* were full of anger, rage, and vengeance at the deaths of their children. The character played by Brenda Murphy, for example, has a recurring dream where she breaks into a hospital nursery and kills all the babies to prevent them from entering the cruel world. The play worked directly against notions of women as implicitly peaceful, forgiving, and kind, and this engendered a lot of discomfort for critics and audiences alike.

Controversy notwithstanding, DubbelJoint retained its funding and continued to produce new works into the mid-2000s, including *Working Class Heroes* (2002) by Brenda Murphy, *Black Taxis*

(2003) by Brian Moore, and *A Cold House* (2003) by Laurence Mc-Keown and Brian Campbell. The company's last two seasons included Moore's *The Session* and Campbell's *Voyage of No Return* (both 2005) and Moore's *The Ballad of Malachy Mulligan* and Gary Mitchell's *Remnants of Fear* (both 2006). In an important departure from the nonsectarian mission of Charabanc, DubbelJoint became increasingly associated with nationalist causes through its premieres at Féile an Phobail, its coproductions with JustUs, and its production of plays written by the ex-republican prisoners Brian Campbell and Laurence McKeown.[19]

Although DubbelJoint became associated with a nationalist voice, the company's original tenants remained constant. Throughout its existence, the company toured politically engaged work, highlighted the stories of ordinary people, performed in locations otherwise without access to theatre, and engaged the North and Republic in a cross-border model that helped to maintain a cultural link throughout the entire island. Its success strengthened the growing independent theatre sector in the North, and its diverse repertoire of classic, dramatic, and comedic offerings served as a model for what other Irish theatre companies could achieve. One of its most significant but controversial contributions to Northern theatre was its support and development of the JustUs Community Theatre Company.

JustUs was created in 1996 by a group of amateur working-class women from west Belfast who wanted to perform their personal experiences of the Troubles for the public. Having seen several DubbelJoint productions at Féile an Phobail, the women approached Pam Brighton to ask her help in producing a play for International Women's Day. This new partnership led to the company's first production, *Just a Prisoner's Wife* (1996), and a new relationship with DubbelJoint. JustUs was made up of politically active nationalist and republican women who wanted a new medium through which to express their voices. Company members included Niamh Flanagan, Anne-Marie Adams, Sue Ramsey, Christine Poland, Orla Adams, Margaret Mooney, and Chrissie Keenan. Many of these women had been politically active in the west Belfast community before founding JustUs. Keenan was married to the Provisional IRA member Brian Keenan, who was a key participant in negotiating the decommissioning of the IRA during talks leading up to the Belfast/Good Friday Agreement. Chrissie Keenan spearheaded the theatre project and recruited many women from west Belfast to become part of the production. Sue Ramsey also had political experience, in leadership positions in Sinn Féin and as an elected Member of the Legislative Assembly on the Northern Ireland Assembly. In 1998, Ramsey made history as one of a handful of women involved in the Belfast/Good Friday Agreement negotiations team. The women who comprised JustUs were politically and socially active members of their communities who looked to harness the theatre as another dynamic medium through which women could stage a politically commanding presence. Whereas Charabanc had certainly addressed political issues in its work, JustUs had the live bodies of political activists and city officials on stage, creating a direct connection between the active, ongoing politics of the conflict and the theatrical representation of it.

Although JustUs occasionally used men as writers and actors, the company was created and managed by women, and its female-centered productions aimed to express the Troubles from a nationalist women's perspective. The company devised original plays based on the personal experiences of community members as well as the shared historical memory of the conflict. As Bill McDonnell asserts, the performances of JustUs "operated as a form of community therapy and political education."[20] JustUs defined its own mission as "empower[ing] the community to tell their own story, in their own words, through the medium of dramatic arts."[21]

The company had another important goal, which was providing women with the opportunity to train and work professionally in the otherwise male-dominated profession of the theatre. McDonnell writes that the company sought "to develop a training programme which would foster the development of women writers and performers."[22] Eoin Ó Broin of *An Phoblacht* promoted that assertion, considering it "important to point out that *Binlids* is not just a play but also a unique drama training programme. DubbelJoint Productions, The Training for Women Network, and Féile an Phobail with assistance from the Open College Network and the Peace and Reconciliation Fund have all assisted in the project, one of whose aims is to provide training and employment for women in non-traditional skills such as script-writing and technical production thus enabling them to gain entrance into what has traditionally been a male dominated profession."[23] In this way, JustUs provided theatre training to a group of working-class women who otherwise would never have had access to these opportunities. The administration of JustUs remained entirely female throughout its tenure, the management committee being composed of Bridie McMahon, Jeanette Keenan, Marie Jones, Sue Ramsey, Margaret Mooney, Christine Poland, Anne Marie Meenan, Chrissie Mac Siacais, and Maureen McGuinness, and the staff composed of Donna McGarry and Anne-Marie Keenan.

The women of JustUs viewed the stage as a platform for political expression. Despite the members' active political participation in Sinn Féin, the Legislative Assembly, and elsewhere, these women were still in a community that limited their political participation to certain categories and to specific actions. In an interview about the importance of JustUs, the founding member Brenda Murphy reflected: "Acting has given us a way of expressing ourselves that we never thought was possible. If there had been a way of venting our frustration and anger like this thirty years ago, maybe we'd never have become involved [in JustUs]. Who knows?"[24] Here, Murphy identifies the need for a new medium through which women could express themselves both politically and personally. Through the vehicle of theatre, JustUs developed a new creative language that was able to cut through the noise of the violence and the stale rhetoric of masculine Troubles politics to give voice and presence to nationalist women whose experiences had historically been ignored.

The company's first production, *Just a Prisoner's Wife* (1995), was a series of monologues. Similar to Charabanc's model, Chrissie Keenan, Sue Ramsey, and others interviewed and researched the personal experiences of women within their community and translated them (with the help of Pam Brighton) into a stage performance. The play charted women's experiences of supporting a family member in jail. During internment, the no-wash protests, and the hunger strikes,[25] the male prison experience was promoted and recorded as one of the most sacrificial and important contributions to the nationalist mission. Although there were women political prisoners who participated in the hunger strikes, their stories were rarely told.[26] The economic, social, and psychological costs that women suffered from losing husbands, sons, and brothers to the prison system were rarely publically acknowledged. As the title *Just a Prisoner's Wife* suggests, women's sacrifices were considered minor compared to the physical bodily sacrifice that nationalist and republican men suffered. This was the first play to articulate the excruciating experience of waiting for family members to be released, and it suggested that women experienced their own emotional and psychological form of imprisonment on a daily basis. Community regulation over prisoners' wives has been explored in films like Terry George's *Some Mother's Son* (1996), Jim Sheridan's *The Boxer* (1997), and Maeve Murphy's *Silent Grace* (2001), as well as in plays like Anne Devlin's *Ourselves Alone* (1985) and Jennifer Johnston's *Twinkletoes* (1993). In her feminist ethnographic study of nationalist women in Northern Ireland, Begona Aretxaga observes: "Waiting looms large in the narratives of Belfast nationalist women: waiting for their children and husbands to come home alive, waiting to see them in prison, waiting for them to be released. . . . Women's waiting becomes an allegory of an imprisoned existence, in the sense that in Northern Ireland the lives of everybody are on hold, that the country is just a big prison."[27] This sentiment is echoed by many women playwrights. In Jennifer Johnston's *Twinkletoes,* Karen remarks about her jailed husband, "It's hard being married to a hero. It's a bit like being in prison too."[28] *Just a Prisoner's Wife* continued the feminist tradition of breaking the silence surrounding women's experience of the Troubles. For the female audience members, it gave legitimacy to their experiences and the knowledge that other women shared their hardships. For the male audience members and the masculine-led politics of the nationalist mission, it served as a wake-up call that women were suffering trauma and hardship on an equal level to men even if they were not jailed at the same rate.

Just a Prisoner's Wife proved a huge success. Although the show was supposed to be performed only once, it was staged more than twenty times throughout different towns in the North. It won the first Belfast City Council award for Best Arts Partnership, signaling citywide recognition of the power of professional and community arts collaboration. It was also the first time that the City Council had awarded a play with a nationalist perspective. Significantly, the production undertook a cross-border tour. The success of the initial show led the women to officially found the JustUs Community Theatre. These auspicious beginnings evoke those of Charabanc, which had also planned to do a single production of *Lay Up Your Ends* until its success led members to officially found the theatre company.

Following the success of *Just a Prisoner's Wife*, JustUs worked again with DubbelJoint to create several successful but also highly controversial productions. Their next play, *Binlids* (1997), was written by Christine Poland, Brenda Murphy, Danny Morrisson, and Jake MacSiacáis, with collaboration from other community actors in the show.[29] Some productions, like this one, included male actors and writing collaborators, but the plays remained committed to highlighting the strength of women's voices and giving a public platform for women's experience of the Troubles. Ó Broin remarked that the focus of *Binlids* "remains on the women. In their multiple roles as mothers, sisters, daughters, soldiers, activists, and endurors there is never a moment when their strength wavers."[30] By showing the varied roles that women played in the nationalist fight, JustUs expanded the community's view of Catholic women and offered one of the first public platforms for the recognition and appreciation of these women's sacrifices.

Binlids took its title from the tradition of Catholics banging garbage can lids on the ground to warn their neighbors that the British military or the Royal Ulster Constabulary were coming. The play traced the history of west Belfast since 1971 through a series of loosely connected vignettes that included dramatic scenes, comedic moments, and rallying songs. Similar to European models of agitprop theatre, the company also used dance, skits, statistics, direct address, and ripped-from-the-headlines verbatim dialogue.

Binlids was the result of six months of research and interviews in the west Belfast community. Several of the scenes were rehearsed privately for members of the community in advance to make sure they resonated truthfully,[31] a practice that Charabanc also often employed. The play staged the daily hardships of living within sectarian violence and had scenes commemorating important moments in Troubles history. Significantly, it highlighted the Milltown Cemetery massacre in 1988 when a UDA man attacked a crowd gathered at an IRA funeral, killing three and wounding sixty. The play also commented on the Corporals Killings later that same year when two British Army officers inadvertently drove into the path of an IRA funeral procession and were dragged from their car, beaten, and shot to death. Like Charabanc, JustUs often devised history-based plays that spanned many years, charting the development of the sectarian conflict and showing the roots of the problem. Ó Broin described *Binlids'* unique combination of personal stories mixed with subjective representations of history as "people's personal memories . . . mixed with political fact and speculation."[32] Although this strategy inflamed unionists who saw these dramatic representations as inaccurate and highly biased, the productions were important, as they reflected the nationalist community's perspectives and experiences of a history that had fundamentally shaped their current views of the conflict.

The set of *Binlids* consisted of four stages and the floor of the auditorium; the acting shifted back and forth from stage to stage and sometimes into the audience itself. Scaffolding towers dotted the room, showing how claustrophobic and dangerous it was to live in west Belfast. A combination of professional and amateur actors played multiple roles and signaled a transformation of character through small costume changes, physicality, and vocal intonation. A bare-bones aesthetic and minimal sets and costumes characterized the productions of JustUs, which were enhanced greatly with light and sound.

The action of *Binlids* was also integrated into the audience, giving them an environmental theatre experience. Actors playing soldiers walked with machine guns through the crowd of spectators, children distributed political leaflets, and processionals bearing coffins moved through the audience. Actors posed as onlookers at protest rallies, transforming the rest of the audience into participants at the rally and blurring the distinction between actor and spectator. As the critic Ben Webster wrote of the production, "When the person beside you cheers at some anti-Brit comment by Adams, you are never quite sure if it is an actor or a member of the audience."[33] The Sinn Féin leader Gerry Adams found the play "inclusive and gripping theatre where the distinctions between the audience and the actors becomes blurred as they mesh together, so that at times it is hard to tell if the person beside you is a spectator or a performer. In *Binlids* everyone can be a player."[34]

Smoke canisters simulated bombs and teargas, and expended cartridges from gun blanks flew into the audience, creating a visceral experience. Brighton explained the reasoning behind her direction: "I wanted the audience to have a sense of events happening all around them—guns going off, sudden darkness—and be physically frightened. This kind of esthetic is not typical in Ireland, which still favors a writers' theatre."[35] Although some critics in New York, where the show toured in 1998, would remark on the tired and passé quality of the show's environmental aspects, many audiences in Ireland had not experienced theatre in this way before.

Binlids begins in 1971, during the start of internment. Between August 1971 and December 1975, the British military and the RUC arrested and detained without trial hundreds of Catholics suspected of being involved with paramilitary activity.[36] The play often broke from the action to give historical information and statistics directly to the audience, sometimes with limited success. For example, in one scene, the women awkwardly tried to integrate historical information about the displacement of Catholics owing to Troubles violence. Breaking from the easy and conversational dialogue of previous scenes, the women say to each other:

> MAIREAD: Did you know that nearly 2,000 Catholic families have been burned out since '69?
>
> SUE: '69. Here hold that child, since August '69 and August '70, 21% of Catholic families living Belfast have been moved from their homes. You know, it was the biggest shift in population since World War 2.[37]

Despite how awkward this integration tended to be, the historical information and statistics were part of the company's efforts to publicize the hidden cost of Catholic civilians during the Troubles.

JustUs often introduced original songs into their plays. In a scene entitled "No Time for Love," the women sing a heartbreaking song that illustrates how the stress and grief of the Troubles have become part of their daily lives. The refrain is:

> No time for love if they come in the morning,
> No time to show tears or for fears in the morning,
> No time for goodbye, No time to ask why,
> And the wail of the sirens,
> The cry of the mornings. (13)

The refrain recounts the uncertainty and anguish that had become associated with early morning internment sweeps. An important characteristic of the work by both Charabanc and JustUs was not only exposing the extreme tragedies of the conflict but also showing how seamlessly and naturally war had become integrated into people's lives. Just as Charabanc's *Somewhere over the Balcony* looked at how the Divis flats neighborhood had become used to the absurd daily machinations of war, *Binlids* looked at how communities are able to absorb war into their daily lives as a means of survival and how much damage can come from this implicit acceptance.

While the song emphasizes the true cost of war on individuals' lives, it also rallies the nationalist community to keep up the fight:

So come all your sisters and brothers who
Give to your people the will to fight on
You say you can't get used to this war,
But that doesn't mean that this war isn't gone.
Just like your people need you,
And the death squads will only get through to
Them, if first they can get through to you. (130)

It is interesting to note that in 1997, one year before the Belfast/ Good Friday Agreement, this song encourages the community to stay strong and to keep up the fight. The song does not echo a war that is winding down; instead, it rallies the community from its complacency, from the everyday banality that the war has become, and asks them to wake up and actively fight.

While *Binlids* takes a hard look at the brutality and injustice of internment and of the British prison and policing systems, it also uses humor to make the work accessible and entertaining. This mixture of dark violence and witty dry humor is a defining quality of Northern theatre. Charabanc, DubbelJoint, and JustUs all used dark comedy in their plays, and this distinctive tonal characteristic continues to be central to the work of many Northern playwrights.

Binlids is thus characterized by vignettes that mix real crisis and tragedy with the everyday humor that allowed women to cope with trauma. Scenes show women supporting and helping one another through the day: grouped together banging bin lids to warn their neighborhoods, working together to solve neighborhood problems such as finding new housing for families whose homes have been burned down, allowing neighbors to use their telephones to track down husbands and sons after they have been interned. In one poignant scene, the character of Claire gently cajoles local women into helping their fellow neighbors:

VERA: Ach, Claire I'm sorry to bother you, it's just I need to use your phone.
CLAIRE: Of course you can Vera, I'm just making a sign to let people know that if they need a phone they can use this one.

> I'm really glad to see you—I've got a family who have three
> wee ones and they were burnt out of Ardoyne this morning and
> I don't want to put them in the Community Center. Will you
> take them?
>
> VERA: Ach Claire, you know Paddy, he's as odd as two left feet.
>
> CLAIRE: Vera, Paddy's in jail.
>
> VERA: Ach, I know but I've to look after his ma and everything.
>
> CLAIRE: Vera these people have only what they're standing up in.
>
> VERA: Claire, you're right, what am I thinking of.
>
> (*to the audience*)
>
> Yesterday she was just a woman with a phone,
>
> Today she's an incident centre. (6–7)

This last line is characteristic of JustUs humor. Vera begrudgingly acknowledges her duty, but not without making fun of Claire's new-found sense of purpose and leadership. The play centers around many of these seemingly mundane but important issues that women dealt with on a daily basis but that rarely received public attention. The play thus sheds light on the plight of the women who were left behind to pick up the pieces as their husbands, son, fathers, and brothers sat in prison indefinitely. These stories were generally not considered worthy of media coverage or dramatic representation.

Women's personal stories of hardship, pain, and perseverance interlaced with humor and optimism again dominate the script. At one point, the women tell a series of comedic stories directly to the audience. Sue talks about her mother's routine during internment when she was only eight: "One incident that I thought was so funny was when they used to raid our house. We had a 50p electric meter and my ma used to only put enough money in to cover the electric until we went to bed. So when the peelers came to raid there was no lights and they found it hard to do a proper search, so after a couple of raids they got so pissed off and brought their own 50p" (15). Another woman recalls a dog that would retrieve all the bricks that Catholic rioters threw at the British soldiers and give them back to the crowd. One day, a protester threw a nail bomb at the soldiers. The dog ran and brought it back to the rioters, who all started running away from the bomb with the dog in pursuit after them. When the bomb exploded and the dog died, the community gave him a military funeral. The British dug up the dog days later for forensic evidence (15). The humor in stories like these highlights the absurdity of the conflict.

Although *Binlids* included male actors and showed the sacrifices and the intense violence that Catholic men often faced, the focus of the play was consistently on women's experiences and accomplishments within the conflict. Begona Aretxaga observes: "In republican culture, men's suffering is inscribed in their own bodies through their fighting; women's is inscribed in the bodies of others: fathers, sons, brother, husbands, or friends. . . . The implications of this economy of suffering that reduces women's historical agency to the passive bearing of testimony have not escaped republican women."[38] *Binlids* showed the physical and emotional trauma that women directly suffered during the conflict, erasing the notion that women's suffering was mediated only through the experiences of men. One scene, set in jail, illustrates the degradations that women political prisoners faced. Bridie, a seventeen-year-old, appears on stage wet and beaten, wearing only a towel. She is forced to bend over a table while she is searched internally. The play also features several important female political leaders during the Troubles. One scene shows Máire Drumm performing a speech to the community to bolster recruitment to the IRA. Drumm, who was the vice president of Sinn Féin and a commander in Cumann na mBan (a women's republican paramilitary group), was assassinated in 1976 by loyalists. The play also celebrates the women hunger strikers whose sacrifices were completely overshadowed by the deaths of Bobby Sands and nine other men in 1981. *Binlids* recovers this lost history by telling the story of the Price sisters who went on a hunger strike in 1973 for more than two hundred days. They were violently force-fed by the British government. In this way, *Binlids* used the extraordinary accomplishments of female activists as well as those of ordinary women to commemorate the wide range of contributions women made to the nationalist fight.

Furthermore, in a departure from standard theatrical representations of the conflict, the play includes many painful scenes that show women not only as victims of the conflict but occasionally as perpetrators of the violence as well. In the most controversial and shocking scene of the play, a group of women encounter a lone eighteen-year-old soldier from Wales and initially converse in a friendly manner with him. The soldier's status as Welsh is particularly poignant for the women since he shares ethnic and religious ties with them. The women attempt to disprove his assumptions that Catholics are barbarians by pointing out that the women of west Belfast collected money for victims of a recent disaster in a Welsh mining town:

PATRICIA: Jesus, Wales. Aberfan[39] I remember, we collected money here for all those poor kids.

MARY: Aye, so do I.

PATRICIA: Sure you'd be too young to remember that.

SOLDIER: I don't believe yous, you wouldn't do that—yous all are animals.

PATRICIA: Where did you get that stuff about us being animals?

SOLDIER: That's what we've been told. That's why we're here to stop you animals from killing each other.

. . .

SOLDIER: I'm a Catholic.

VERA: Well now we've got a lot in common, you're a Celt, so are we, you're a Catholic like us.

SOLDIER: But you're not Catholics—you're Fenian scum. Its not the Catholics or the Protestants that cause the problems; its ye Fenians.[40]

Although the soldier is both Catholic and of Celtic origin, he has been told by the British military that Northern Irish Catholics are barbaric, violent animals who bear no relation to his own religious or ethnic background. The women attempt to use reason and persuasion to convince the Welshman that he has joined a military that does not support or respect his people:

PATRICIA: A Welsh man in the British Army, not very Welsh of you, is it? The English don't like the Scots, the Irish or the Welsh, you wee fuckin' moron.

SOLDIER: The mines are closing and it's a living, you can get fed and waged and you get to see the world. (26)

The women point out the soldier's ignorance and hypocrisy in joining the British Army, but the play also paints the soldier in a sympathetic light, showing how the military is often filled with the poorest men who have the least options.

The scene then descends into the most complex and highly disturbing moment of the play. As shown above, the women use both emotion and logic to connect with the Welsh soldier and to make him realize that he is just as much of a victim and pawn in the British war as Northern Catholics are. The women convince him to sit down and relax. Once he does so, the women stealthily take his gun, and an IRA man enters the scene and shoots him point blank in the head. The scene that began with the women emotionally connecting to and mothering the young soldier unexpectedly turns into a cold execution. The scene counters notions of women as innately peaceful and instead illustrates how they were complicit in Troubles violence in both direct and indirect ways.

The scene is further complicated by being sandwiched in between two scenes that show a young Catholic, Liam, being tortured by British soldiers who are attempting to extract information from him about members of the IRA. The stage directions demonstrate the visceral brutality and violence:

Liam has already received quite a beating so it's not long before his limp body tries to relax. Every time he does so, he is punched in the ribs, kidneys, lower back and then forcibly returned to the same position. Liam's muffled sounds of protest are getting weaker and weaker, along with his body. When his two jailers are quite sure that he has been physically exhausted, they introduce white noise. The introduction of the noise (which is a high pitched hissing sound like that of compressed

air being released) startles him at first. Soon after, it agitates him, as
if there's something in his ear he can't get out. (18)

Liam's torture and interrogation preceding and following the scene
with the Welsh soldier juxtaposes the women's cruelty against what
is happening to their own men. By placing the murder of the Welsh
soldier in the middle of Liam's torture, the play arguably repositions
the women's actions as justified given the brutality that their community is experiencing.

Justification for republican violence and retaliation is further
reinforced later in the play through another song called "Ballad of
an Internee's Wife." The song recounts a wife's experience of visit-
ing her husband in prison, the humiliation of the strip searches she
must endure in order to gain access to the jail, and how her husband
is beaten and broken down by prison guards. The last line of this
arresting song is: "I've come to know his jailers and I know what
must be done. For the only voice they'll listen to comes from behind
the gun" (29). The song suggests that politicians are not helping
and no one outside of the North is listening to the pleas for aid from
the Catholic community. The lyrics position Northern Catholics as
completely alone and unsupported, forced to take action through
violence. This song along with the Welsh soldier scene illustrates how
women in the Catholic community have been radicalized: women
have resorted to violence in order to be heard, protect their families,
and empower themselves within a hostile state. Not surprisingly, the
section with the Welsh soldier drew strong critical reaction from the
unionist community, which pointed to it as evidence of republican
brutality and immorality.

The play achieved some balance to the controversial Welsh soldier scene by including moments that showed compassion for the
declared enemy. The Corporal Killings had been captured on television cameras and broadcast widely, becoming an especially shocking and brutal representation of republican mob violence. In *Binlids*,
a mother and daughter discuss their complex emotions relating to
those murders. The daughter is confused and internally conflicted:

DAUGHTER: I can't understand why I feel like this. I'm confused
about what I think I should feel. Why do I. . . . Why am I feeling sorry for those soldiers—I know—I don't know I'm afraid
to give them sympathy—I mean they were soldiers—I'm afraid
to say I'm sorry they were killed.

MOTHER: The day you stop feeling like that is the day you should
start worrying. . . . Granny was a republican all her life. One day
a soldier got shot outside her front door. She went out and put
a pillow under his head and said a prayer over him. She got a
lot of stick from people . . . she told them she didn't care what
they said, he was somebody's son. That made me proud of her.
I knew then I was on the right side. (75–76)

The mother's response attempts to show that one can have simulta-
neous compassion for the enemy as well as loyalty to the fight. The
empathy positions them as ordinary individuals stuck in an impossible and terrifying war.

Scenes like this one countered the British propaganda machine
that for centuries had promoted the image of an atavistic and
innately violent Irish in order to justify the violent suppression of
uprisings. During the height of the Troubles, the British media further perpetuated this narrative. It argued that the British military
was in the North not as an occupying force but as a means to protect
the Irish from themselves and to bring peace and civilization to a
barbaric population. In contrast to this dominant narrative, *Binlids* wanted to show that the people who were directly involved in
the IRA and in the fight against the British were ordinary citizens
who, in any other situation, would have led conventional, peaceful
lives. Nationalists and republicans argued that it was circumstances
rather than an innate tendency for violence and hatred that had led
schoolteachers, shopkeepers, and bus drivers to lead brutally violent
and dangerous lives. In fact, Pam Brighton made sure to note in her
interview with *Back Stage Magazine* that Sinn Féin "is made up of
people who, under other circumstances, would be academics and
social workers."[41]

Binlids exposed this propaganda war by showing how Catholics were portrayed by the media, both British and Irish. In a direct address to the audience, actors read verbatim passages from real newspaper articles such as *The Irish Independent*, *Daily Star*, and *Daily Mirror*, which described the republican movement as barbaric, violent, and animalistic:

> In every country where a television service operates, millions of people saw the real face of Provisional involvement—a compound of hate, ferocity and animality, which removes its members almost from the human race. If this is the face of nationalism then lets forget about nationalism. It changes humans into animals. The Provisional have caused many here to ask themselves if they would agree to accept the North back if it were offered to them and come up with a definite answer, then NO. (76)

This passage suggests that the war has turned so savage that the Northern Catholics have lost credibility in the eyes of the world. The Republic of Ireland shuns the violence and vitriolic nature of the North, undermining the goal of reunification with the south. As articles such as this were read to the audience, the stage filled with a chorus of actors who chanted after each quotation: "That's not us, that's not us, that's not us." Whereas the media tried to make the conflict black and white, victim versus perpetrator, innocent versus guilty, the play complicated these reductive narratives. This scene rejected simplistic notions of the conflict presented by a media that fixated on the brutal violence and neither understood nor presented any of the compassion, the conflicted emotions, or the daily realities of ordinary citizens. During their New York run, the cast member Brenda Murphy told National Public Radio that the show was "a chance for people to hear a story of the other side. We were described in the papers as animals, scum. We're not animals. We're not scum. We're resilient people, and we are here, and we survived it. And we're just telling our story."[42]

The play ends by showing the cacophony of competing voices and opinions within the nationalist community. The last scene of the play is entitled "Public Row about the Troubles"; the name alone signals an acceptance of allowing opposing voices and opinions to be aired within the nationalist struggle.

> SALLY: I'm sick and tired of it. Everybody I know has had somebody jailed or injured in one way or another. . . . I'm friggin' fed up, sick to death with hospitals and jails and funerals, seeing young ones lying in coffins, mothers and fathers broken hearted. Lives destroyed. Bodies maimed. I'm sick of the whole bloody lot, the IRA, the Brits, the Orangies. . . .
> ANNEMARIE: The only thing they understand is war.
> CONOR: The Brits will be out of here in two years, they know they can't win.
> MARC: You'll never bomb a million Protestants into a peaceful united Ireland. You don't talk to your friends to make peace, you talk to your enemies.
> MAIREAD: What way will our kids grow up if all they know is war. I know we didn't create the war, but we owe it to our kids to create the peace.
> BRIDIE: Peace. Yeah, but not peace at any price. (78–80)

The competing opinions stress that the Catholic community is made up of a diverse group of people who do not conform to media representations as single-minded, entrenched, violent, or animalistic. The last line of the scene, "not peace at any price," sums up the main argument of the play: the nationalist and republican communities want peace, but not at the expense of completely dismissing the basic civil rights of the Catholic community. This is further reinforced in the play's final lines, which quote a famous speech by Gerry Adams in which he declared: "We will pay a high price for peace but we will never go back to being treated as second-class citizens in our own country. We will build a new future for all of our people, Catholic, Protestant and dissenter based on equality and the principals of democracy of freedom and justice, we will move forward. Beidh ár lá linn [Our day will come/Our day will be with us]" (80). The play thus ends on a positive note of renewed nationalist vigor tempered with hopes for a peaceful future.

Tom Maguire has argued that *Binlids* played a role in the peace process leading up to the Belfast/Good Friday Agreement by showing that the conflict is a result of specific historical circumstances that can be changed in the present:

> By demonstrating the ways in which the community has evolved in response to its changing context, there is a differentiation between the past and the present. This is a way of showing both that the present is not inevitable but the result of specific historical processes and that the present moment is not the same as the past and therefore presents an opportunity for doing things differently. By making manifest the changes within the community and in the community's external relationships, it articulated the possibility that the conflict is the product of specific historical circumstances which now can be changed. On this basis, the play can be seen to have had a role in the process of peace-making for this community at the precise point of its staging in 1997.[43]

This reading, however, seems to contradict many of the lessons communicated in the play. Several of the scenes in *Binlids*, including the play's final scene, rally the community to continue the fight. The play does not reflect a community that is inevitably moving toward peace, but one that is reengaging with the past to make sure that the issues they fought for are not subsumed or weakened by peace negotiations. A more accurate reading of the play would be as a warning to those engaged in negotiating peace that the history and sacrifices of the nationalist community must be acknowledged and their story interweaved into the peace talks; otherwise, the community will continue to fight.

This interpretation is supported by the historical context in which it was performed. An IRA ceasefire was in effect while *Binlids* was in rehearsal and as it toured. Audience members watched the play hopeful for peace but also wary of the compromises that each side would have to make. Northerners were distrustful of each side maintaining the peace and concerned that issues that each community had fought for would be nullified by any agreement at the state level. Terence O'Neill summed up the nationalist position clearly (as well as the overall argument of *Binlids*) when he told the American newspaper *The Irish Echo*: "Reconciliation is everybody's goal but if that reconciliation is going to kick in behind the peace, the nationalists are going to have to be listened to. It is a very important component of the whole process, that these anxieties, bad memories, and fears be recognized and released and understood."[44]

The political climate of the North in 1997 during the peace talks called for moderation, calm, and nonincendiary speech. The play, however, was extremely controversial, taking an uncompromising and often shocking look at injustice against the nationalist community. It was thus interpreted by some as counterproductive to the larger political project of peace that permeated the North. Many viewed *Binlids* as rejecting the call for moderation and moving beyond the trauma of the past. Indeed, controversy surrounding the play captured the growing tension between whether people need to leave the past behind without receiving official justice or whether the tragic events of the Troubles needed to be publically and formally dealt with before individuals could be expected to move on. The production thus reflected a very specific and complex historical moment in which two warring factions were on the verge of peace but entirely certain that everything they fought for would be sacrificed in its wake.

Because Catholics feared their stories and histories would be lost to this dominant peace process narrative, *Binlids* was purposefully polemical and propagandistic with an aim to educate audiences and give voice to an underrepresented portion of the population. A program from the 1998 production directed the audience toward facts that emphasized how the Catholic population in the North was constantly under siege:

> The state forces of heavily armed paramilitary Police (the Royal Ulster Constabulary/RUC) and the British Army currently stand at levels where there is one armed member of the state forces for every 3.7 Catholic males between the ages of 16 and 45. The RUC

maintain 161 fortified military bases with the British army occupying 135 bases, the vast majority of which are located garrison style in nationalist districts. The city of Belfast houses 56 military installations making the nationalist area of West Belfast one of the most heavily militarized areas in Western Europe. It is against this background and the accompanying conflict that *Binlids* the play is enacted.[45]

The program was filled with photographs of British soldiers lining Catholics up against walls and strip-searching them along with images of the RUC shooting, hitting, and arresting Catholics. Gerry Adams also wrote a program note, underscoring IRA and Sinn Féin endorsement of the show.[46] Shane Connaughton, who helped develop the script, further emphasized the nationalist ideology of the production by including a program note that read: "If you hate the thought of Irish Unity, don't see this play. If you don't want to think or feel, don't see this play. In short, if you are afraid of having your mind changed, then stay at home."[47] Thus the audience was warned from the moment they were handed the program that this play would chart the story of the nationalist minority in highly biased terms. As Pam Brighton said of the show, "West Belfast is a political community and to tell the story truthfully, the piece had to be one-sided. That's not to say it isn't impeccably honest. But the play was conceived in response to British propaganda against Irish Catholics, whose stories have never been told, and [British] demonization of the IRA which they view as an evil terrorist group."[48]

Many in the nationalist community viewed the work of JustUs as the expression of a subjugated minority whose story had been repressed by the British and Northern governments and the unionist-controlled media. Terence O'Neill, who wrote the songs for the production, told *The Irish Echo* that *Binlids* was an important contribution to and preservation of the oral history of the North: "There's a challenge for recognition involved even to the extent of admitting that we even have a story to tell here. We constantly have to keep proving that we're real and that what we're doing is authentic, and that we have a place in the scheme of things."[49] Similarly, Gerry Adams saw the play as an expression of a minority working-class Catholic experience that had been consistently ignored and repressed:

> *Binlids* is an important play also, because it represents a piece of the jigsaw which has been missing for some time. When I say that it has been missing I mean that it has been kept until now to one side, out of the sight and on the margins. With the rest of us, struggling to be heard. Now it has a voice. A creative voice testing its range and rhythm and trying to sing out for itself in explanation of its existence and celebration of its survival. Telling its own tale. It appears to me that part of the process of making peace includes and needs people reclaiming their own stories and telling their own tales. . . . It is partisan but it is also history relived with all its memories remembered and its myths reborn in a way which makes some sense of it all.[50]

Adams argues that peace for Northern Ireland is not possible until the voices of the repressed are heard and recognized. He saw the theatre as a powerful medium of creative expression that could legitimize marginalized voices in the North. He and Sinn Féin recognized early on the value of the arts in helping to publicize and spread a nationalist ideology in the North and abroad and thus often lent their voices and financial support to nationalist community cultural projects like *Binlids*.[51]

The importance of promoting the nationalist story was further exacerbated by the media's tight control on Troubles narratives. Because the mainstream Northern media was primarily run by Protestants, it historically did not report on Catholic inequalities. Catholics were thus doubly denied a public voice through the media as well as through the Protestant-controlled government. Especially important was the island-wide broadcasting ban on IRA and Sinn Féin voices from 1988 to 1994. Republican faces were shown on television but their voices were not allowed on TV or radio; instead, their words were voiced by an actor, denying republicans agency, ownership, and the emotion behind the words they expressed. *Binlids* paid homage to this history in a reversal of the historical practice when an actor, dressed as Gerry Adams, mimed the words to a recording of the real voice of Adams.

However, the argument that the republican working classes had long been denied a public voice was challenged by the mainstream press. Malachi O'Doherty of the *Belfast Telegraph* argued that *if* Catholics had historically been denied representation in the media, the Troubles helped to remedy this imbalance: "I have asked this before of DubbelJoint Productions: What is the point in going into a community and affirming its most venomous prejudices? If you see west Belfast as a community without a voice; if you imagine that the old republican story has not been heard; if you see the people of west Belfast as cowed and ignored, then there is an argument for enabling those who are passionate about that story to tell it starkly and simply. But there is no case to be made for these things."[52] It is true that during this period Irish nationalists gained international sympathy and recognition for their civil rights demands, and the republican cause was aired on Irish and British televisions nightly. Catholics told the story of the nationalist struggle through film, theatre, novels, poetry, music, and other artistic forms. Critics have argued that Northern Catholics have been much more successful than their Protestant counterparts at promoting and educating audiences about the injustices within their community.[53] For example, the majority of feature films made about the Troubles (both from Hollywood and Ireland itself) show Catholics as victims of an unfair and brutal political system, whereas unionist experiences are rarely showcased. Despite the cultural stereotype that the arts remain under the purview of the Catholic community, many Protestants have held prominent positions the arts, especially in Northern theatre: Charabanc was founded by several Protestant women, and Marie Jones, Christina Reid, Gary Mitchell, and Stewart Parker all come from the Protestant faith.

When O'Doherty dismissed *Binlids* as a story that has been told before and when he contends that the Catholic population has adequately promoted its experience, he completely dismisses the unique fact that the play was written, produced, and performed in large part by Catholic nationalist *women* who had not had their stories, experiences, or perspectives told within the larger grand narrative of the Catholic Troubles experience. As Ó Broin wrote in defense of *Forced Upon Us* (1999):

> JustUs, the West Belfast based community theatre group, is not just about making plays. It is also about empowering local women to express their own sense of selves and build their skills in order to improve their employability. On the night I attended *Forced Upon Us*, the vast majority of the audience was made up of women of the same generation as that of the women from JustUs. Viewing their own friends and peers dramatize their life experiences also has a validating effect on the audience, again a constituency usually excluded from history, theatre, and politics.[54]

Both *Binlids* and *Forced Upon Us* were projects to correct misperceptions about the Catholic minority that had been popularized by the media for decades. It was also an attempt to insert women's experiences into the narrative of the sectarian conflict with the understanding that women's voices were central to the success of the peace process. As Pam Brighton argued, "*Binlids* in its re-enactment of a community's traumas, in its ritual rejection of the media's distortion of that experience, has a great deal to offer the peace process. It attempts to lay bare the republican experience of the past thirty years and if the peace process is to gain meaning, this experience has to be understood. *Binlids* was not seeking a balance within itself but seeking a balance in the overall perception of what makes west Belfast tick."[55]

The issue of whether art with a clear sectarian viewpoint has a place in Northern culture and a legitimate role to play within the conflict is at the heart of Northern theatre history. Since the establishment of the Northern state, politically engaged theatre has been repressed, censored, and rejected by the government, critics, and audiences alike. There is a cultural attitude that art with a political agenda is biased, sectarian, and propagandistic and thus naturally inferior in artistic and creative worth. Politics essentially sullies, dulls, or destroys the integrity and artistic value of theatre in the North. Art, on the other hand, that is "balanced," "evenhanded," and promotes cross-community experiences and cooperation is elevated and privileged above all else. This is seen in the wide embrace of Charabanc versus the sharp rejection of JustUs. Charabanc enjoyed widespread support throughout the North and Republic in part because it advocated cross-community partnership and a nonsectarian agenda.

Despite the North's historical and continued rejection of agit-prop theatre, incendiary drama, and one-sided plays, these stories can serve an important and productive role in society. Wendy Heresford writes, "One of the standards against which political theatre is judged is whether a performance shakes the audience out of complacency and unsettles easy identifications." Sympathy, compassion, and identification engendered from victimized characters in plays, Heresford points out, can often "function as an alibi for a lack of action."[56] In other words, audience members feel they are not responsible for the suffering or victimization they are viewing and instead allow their sympathetic emotions to act as an acceptable alternative to action. Instead, writes Heresford, "to move audiences to consider ethical questions and political action, political theatre must alter the relationship between the audiences and the subject(s) presented."[57] To encourage audiences to transform their sympathy and emotion into direct action, JustUs used shock and rage to propel audiences from their seats. Their plays were not fashioned to produce balanced and thoughtful conversations, but to provoke physical action in the nationalist community and direct political change in the North. When presented by women, this kind of work went directly against conservative notions that women's voices and bodies should be private and unobtrusive, and the gendered dynamic of JustUs arguably magnified the backlash against them.

Binlids sold out during its initial run at Féile an Phobail, and it was restaged for another Belfast run in February 1998. In October it traveled to New York for a three-week off-Broadway run. The show was performed at the Angel Orensanz Foundation Center for the Arts in Manhattan (a former Jewish synagogue that had been transformed into a performance space). The Belfast City Council, the Northern

Ireland Voluntary Trust, and the Training for Women Network all contributed funds to help bring the production over to New York. The Training for Women Network sponsorship signaled the recognition JustUs received as advancing women's professional training in the arts. However, because of the controversy surrounding the production, the Arts Council of Northern Ireland declined to give any money to sponsor the New York tour. The *Binlids* actor Niamh Flanagan said in response to the Arts Council's denial, "They don't like political drama." Terence O'Neill, who wrote songs for the production, added: "But it's more complicated than that. There's a situation with funding agencies in the Six Counties. There's a political agenda at work all the time. If it's perceived that the work is critical of the state, nine times out of ten you will be refused funding."[58]

Despite limited financial support from home, the production had an international political impact. It initiated a three-year cross-cultural exchange program between Belfast and the United States, which was intended to be "a non-secular [*sic*], apolitical vehicle to promote better understanding of the Irish culture and social cohesion within the Irish American Community and with Northern Ireland."[59] The first step of the exchange program was sponsoring and coordinating the *Binlids* run in New York. The play was an unusual addition to the rest of the Irish theatre being performed in New York that year. Commercial hits celebrating Irish culture such as *Riverdance* and critically acclaimed dramas such as Martin McDonagh's *The Beauty Queen of Leenane*, Conor McPherson's *The Weir*, Frank and Malachy McCourt's *A Couple of Blagaurds*, Jim Nolan's *Moonshine*, and Marie Jones's *A Night in November* all graced the New York stage. The rough aesthetic and agitprop style of *Binlids* was in stark contrast to these polished, expensive productions that celebrated less controversial accomplishments of Irish culture.

Binlids was generally well reviewed by foreign critics. Jim Woods of BBC radio called it "a truth commission allowing people to have their histories publically recognized. That was their truth, their world view, articulated in their own terms with professional accomplishment, clearly, coherently, and most importantly publically."[60]

American reviews often included in-depth interviews with the cast
as well as history about the Troubles, allowing their readers to better
understand the controversial production within its historical context.
For the most part, foreign critics did not condemn *Binlids* for being
biased or unbalanced. Instead, they accepted the play for what it was:
the voice of one particular community.

Whereas *Binlids* was well received by foreign critics (who were not
burdened by the same complex political and historical ties that critics
from the North contended with), it was dismissed by many at home
as propaganda. The production was viewed by unionist reporters and
politicians as highly antagonistic, and they called for public debate
about the role of art within the peace process. One repeated criticism
was that the play failed to address the cost of the IRA on Catholic
lives. This arguably left the audience with the inaccurate view that the
only paramilitary violence that affected Catholics was loyalist, when,
in fact, the IRA was known to brutally police its own community. Just
as critics condemned DubbelJoint's *A Mother's Heart*, the critic Ben
Webster accused *Binlids* of being only superficially balanced, when, in
fact, it downplayed and justified republican violence:

> They have been careful to include a couple of incidents [of repub-
> lican violence] yet this hardly amounts to "balance" when the vio-
> lence—unlike with the many British atrocities shown—is narrated
> rather than enacted. For example, the action in the infamous cor-
> porals incident is cut short at the very point in the funeral when the
> two men were about to be beaten and murdered. The play swiftly
> switches to the aftermath of the killings, with a young eye-witness,
> played by Ramsey, describing how the corporals drew their guns,
> thereby apparently inciting the crowd of mourners. Another char-
> acter then pronounces that the crowd's response was "spontaneous,
> an act of self-defense."[61]

Tom Maguire believes that critical response to *Binlids* was so harsh
in part because viewers assumed that art that engaged the Troubles
should take an evenhanded approach.[62] Sectarian stories are not considered to be authentic or accurate because they do not include all

perspectives on the conflict. *Binlids* was decidedly and purposefully one-sided and thus denied the label of "authenticity" by some critics. Pam Brighton responded to attacks on the production's sectarian viewpoint with the assertion that the show's authenticity was born out of the true stories and experiences of the nationalist community. Maguire agrees with Brighton, arguing that "the basis of the production's claim to authenticity is shifted, rooted in the authority of individuals and communities to speak from and act out (of) their own experience."[63]

Similar to the critical reaction to *A Mother's Heart*, many of the Northern reviews were highly politicized op-ed pieces that were sectarian in nature. Toby Harnden dismissed the play entirely in an article provocatively entitled "Arts Council Funds Play That Jokes IRA Killings." He called the show "a powerful piece of propaganda; a poor piece of theatre."[64] A common tactic that unionist critics employed was to attack the artistic aspects of nationalist productions (such as the acting and writing) and to reduce the plays to political propaganda. By essentially removing a performance from the venerated category of "art" or "theatre" and by placing it within the more debased category of "politics," critics arguably felt safer and more justified in attacking the productions. Harden's article went on to list only the cast members who had IRA involvement in the past, stating that the play was "co-written by Danny Morrison, a former Sinn Féin leader jailed in 1990 for an IRA kidnapping. The cast includes Mairéad Ní Adhmaill, whose husband Felim is serving a 25-year sentence for possession of explosives, and Sue Ramsay, a Sinn Féin Councilor." The article also reported in disgust that the audience laughed and clapped when the Welsh soldier was shot and killed. Not surprisingly, as the review's title suggests, the piece also attacked issues of public funding. Harden was especially outraged that public funding marked for what was termed "peace and reconciliation" had been used for a politically sectarian piece of theatre: "Government subsidies and money from the European Union Fund for Peace and Reconciliation have been used to fund a Belfast community play which includes jokes about the IRA Brighton bombing and the shooting of soldiers."[65]

The media frenzy over the production and the attacks specifically on issues of funding led Philip Hammond, a funding officer of the Arts Council of Northern Ireland, to defend his organization, clarifying that the Arts Council had not specifically funded *Binlids*. Instead, the Council had given DubbelJoint its yearly funding scheme of £77,000 and had given the West Belfast Festival (which staged the play) £10,000 toward its operations. In response to the controversy, Hammond stated: "What we are concerned with is purely artistic standards. We are not in the position of censoring anyone. What they are expressing is their prerogative."[66] Like the unionist critics, the Arts Council focused on the artistic merits of the production in order to attempt political neutrality, a tactic that would explode into controversy with the next DubbelJoint and JustUs production.

The debate over whether government funding should support sectarian art overwhelmed *Forced Upon Us* (1999), which premiered at Féile an Phobail in August 1999. This time the Arts Council arguably bowed to increasing public pressure and refused outright to fund the production. *Forced Upon Us* begins in 1999 with the rape of a young Catholic girl who is afraid to report the assault to the Royal Ulster Constabulary. The young girl's fear of the very organization that is supposed to be protecting her causes her father to yell out in anguish, "Sweet Jesus—what kind of a country do we live in? How the fuck are we supposed to live like this? How the fuck are we left in this state? How?"[67] This desperate plea is the catalyst for the rest of the play, which then explores the historical conditions that have left present-day Catholics in such difficult circumstances. The play goes back in time to cover the early part of the twentieth century during the building of the *Titanic*, the signing of Ulster Covenant,[68] and the formation of the Ulster Volunteer Force (UVF).

Controversy came in large part from the shocking opening scene of a rape victim unable to report her abuse, followed by an even more gruesome scene when a group of Protestant ship workers attack a Catholic worker, tie him to a lamppost, pour paint thinner over him, and set him on fire. As demonstrated by these opening scenes, *Forced*

Upon Us never shied away from graphically describing or depicting violence on stage. One scene narrates the story of two Catholic men pulled from their beds at random by the B-Specials.[69] The men are brutally beaten, genitals ripped off, bones broken, skin torn by barbed wire, and left to die in a field. Another scene describes the burning of homes by the UVF, and another shows the cold-blooded execution of Catholics by the police force:

> (*Men run down the ramp to opposite platform, which is Donnelly's pub. They enter pub to find Mrs. Donnelly with her daughter who she pushes under a table as the men troop in and begin to wreck the place. They are all screaming at her to tell them where her husband is. Mrs. Donnelly starts to cry.*)
>
> MRS. DONNELLY: Please, please stop. Please! My husband is not here, I swear to you he is not here.
>
> (*Touches Nixon's arm as he is standing with gun in hand.*)
>
> MRS. DONNELLY: Please sir, are you in charge? Please tell them to stop. My husband is not here.
>
> NIXON: Do not touch me.
>
> (*He shoots her twice in the stomach and walks out followed by his men.*)[70]

Like *Binlids*, critics again were split down sectarian lines; many called the production highly offensive, grotesquely exaggerated, and sectarian in nature, whereas others lauded the production for exposing the continued repression of Catholic voices and bodies. Malachi O'Doherty of the *Belfast Telegraph* summed up the Protestant view succinctly: "It is a sectarian play which sees all modern history in Northern Ireland as the suppression of Good Catholics by Bad Protestants."[71]

DubbelJoint had already experienced calls for its funding to be cut with *A Mother's Heart* and *Binlids*, thus it was not entirely surprising when the Arts Council of Northern Ireland withdrew its funding before the production even premiered. The refusal to fund the play was polarizing. One side condemned the use of public money for art that promoted a specifically nationalist agenda, whereas others accused the Arts Council of politically motivated censorship against the Catholic population.

DubbelJoint produced the show despite the loss of funding and then promptly sued the Arts Council for censorship. Brighton called the Council "a quango, nobody knows who appoints them, there is no public accessibility to their decisions, there is no forum in which we can appeal this decision outside them and beyond them—it is a most extraordinary decision."[72] The controversy, which played out in the court of public opinion, certainly helped pack the auditorium, and *Forced Upon Us* played to sold-out houses. DubbelJoint and JustUs would later use the controversy in marketing materials to attract audiences to their touring productions.

The Arts Council ultimately denied any wrongdoing, arguing that its decision was based purely on the script being "deemed not of a sufficiently high artistic standard to warrant a huge injection of public subsidy."[73] The Arts Council public relations officer Damien Smyth accused his critics of hypocrisy: "It is safer to cry 'They've censored us' than 'They think we're rubbish.'"[74] Owing to the uproar, the Arts Council released its anonymous reader notes on which they had based their funding rejection. The readers judged the play to be: "a propagandistic play [that] could only serve to deepen existing prejudices," "distasteful," and "exploitive," concluding that "as . . . an exposé of the force's [RUC] bias, it is very poorly realized."[75] Brian Ferran, the Arts Council director, said that the three external examiners agreed that the play's "characters were wooden—'cardboard' I believe the word was used. It was also deficient in structure, and the quality of the writing was as bad as anything the assessors had ever read."[76] Here, the Arts Council reflected the widespread fear that sectarian art would naturally "deepen existing prejudices," essentially reinforcing and promoting further division. However, the goals and intensions of JustUs and DubbelJoint were to recover the repressed history of the conflict in order to confront it, acknowledge it, and address the issues that gave rise to it. This approach cuts to the central core of current debates in the North about whether the past needs to be confronted and documented or whether people simply need to move forward without rehashing an entrenched history that appears impossible to resolve.

Although the Arts Council claimed that it was denying funding based on artistic merit rather than sectarian ideology, a more realistic explanation may have involved new standards associated with the Belfast/Good Friday Agreement. *Forced Upon Us* was produced in the direct aftermath of the Agreement when a renewed atmosphere of tolerance, cross-community participation, and nonsectarian narratives were being advocated at the highest levels of government. The North had also received hundreds of millions of pounds from the European Union to encourage "peace and reconciliation" and "cross-community partnerships."[77] *Forced Upon Us* can be seen as oppositional to these directives for nonpartisan and nonincendiary speech and could possibly have violated the spirit in which funds had been designated, fueling public outrage.

Debate over whether sectarian art should be funded consumed the press. *Fortnight Magazine* published a multipage article that included commentary from all perspectives. Just as in debates surrounding *A Mother's Heart*, the issue of whether art that engaged the conflict must be balanced and objective was at the center of the dispute. Malachi O'Doherty of the *Belfast Telegraph* derided the play as "disappointing," "nasty," and "sectarian": "if it is supposed to be evidence of reflective thinking in a more politically mature republican culture, then we are in trouble." O'Doherty went on to dismiss the work as political propaganda because "explicit party political propaganda is surely always bad drama."[78] Whereas Catholics argued they were telling a truthful history of their experiences through an artistic medium, Protestant critics like O'Doherty repeatedly argued that JustUs productions were not pieces of art but poorly disguised political attacks, spewing propaganda and threatening the peace process. In his review, O'Doherty defines political theatre as inherently lacking artistic quality, implying that nonpolitical drama with an evenhanded approach has higher artistic merit.

In contrast, nationalist publications denied that stories about the Troubles had to be objective or show both sides of the conflict, arguing that there was inherent value in partisan stories. Ó Broin defended the production in his article "A Clear Case of Political Censorship." He argued that the play "does not pretend to be an objective historical document of the complex and turbulent period it deals with. Rather it offers the audience an interpretation in tune with the feelings and historical memory of the community who will make up its primary audience." He went on to declare: "The play also attempts to write a number of omissions into the local historical dramatic and political canon, namely the experiences and needs of nationalist working-class communities from Belfast. And in doing so, it provides all theatre goers with an insight into a particular Belfast community, both past and present, who are usually absent from public view."[79] Others took a more strident approach. The writer and actor Shane Connaughton declared: "The idea that funding is conditional upon Arts Council 'external assessors' liking a particular script is a Stalinist criteria hitherto unpracticed by the council."[80] On July 30, 1999, Connaughton, Marina Carr, Frank McGuinness, Marie Jones, Peter Sheridan, and Trevor Griffiths were among a group of leading Irish artists to publish an open letter in the *Irish Times* that called the withdrawal of funding a political act that trampled on freedom of expression.

Just as the ceasefire and the tense months leading up the Belfast/Good Friday Agreement colored audience reception of *Binlids*, the political context again had a significant impact on the North's interpretation and reaction to *Forced Upon Us*. An important part of the peace process and of the Agreement was the renaming and reorganization of the police force. The sectarian name of the Royal Ulster Constabulary,[81] its role in brutally suppressing the Catholic population, and its long history of abuse and corruption caused the organization to be given a neutral and nonsectarian label in 2001: The Police Service of Northern Ireland (PSNI). In addition, reforms mandated by the Agreement included that the police force recruit an equal number of Protestant and Catholic officers to balance out a force that historically had been composed of more than 90 percent Protestants.[82] *Forced Upon Us*, which is largely a scathing critique of the RUC, was performed in 1999 when a lot of these changes to the force were being debated and worked through as part of the continuing transition to peace. Thus attacks on the merit, quality, and subject matter of the play were filtered, in part, through the lens of an ongoing political debate about the future, form, and structure of policing in the North.

Like Charabanc, DubbelJoint and JustUs looked to the past in order to understand how contemporary sectarian divisions were molded by history. The three companies looked uncompromisingly at how continuing prejudices repressed the working classes and perpetuated violence. They decentered the Troubles from a male-centric to a female-centric experience, brought theatre into working-class communities, trained women with new professional skills, and empowered women's voices. Charabanc was also important as an incubator for Marie Jones and Pam Brighton, who were then able to found DubbelJoint. DubbelJoint continued Charabanc's tradition of cross-border touring while expanding the form, genre, and content of its theatrical offerings. The company was then able to use the security of its reputation and its firm positioning within the Irish theatre scene to take new risks by staging coproductions with JustUs. It is fortunate that in 1996, one year after Charabanc officially disbanded, JustUs performed its first production, *Just a Prisoner's Wife*, continuing the tradition of women playwrights and actresses devising original work about their lives during the Troubles.

In the 1980s, Charabanc was fully embraced by critics and audiences for productions that emphasized the commonalities between Catholic and Protestant women's experiences. In the 1990s, although DubbelJoint initially established itself as a company that produced politically astute and balanced work, its increasing association with Catholic narratives quickly gained it a reputation as a nationalist theatre company. Likewise, the tenure of JustUs was defined by controversy and polarizing sectarian dialogue. Despite these differences, all three companies secured a new respect for women on the Irish stage and forged new models for politically engaged theatre. Instead of accepting the status quo and waiting for their shows to be produced at the Lyric and other established Belfast venues, these women wrote, directed, performed, and produced their own work. Whereas so many politicians and state officials had failed to make a lasting impact on the sectarian conflict, the companies' cross-community and cross-border paradigms served as inspiration for what the performing arts could accomplish within the Troubles.

Thus the 1990s was a dramatically different landscape than the early 1980s, which had been dominated by male theatre boards, one-dimensional female characters, a lack of opportunities for women theatre practitioners, and a dearth of productions written by women playwrights. Instead, with the major advancements of Charabanc, DubbelJoint, and JustUs, supportive venues such as Féile an Phobail, and seminal productions of plays like Anne Devlin's *Ourselves Alone* (1986) and Christina Reid's *Tea in a China Cup* (1987), Northern Irish theatre of the 1990s was characterized by a growing independent theatre sector and a new standard for women's writing and participation in the theatre. The impact that these artists had within the historically male-dominated tradition of Irish theatre was even more extraordinary given the level of violence, sectarian politics, and repression of women's voices and bodies during the Troubles. Together, Charabanc, DubbelJoint, and JustUs forged a lasting space for women's politically and socially active voices on the Northern stage and created a tradition of women's activism through the theatre that transformed the makeup of the Northern theatre sector.

PART THREE

The Post-Agreement North, 1998–2012

6

Borderlands and the Rural North

Abbie Spallen

Abbie Spallen is a self-professed outsider. Raised in the border town of Newry, her identity has been informed by the liminal position of the border regions, which were often the sites of intense conflict during the Troubles. The Northern borders were heavily patrolled by the British military in order to prevent paramilitary members from moving in and out of the Republic, and citizens of this area were subject to heavy monitoring. The symbolic split identity of the border was often literally embodied: family members lived on opposite sides and farmers' land was historically divided by partition. The border region essentially acted out the core disagreement of the Northern conflict on a daily basis: the liminal and contested status of whether the land was British or Irish. Northerners could look across to the south and see a landscape that was identical to theirs; however, it had a foreign currency, different laws, independent sovereignty, and no meaningful violent conflict. This sense of alienation was exacerbated as the center of politics and commerce was and continues to be Belfast, and the border areas remain among the poorest in the North. The region thus often feels doubly excluded from the state's urban center of power and from life in the Republic.

Spallen, like the borderlands, has often felt like "not one thing or the other." She remains "fascinated with the border because there is a different sense there. You grow up in neither one nor the other. You are in the North . . . and yet being so close to [the Republic] . . . you are really close to it but you are not part of it . . . and I think that informs a lot of people from that area. It's a very closed-off area." Growing up, she found the small-town life of Newry quite conservative and cloistered. Creative and artistic pursuits were neither encouraged nor considered real professions, and she often found herself alienated as a Northerner, as a member of the rural border region, and as an actress and then playwright. However, Spallen feels that "it's important to stay on the outside."[1] Her marginalized status has been essential to her ability to view her community with a critical and creative eye and to write about the changes she has seen in the recent decades. Three of Spallen's plays, *Pumpgirl* (2006), *Strandline* (2009), and *Lally the Scut* (2015), are set in small, conservative border towns, and the characters are based on an amalgamation of the personalities Spallen saw in her community growing up. Her work calls attention to a minority rural experience and presents the voices, bodies, and perspectives of a community that is rarely seen on the Northern stage.

Spallen left Newry at the age of twenty-six to be an actress, living primarily between Dublin and London. She appeared in productions for the Lyric, Replay, and Rattlebag, as well as in Charabanc's *A Wife, a Dog, and a Maple Tree* (1995), and DubbelJoint's much-lauded *The Government Inspector* (1993). She based her decision to start writing on "the knowledge that I was going to end up playing mammies for the rest of my life. There is a serious lack of roles for women. . . . I just became more disillusioned."[2] Spallen began writing her own plays to create more opportunities for herself and other actresses, mirroring the initial impulses of the Charabanc women.

Spallen first started to write in the late 1990s when she accompanied a friend to a playwriting workshop. Her first play, *Abeyance* (2001), about ghosts haunting a home in Belfast, was the result of that effort and demonstrates the importance of training and educational opportunities in developing women playwrights who otherwise might not view the historically male-dominated theatre as a viable professional option. Spallen wrote her second full-length play, *Pumpgirl*, while acting in Shay Healy's *The Wiremen* (2005) at the Gaiety Theatre in Dublin. She sent the script to theatres in Ireland and the United Kingdom. London's Bush Theatre and a few other producers in England responded quickly and enthusiastically. However, Irish theatres were not as encouraging, and many failed to respond at all: "I sat for two years in Dublin while all this was happening, and all I could hear was that (a) there were no new writers in Ireland, and (b) there were no female writers in Ireland. I was both. . . . Anne Devlin, Christina Reid, Marie Jones. Women's voices have always been there. Maybe people haven't wanted to hear what we want to say."[3]

Pumpgirl premiered at the 2006 Edinburgh Theatre Festival and then transferred to the Bush Theatre later that year.[4] The production was a critical success, and Faber & Faber published the play, an essential step toward ensuring that her work would receive more productions and greater recognition from both the theatre and academic communities. The Bush production and the play's publication attracted the attention of the Manhattan Theatre Club, which staged an acclaimed production in 2007.

After successes in London and New York, the Lyric Theatre produced a short Irish tour in the fall of 2008. The three-person show, which required no sets, was an inexpensive production to tour while the Lyric's main theatre building was being renovated. *Pumpgirl* was nominated for the category of Best New Play by the *Irish Times* Theatre Awards in 2009, and a film version was made that same year, directed by Charabanc's Carol Moore. Spallen speculates why it took two years for an Irish theatre to produce the play, and then only in such a limited run: "That question needs to be put to the theatres in Ireland. The play was sent out to each and every one of them. . . . It's not for lack of trying. It's not me ignoring Ireland."[5] Seeming disinterest from the Irish theatre community and the immediate support for *Pumpgirl* by foreign theatres reinforced Spallen's belief that she should focus on getting produced abroad, and she moved to London in 2010.

In doing so, Spallen joined a long history of Irish writers who move abroad: "It saddens me sometimes . . . it's something that has happened again and again. Writers have to leave Ireland. It has been going on for hundreds of years."[6] However, she feels that she has been given more creative freedom and artistic control from British theatre companies. She finds also that in the small theatre community of Ireland, "it is who you are and who you know. In London, people read my work before meeting me."[7] In 2010, she advised her fellow playwrights: "Until things change further, get out. That probably sounds quite nihilistic and depressing but I wouldn't lie to anybody and say you're going to have a ball. The only way for things to change is for people to say that, instead of pretending everything's tickety-boo."[8]

The North's initial lack of support and recognition for one of their most talented playwrights did not go unnoticed by some critics. In a glowing review for the Lyric's production of *Pumpgirl*, *Culture Northern Ireland*'s David Lewis wrote: "Like [Owen] McCafferty, Spallen's work was produced first outside of Ireland, enjoying success in London and New York, before returning home. Let's hope that this production and new productions from McCafferty and Lucy Caldwell at this year's Belfast Festival at Queen's, herald the end of NI's most gifted playwrights being forced into exile. Perhaps the powers-that-be at NI's producing theatre companies will wake up and start investing in our widely recognized playwriting talent, before they sell another generation of writers and theatre-goers short."[9] Similarly, the *Belfast Telegraph* started out its review of *Pumpgirl* by asking, "Why does it take so long to see a local play staged in an Ulster theatre? And are there really so few female dramatists in Northern Ireland?"[10] Therefore, although these issues have been raised by the media, academics, and even theatre companies themselves, there seems to be a disconnect between awareness of the issue and the knowledge of how to fix it.

The gravitation of talent toward London is partly due to its having far greater opportunities for theatrical productions. Given the size of its economy, its audiences, and its theatre industry, it would be hard for Ireland to compete on that scale. However, it is not just greater opportunities that have encouraged many playwrights to move abroad. Spallen has also found British theatres to be more welcoming and easier to navigate than Irish ones. She describes working for British theatre as "less fussy" and with "fewer strings attached." Furthermore, dramaturgical qualities that have been applauded in London—"honesty, openness, and a forthright outspoken[ness]"—are the very things for which she has been criticized in the North.[11] When the Lyric produced *Pumpgirl* in 2008, a letter was written to the *Irish News* stating that the play was "gratuitously sensationalist," "overflowing with foul language and course sentiment," and should not be shown.[12] Indeed, before the show opened, the *Belfast Telegraph* reported that "there have already been rumblings about the strong language and loose morals of *Pumpgirl*, and Spallen wonders if there might be protests outside the theatre." In the same article, the playwright commented, "I'm sure the play will rattle a few cages. Let's face it, Northern Ireland isn't exactly at the forefront of liberal thinking. But it needs to realize that the rest of the world has moved into the twenty-first century. Maybe I'll have my very own picket on opening night. I'd really know I was home then!"[13] Conservative cultural values combined with hypersensitivity regarding political issues makes for a challenging artistic environment and limits the forms and subject matters that artists can address if they want to see their productions staged in the North.

Spallen has found an outpouring of support for her work abroad and has been frustrated by the fact that Irish critics and theatres say that there "are no new female writers in Ireland, and it's just oul' blather. . . . It's as if they keep saying these people don't exist, then they don't have to go out looking for them. The fact is English theatre companies and American theatre companies are tripping over Irish playwrights. What is going on?"[14] In London, Spallen has received commissions from the Royal Court, National, and Tricycle theatres.[15] In addition, her plays have been produced at the Bush Theatre (London), the National Theatre Studio (London), the Traverse Theatre (Edinburgh), the Manhattan Theatre Club (New York), and 59East59 (New York). Her one-act play *Shaving the Pickle* premiered at the 1st Irish Festival in 2008 in New York, and several regional theatres in the United States have staged *Pumpgirl*, including Chicago's A Red Orchid Theatre in 2009 and Philadelphia's Inis Nua in 2011. A Red Orchid Theatre also produced *Strandline* in 2014. Her accolades include the BBC's Tony Doyle Award for screenwriting (2007), the Susan Smith Blackburn Prize (2007), the HALMA Foundation Award for Excellence in the European Arts (2010), and the Clare McIntyre Bursary from the Royal Court (2012). Significantly, in 2016 she was awarded the prestigious Windham-Campbell Literature Prize from Yale University.

As her work continues to be lauded by foreign theatres, academics, and critics, Ireland has begun to recognize Spallen's importance as a playwright. She was awarded the Stewart Parker Award in 2009 and that same year the Dublin-based Fishamble Theatre premiered *Strandline*. In 2014, she received a Major Individual Artist Award from the Arts Council of Northern Ireland, the largest individual award that the council grants. Tinderbox also commissioned a new play, *Lally the Scut*, which premiered in 2015. It was lauded by *The Irish Times*'s Fintan O'Toole as "brave, brilliant, darkly hilarious," and it was his pick as "Irish play of the year."[16]

Perhaps most symbolically, in August 2012, the Lyric appointed Spallen their writer-in-residence. The Lyric appointment was a hard-won achievement, one that Spallen embraces as evidence of how Northern theatre is slowly becoming more inclusive. She reflects, "I may have felt that my work was more welcome outside Ireland in the past . . . [but] I have to say that the Lyric has been one of the exceptions, and I see this now as a vote of confidence in my work from a theatre that has in fact supported me in the past."[17] The Lyric's renewed interest may also stem from a complete overhaul and restructuring of the theatre, which was completed in 2011. The renovated building now includes spaces and programs devoted to developing new playwriting. Richard Croxford, formerly artistic director of Replay, was appointed the head of the Lyric in 2008, bringing a new commitment to staging and developing new works. These changes at the Lyric suggest that a progressive and more inclusive approach is being forged, perhaps one that will now include more indigenous women's writing.

Spallen's work engages questions of how the legacy of sectarian violence and the current-day peace process have affected the political, economic, and cultural lives of Northern citizens. *Pumpgirl* (2006) was written at the height of the Celtic Tiger and after a period of growth and relative calm in the North. The Celtic Tiger was a period of rapid economic development in the Republic of Ireland from the late 1990s until 2008 when Ireland experienced a massive financial collapse (along with the global economy). Because the North was tied to the currency, laws, and economy of the United Kingdom, it did not experience the same influx of wealth and development during the Celtic Tiger years. Yet the North did benefit from spillover effects across the border such as increased tourism and consumer spending, both of which supported a building boom, particularly in Belfast. The rural North, however, was left behind in terms of money, jobs, and opportunity.

Pumpgirl, set in an unnamed Northern border town, follows the lives of Sinead, a housewife, her husband Hammy, an unemployed racecar aficionado, and Pumpgirl, a local petrol station attendant. This three-character monologue play brims with the complicated inner lives of its characters, exploring the emotional and psychological effects of poverty and violence.[18] Sinead lives a small and suffocating life, trapped in the domestic roles of wife and mother. She dreams of leaving her husband and experiencing life outside of a small town. Out of boredom and desperation to feel loved, she has an affair with a man she meets at the local market. When she learns that she is pregnant, she tells her lover, who angrily beats her, leaving her in the dirt, torn and bloody. Hammy, Sinead's neglectful, emasculated, and woman-izing husband, is obsessed with racing cars. He frequents the petrol station where Pumpgirl works and uses her for quick and meaningless sex. Without a steady job, his only purpose in life is racing cars, trying to get an adrenaline rush so he can feel alive amidst a broken marriage and unemployment in a dead-end town. Pumpgirl, a town outcast with her butch haircut and dirty work overalls, rejects all that is femi-nine. She has seen how the roles of wife and mother trap women in her town, and she scorns femininity, associating it with that which is weak. She prefers to hang out with the guys at the petrol station and with Hammy, with whom she is in love. However, Pumpgirl pays a price for her refusal to inhabit the feminine sphere. Hammy and his friends pick up Pumpgirl one evening for a joyride and end up gang-raping her in the back of the car.

Both Sinead, who has dutifully followed the proscribed roles of wife and mother (until her rebellious affair), and Pumpgirl, who has rejected traditional notions of femininity, are trapped in an impoverished town and are violently used and rejected by men. Despite their different choices or positions in the contemporary rural landscape of *Pumpgirl*, women's options are ultimately limited and the end result is tragically the same. Furthermore, women's limited social positioning is exacerbated by men's emasculation. Unemployed, mired in poverty, and without an active conflict through which to define themselves, the men in the play are angry and directionless, channeling their frustrations through the sexual exploitation and subjugation of women.

Pumpgirl's real name is Sandra, yet few call her by her proper name. Instead, she is defined by her dead-end job in a rundown petrol station. Pumpgirl revels in the masculine nature of her job. She participates in female-bashing with the men around her, completely seeming to disavow that she herself is female. The traditional exchange between Hammy and Pumpgirl whenever Hammy comes into the garage demonstrates Pumpgirl's complicity in the misogyny that surrounds her:

> "How's the cunt?" says I, meaning his wife. It's always the same.
> "Still a cunt," says he, and we laugh.
> "How's the cunt?" says he, meaning my cunt.
> "Still a cunt," says I. It's our wee game.
> There isn't a person in the whole world I can talk to like Hammy.
> I'm that glad he's my friend.[19]

However, Pumpgirl's refusal to accept traditional feminine roles makes her the town outcast—the women make fun of her and the men, simultaneously attracted and repelled, treat her as an intriguing freak, someone they can use for their own amusement and then discard. Pumpgirl occupies a dangerous space between the proscribed masculine and feminine worlds. Refusing to comply with the feminine one and never being accepted by the masculine, she is isolated, denied entry into either. Spallen suggests that an atmosphere that has stifled and trapped women in traditional roles has led Pumpgirl to deny any association with womanhood. However, although she scorns traditional gender roles, she has unwittingly fallen into one: that of Hammy's submissive mistress who subverts her own needs and desires to those of her man.

Judith Butler's scholarship on the performative nature of gender resonates within this play. Butler argues that gender is a socially and culturally constructed concept that is created through repetitive, stylized performance.[20] Individuals mimic heteronormative conventions of gender, aspiring to replicate an archetype that can never be fully achieved: "Gender is an impersonation . . . becoming gendered involves impersonating an ideal that nobody actually inhabits."[21] The performative nature of gender has an important theatrical quality to it. Societal rules and expectations direct individuals to conform to predefined notions of gender in a similar way that a script directs an actor onstage: "The acts by which gender is constituted bear similarities to performative acts within theatrical contexts. . . . Actors are always already on the stage, within the terms of the performance. Just as a script may be enacted in various ways, and just as the play requires both text and interpretation, so the gendered body acts its part in a culturally restrictive corporeal space and enacts interpretations within the confines of already existing directives."[22]

Because gender is a socially constructed and enforced idea, expectations of gender vary according to culture and time period. Violent sectarian conflict can produce extreme and restrictive concepts of gender around which society is organized. These gender norms also serve to legitimize and reinforce the underlying principles of the conflict. This was a primary argument of women playwrights starting in the 1980s. The Charabanc and JustUs theatre companies emphasized how the conflict has restricted women's roles and participation within narrow definitions of what is proper for women during wartime. In Spallen's *Pumpgirl* and *Strandline* (as well as Stacey Gregg's *Lagan*, Jaki McCarrick's *Belfast Girls*, and other post-Agreement plays), women break out of restrictive gender norms only to be brutally punished. In post-Agreement drama, adventurous women are judged to be too promiscuous, not motherly enough, too ambitious, and unfeminine. In each play, women are pushed back by larger societal forces into restrictive and outdated gender identities that no longer reflect the realities of contemporary society. Furthermore, the hypermasculine ideals that expected men to fight for and defend their communities have become destructive and redundant during peacetime, disorienting and angering the men in these plays. Pumpgirl's rejection of feminine dress highlights the tenuous and performative nature of gender, and her repudiation of anything traditionally feminine signals that traditional roles for men and women are beginning to fracture in peacetime.

In contrast to Pumpgirl, Sinead is initially positioned as the quintessential housewife. She has married her hometown sweetheart and become the dutiful wife and mother. Spallen presents Sinead as a smart, capable, and intellectually curious woman who is stuck in poverty and a loveless marriage. She sits at home, going through the motions of raising children, suppressing her ambitions, and boiling in a hatred and anger that defines her existence. In this way, *Pumpgirl* departs from a long tradition of Northern Irish plays that portray women as perfect mothers and wives, concerned entirely with peace and a positive future for their children. Tom Maguire observes, "These women figures remain behind loyally awaiting the return of their absent husbands, essentially passive victims, brides awaiting fulfillment through the love of the right man."[23] However, Sinead is a woman deeply conflicted about her role as wife and mother. Although she provides all the appropriate care and nourishment for her children, she does so in a robotic manner: "I tidied the house . . . waited smokin' cigarettes for the two kids to arrive, and then fed, washed, minded, said 'Aye right' and 'Don't pull the dog's tail' and the other pieces of robot crap that tumble out of the mouths of mas" (37). Spallen discredits the image of the passive, content wife and mother and instead shows how oppressive and debilitating these roles can be.

Sinead's negative relationship with motherhood is also one that Helen Lojek identifies as a trend in Northern women's writing. Pregnancy and motherhood are often associated with entrapment, and

Lojek lists several examples of female characters in Northern drama who fear the consequences of having children:

> Sarah in Christina Reid's *Tea in a China Cup*, learning her daughter has begun to menstruate, declares, "God help you child, this is the start of all your troubles." Sandra in Reid's *Joyriders* refuses to romanticize motherhood and deliberately avoids Belfast's Botanic Garden because it is the site of sexual activity that resulted in a friend's unwed pregnancy. Karen, in Jennifer Johnston's 1993 *Twinkletoes*, reflecting on her seventeen-year-old daughter's pregnancy and upcoming marriage wonders, What about her freedom now? . . . In Northern Irish drama, escape from the trap of motherhood is persistently associated with emigration to England. . . . Married or unmarried, mothers or not, women are freer in England than in Northern Ireland. The themes carries through the plays by Devlin, Reid, and Jones, and reflect real-life choices made by Reid and Devlin.[24]

This same trend that Lojek identifies in late-twentieth-century plays can be seen in more recent writing, which shows young women rejecting (sometimes violently) any association with motherhood. In Stacey Gregg's *Lagan* (2011), a young unwed teen must travel to England for an abortion. In Lisa McGee's *Girls and Dolls* (2006), two teenage girls kill a local toddler and then bury her body in the woods. In Spallen's *Strandline* (2009), Máirín viciously rejects her role as stepmother to Tríona, hurling abuse at the young woman. Few recent plays show positive images of motherhood, and most position childhood as a fraught and dangerous condition.

In *Pumpgirl*, Sinead, the imprisoned mother and wife, has developed an active fantasy life in which she imagines breaking free of her husband and acting out her violent desires: "I can feel the first of his low snores beginning to form from the pillow beside me. His bottom lip odes in and out with each snore, like a baby's. I used to think that was cute. 'Your honour. It was the way his bottom lip puckered when he snored that made me put the hatchet through his head.' How's that for a country and western song, Hammy? I could call it 'And I'm

Praying for a Female Judge'" (18). Sinead believes that only another woman could possibly understand what it is like to be trapped in a suffocating and loveless marriage. She never suggests leaving Hammy or her children, going back to school, or moving to another town. These are not options for her; she quite simply has nowhere to go and no skills to draw on, and she is too entrenched in the proscribed societal expectations of woman as wife and mother to imagine herself outside of those roles. Even her violent inner daydreams are only fantasies—something to imagine in her subconscious in order to calm her rage but never something that she acts on.

Spallen shows that women are not the only victims of poverty and limiting social norms in Northern Ireland. Hammy has been out of work for a long time, collecting the dole (unemployment) and secretly cleaning out a chicken hatchery for extra money. He is a local boy who never left town and is stuck without an education and few jobs from which to choose. He is emasculated by his inability to provide for his family and resorts to highly dangerous activities to remind himself that he is alive. Instead of repressing and internalizing his emotions as Sinead does, Hammy acts out physically by racing cars and sleeping around. Hammy treats women like racecars: there for his own pleasure and expendable after the ride is over. In fact, all the men in *Pumpgirl* view women as expendable sexual objects. Hammy describes riding in the car with his friends and competing with one another about how many women they are sleeping with:

> Shawshank's all pally-wally, sayin' to me stuff about women, women he's had. Conversation goes on and on and becomes a bit more of a competition. He's coming' out with some Fantasy Island bullshit guff about some PE teacher he's riding in Lisleagh. McManus starts chippin' in about this mother and daughter combo he's taking' turns with in Culloville. Shawshank comes right back at him with some housewife he's left not two hours ago with a smile on her face like Liberace in a locker room. Doot's throwin' in his 50p, too, some English bird, manager of Dixons, gets him free blank videos, but they don't stay blank long. (25)

Hammy and his friends see women as conquests. None are faithful to their wives, and they see women only in relation to their sexual availability. As Sinead sums up perfectly, "In this town you're either a slut or a snob, no inbetweens" (27).

In *Pumpgirl*, men use sex as a weapon to prevent women from deviating from tightly regulated gender norms. Sex is linked to violence in one of two ways. Sex is presented as direct violence (that is, rape), or past violence is conjured up during the act of sex, inextricably intertwining them. The make-out spot where Pumpgirl and Hammy have sex is the location where two Protestants were killed fifteen years ago. Pumpgirl notes that their families still hang wreaths and flowers at the site of the killings. While making out under the tree of the dead Protestants, she notices there are some scratches on the ceiling of Hammy's car, which remind her of a local car accident:

> Hammy pulls the front seat down and lies on top of me. I don't move much. While I'm lying there, watching my feet flappin' away just either sides of his ears, there's these marks I can see in the plastic on the ceiling of the car . . . [they remind] me of this story I was told of this car that had gone into the bog up round Camlough. The people had been trapped inside. The car sank with them in it and they were there for ages, stuck, air running out, but no one could see it from the road except maybe the number plate and only if you were lookin'. And when the car was dragged out they found marks in the ceiling, like animal scratches, and bits of the beigy white roof-plastic under the fingernails of the people inside. They'd tried to claw their way out of the car while they were dying in the dark. (20)

As Hammy "makes love" to Pumpgirl, all she can think about is the horrific drowning deaths of some local residents. Violent death is thus linked to sex even before Pumpgirl's gang-rape. The image of a person clawing at the ceiling of a sinking car also parallels the situations of Pumpgirl and Sinead, who are both stuck in poverty, trapped and essentially drowning in a society that suffocates women's ambitions. Pumpgirl again focuses on the scratches in the car ceiling when she is gang-raped later in the play. As Hammy's friend McManus is forcing himself on her, Pumpgirl says, "And I can't help thinking of the people whose car went into the bog. My head is moving back and forward and I'm looking at the scratches on the roof above. Four people on a night out in Warrenpoint. Four people scratchin' on the roof of a car. Broken fingernails, silent screams, stiletto shoes and Saturday-night boots banging against black squeezing windows" (35). As Pumpgirl imagines the violent deaths of those who drowned in the car, the "broken fingernails" and "silent screams" are also those of Pumpgirl being raped. Spallen thus presents sex as a form of violence, suffocation, and death for women.

Even Sinead's steamy affair with a man from the local market is interwoven with the telling of Pumpgirl's sexual attack; thus, in the audience's mind, Sinead's affair is linked with violent rape. Sinead and Pumpgirl alternate telling their stories to the audience. Sinead meets a handsome man at the local market who charms her with banter. She brings him home, and they have sex. It is the first time in years that she feels alive, youthful, and excited: "He undresses me with so much love, so much kindness, that I want to cry . . . and I think for seconds, maybe even a minute, I'm going to be able to forget about being someone's wife, a man or just a woman doin' something that's bad . . . there's a gap. Just enough. A gap that's filled with nothing. I get my moment. I lose myself as the fear, the grief, the loneliness, the hate on the washing-line, and the solitude slips from my mind" (33–34). Interlaced throughout Sinead's description, Pumpgirl slowly recounts her rape. Hammy and his friends, Shawshank and McManus, pick up Pumpgirl from work to go to Shawshank's house. Pumpgirl becomes ill and goes to lie down in Hammy's car. The men come outside and take turns raping her. She recounts: "Hammy stands watching as Shawshank's mouth is pressed against mine. . . . My face is pressed into the back of the seat now as he turns me over . . . I'm turned round again, and this time it's McManus. Hammy's standing behind him with this mad face on and I can't help feeling I've done something wrong. . . . Hammy is the last, and when he stops he rests his head beside me and he looks so sad I whisper in his ear, 'It's okay'" (34–35).

Slowly as Sinead and Pumpgirl unveil their stories, it becomes clear that the person having the affair with Sinead is the same man who instigated the gang rape of Pumpgirl—Shawshank. The ex-convict was recently released from Maghaberry Prison, one of the hardest and most notorious penitentiaries in the North, known for housing republican prisoners. Although the play does not explicitly name Shawshank as a former paramilitary prisoner, it does position him as the product of an infamously violent prison system, suggesting that he too may be a casualty of a stark Troubles past. Thus Sinead unwittingly has sex with a vicious rapist, and Pumpgirl is abused and raped by three men, one of whom she thought loved her. In this way, both forms of sex—one consensual, one rape—are presented as violating and false.

By the end of the play, Sinead's affair turns from a casual one-night stand into a tragic lesson about straying from one's "proper" sphere: she becomes pregnant with Shawshank's baby. The poverty and entrapment of caring for two children plus a neglectful husband has now been exacerbated with yet another child. This situation is only intensified by Shawshank's reaction to the pregnancy. Sinead returns to the market to tell him that she is pregnant, but before she is able to, he assumes she knows about the gang rape. He takes her out to a deserted road and beats her. When she reveals the pregnancy, he simply laughs, leaving her bloody and bruised on the side of the road. Sinead has to walk miles back to town with torn clothes and bloody skin: "After he left me in the lay-by I had to walk for miles before one stopped. Walkin' along the road like a drunk woman with my tights in shreds and blood on my knees. . . . And I'm sad. I feel sad, and I feel frightened in my ripped clothes and I feel like a fool . . . my legs are shaking as I make my way into the safety of my home" (59). The image of a bloody woman with her clothes in shreds, walking along the side of the road after having been thrown out of a man's car, eerily evokes that of a rape victim, reframing the initial sexual encounter from a casual extramarital fling to a more sinister act of exploitation. Through his fists and his indifference to her pregnancy, Shawshank has shown Sinead what happens to women who transgress the marriage bond.

The play ends with Sinead submissively returning to the domestic sphere. She returns home, bruised and bloody, and resumes her domestic activities, making tea for Hammy and the children: "And I'm sad. I feel sad, and I feel frightened in my ripped clothes and I feel like a fool. He just got into the car and drove off and left me. Laughed at me, picked up his belt and screeched off in the car . . . my legs are shaking as I make my way into the safety of my home. . . . I make my way into the kitchen and get out a pot from the cupboard above the cooker. . . . Hammy and the kids'll be home soon and I start to make the tea" (59). Her trauma is subverted to her duties as wife and mother, and she represses her sadness and fear, pushing it down into the same deep, dark space where she hides her daily frustrations and anger as a housewife.

Pumpgirl's transformation after the gang rape is even more disturbing. Calm and submissive, she returns to work the day after the assault and, disturbingly, seems to accept a level of responsibility for the rape. In addition, when she sees Hammy with his family out at the shops, she tries to let him know that she is not angry: "I'm wonderin' should I go up to talk to him, but his look says not. . . . I'm trying to say 'It's okay but I miss you' with my eyes" (42). Pumpgirl's unsettling acceptance of the rape is rendered even more troubling by her sudden feminine dress. In the days after the rape, Pumpgirl wears a skirt and sandals, having "put the baseball hat in the bin" (41). She discards her entire physical identity, conforming to traditional feminine dress.

Whereas the women internalize their fear and guilt and silently move back into the constricted roles of womanhood, Hammy, in contrast, is emotionally unable to deal with his role in the rape and acts out with violence. He osculates between incredible guilt that he took part in the rape and anger that his friends took advantage of "his" woman. When he sees Pumpgirl in the street and a man accidentally bumps into her with his shopping cart, Hammy reacts with anger toward Pumpgirl, toward the man, and ultimately toward himself: "And she looks hurt, she does. And I want to smash her face in. And I want to smash his face in too, the bastard with the trolley, but most of all I want to put my own face through the glass in front of me, again and again back and forward, and lacerate my head to bits" (43). Hammy has a nervous breakdown after the rape, acting out his confusion and rage through destructive acts. He drives by the pet-rol station several times a day afraid that Pumpgirl might report the rape. He races his car and ends up crashing, smashing his head into the front window. He finds Shawshank at a bar and sets his truck on fire in retaliation. Hammy realizes (to a very limited extent) that he has played a part in making Pumpgirl's hard life even more difficult. Hammy is in a bar one night and sees Shawshank and Pumpgirl's alcoholic father: "I stayed for just the one in the bar after all. Just lookin' at her da and lookin' at the lads and lookin' at my hands and thinkin', 'Some people just get a raw fuckin' deal in life.' And amn't I the fuckin' master-dealer? Shufflin' away like the bastard and flickin' them raw-deal cards in the Pumpgirl's face?" (40). This is the closest that Hammy ever comes to acknowledging his role in the rape as well as recognizing that Pumpgirl, like many in town, is someone who is vulnerable. As he drives aimlessly in his car, afraid that Pumpgirl will report him, he says, "No I don't think she'll say anything, so I should be breakin' easy, but I'm not. Because she's not the real problem, is she? Is she? I'm not breathin' easy at all. I'm barely breakin' at all" (52). Hammy slowly begins to understand that the people of his town are all products of the poverty, violence, and suffocation of rural, post-Agreement life.

Increasingly distraught, Hammy drives to his job at the chicken hatchery to powerspray chicken droppings off of the coops. The hatch-ery job represents the desperation and debasement that poverty has led him to. In an act of frustration and anger, he takes the water pump and sprays high-velocity water around the entire yard, shower-ing chicken feces everywhere and snapping the heads of chickens who get caught up in the spray:

> One bird hits the wall with such a force that its neck snaps and there's this strangled noise as I have it pinned to the wall with a giant jet of water. I'm screaming at the top of my lungs this fucking animal yell and I'm smashing everything around me. Boxes upon

boxes of eggs splattered to fuck and panic-stricken birds runnin' about trying to escape from me and my mighty weapon. And I start to laugh. I slide down the wall with the water gun in my hand just dribblin' now, and I'm laughin' so hard I think I'm gonna pass out, and I sit there for what seems like hours, every now and again laughing with the hilarity of it all. (54–55)

Like his wife, Hammy is so broken down by his position in life that all he can do is laugh. It is a laughter of defeat and also of recognition that his life is full of despair and dead ends. Hammy has "spent three and a half years of spinnin'" (38), unemployed, frustrated, and unable to move forward: "treadin' water in the deep end" (45). In his haze of anger and guilt, Hammy recounts a dream where he is drowning, mirroring his waking life: "I'm being sucked down into this massive plughole . . . and everyone else gets out of the pool easy, but I'm trapped in the fuckin' grossest slipstream of a current in the world" (46). After leaving the chicken coop, Hammy climbs into his prized Toyota Celica and commits suicide by carbon dioxide poisoning.

Women and men are not the only victims of a violent post-Troubles landscape. Children are often neglected, punished, or threatened with violence in Spallen's work. Although the next generation has grown up in peacetime, Spallen's young people are still harmed by the lingering effects of the Troubles. When Hammy rebuffs Pumpgirl after the rape, she decides to exact revenge. She lures Hammy's children to an old abandoned house on the outskirts of town. As Hammy's youngest son, Darren, perches over a huge hole in the floor of the dilapidated house, Pumpgirl contemplates pushing him in:

He's climbin' round the edge of the big hole in the floor, hangin' on to the old ivy roots and I go and stand behind him, quietly. . . . I'm close enough to him now, but he's no idea I'm there. . . . We stand there for about a minute that's just like an hour with him near breaking his neck twisting round his head first to one side then to another trying to see who's behind him and the whole time I'm leaned over him with my face about two inches from his. Just watchin' his wee face twichin' and jerkin' with the panic and the wee hands grapplin' and twistin' and tryin' to hold on to the roots. And it's deep, that drop behind him. Very deep. (56)

The play ends with Pumpgirl sending the children back home unharmed and Sinead unwittingly laying out tea for her family, unaware that Hammy has committed suicide. In contrast to the mill-workers of Charabanc's *Lay Up Your Ends* who march back into the factory singing (although they have lost the strike), Spallen shows women who have been broken down, too exhausted to rebel against societal expectations. Furthermore, the discomfort of searching for new meaning and identity in peacetime has made the male characters in *Pumpgirl* cling more desperately to the past, unwilling to let go of the strict gender roles that defined their nationalist fight.

Reviews for the three productions in London, New York, and Belfast were positive. *The Observer* called the 2006 Bush Theatre production "enthralling," and the *Evening Standard* declared that Spallen's writing was full of "terrific zeal." *The Independent* agreed, remarking that "Spallen structures her play like a piece of music, seamlessly slipping between subject and counter-subject, orchestrating faster and slower movements, themes in a formidable coda."[25] The *New York Times* called the Manhattan Theatre Club's 2007 production a "fiercely observed, unflinching play." The review went on to praise Spallen's writing, declaring that "Ms. Spallen's penetrating language and unsentimental view place it among the most powerful" contemporary plays coming out of Ireland. "No bog of plummy prose or nostalgia for her. Adding a fresh, female voice to the boys' club of Irish playwrights, she infuses her monologues with slightly dated pop culture references that make her characters contemporary while revealing the tacky limits of their horizons."[26] The Irish reviews were similarly flattering. *Culture Northern Ireland* declared that Spallen's writing "sparks and fizzes, with sharp lines and terrific jokes."[27] Spallen's intelligent and critical voice exploring the marginalized rural North deeply resonated with critics and audiences alike, and similar themes would again become the core of her next play, *Strandline*.

A strandline is the high-water mark that the tide makes on the shoreline after the water retreats. Debris from the ocean is often deposited on the strandline, leaving seaweed, driftwood, and human trash. The play's title suggests that just as the waters retreat during low tide to reveal hidden trash and debris, the Troubles has retreated from this small town to reveal dark and terrible secrets in its wake.

The play begins with the wedding night of Tríona, Tom's daughter and Máirín's stepdaughter. The chaos of the wedding with drunken revelers, dancing partygoers, and an inebriated, belligerent bride compliments the dark storm that is brewing offshore and causing rough waters. In the opening scene, Tom drowns trying to save a group of tourists who have capsized. Three people watch from shore: Eileen, a local woman whose husband has been out of work for years; Sweeney, a precocious and opinionated thirteen-year-old boy who is described as "part bore, part mystic, part idiot"; and Máirín. The three observers worry that if the visitors drown, it will destroy the little tourism that had been coming to their economically depressed town. Staring at the ocean, Sweeney tells the women, "I heard tell they were foreign. Not immigrants like but tourists. Real tourists. Bona fide. Put us back that will now. Even further like."[28] This one casual exchange references the economic and social issues that the town is facing: the influx of immigrants who bring a wave of ethnic diversity to the region for the first time, and the lack of tourism given the economic depression. In the boom days of the Celtic Tiger, Clodagh, the town matriarch, had built and sold a large housing development, and tourists had brought business to the community. Today, however, the town's inhabitants can barely find work. Thus from the very first moments of the play, the town's recent economic decline after decades of increased prosperity and tourism is shown to be a central issue in the community. As in *Pumpgirl*, lack of jobs and opportunities have trapped the residents and exacerbated divisions within the town.

Whereas the poverty in *Pumpgirl* is palpable and affects all the characters in the play, in *Strandline* there is a tense divide between the impoverished seaside village that has limited job opportunities and the financial and professional accomplishments of Máirín, whose success in London has continued since she returned home. Máirín's *"classy, expensive, arty [look] sets her apart"* (9), and her house, where the majority of the play takes place, is a symbol of the wealth that she has achieved, marginalizing her from the rest of the struggling town. The stage directions describe the home as *"magnificent"* and *"a minimalist dream"* (18). One wall is entirely glass, and the view overlooks the ocean. In the main living room, there is a large weaving loom, a constant reminder of Máirín's status as an artist and of her financial success. On the wall hangs one of her hand-woven tapestries that is *"modern, yet containing traditional elements"* (18). She has made her money by taking the traditional Irish craft of weaving and creating luxurious tapestries to sell to wealthy collectors in London. As a result, Máirín *"is stinking rich. There is also the feeling, however, that the place is soulless"* (18). Here Spallen suggests that a loss of heart and compassion has accompanied the accumulation of Máirín's riches. This is, perhaps, a comment on the Celtic Tiger phenomenon, which brought great wealth to the island along with greed, overconsumption, and greater class divisions. In a 2007 interview with the *New York Times*, Spallen referred to the Celtic Tiger, saying: "The country is almost like a lottery winner, and there are problems that come along with that, almost like a frightening slipping away of humanity. . . . With great wealth can come an uneasiness about self and an uneasiness about identity."[29]

Although Máirín has gained financial success and social status, the play contends that she has lost her empathy, her heart, and her connection to her Northern roots. This emotional state is portrayed through her contentious and bitter relationship with her stepdaughter. Máirín's rapport with Tríona is marked by aggression and blame. In the first scene, Máirín exhibits outright hostility to the bride on her wedding day, calling her a maggot and trying to hit her with a shoe. Máirín is a woman who has begrudgingly inherited a child and is unable or unwilling to mother. In Tríona's view, Máirín "stole" her father away from her and created a new home, erasing the marks of Tríona's biological and caring mother: "You threw me out of my home. . . . Turfed me out on my ear. . . . You . . . made it so as I couldn't stay here.

You did. . . . Every time I scratched myself you were there. Sniffin' around like an oul' cat lookin' meat. Your oul' face in mine. Tidyin', rearrangin'. You'da stuck me under the stairs with the Hoover if you could. Life was dandy till you came along, nice wee house, my ma's things about. All pink and ribbons and . . . you could smell her on the cushions still" (47). Dedicated to her career and her relationship with Tom, Máirín was uninterested in mothering and thus exiled Tríona from her own home. In addition, Máirín razed the cozy modest house of Tríona's mother and, in its place, built a modern and soulless monstrosity that exudes money and pretension rather than warmth and love. Her disinterest in fulfilling the role of "good mother" has made her a pariah in the town and alienated her from her community.

Indeed, Máirín's professional success and ambition seems to have derailed her from "proper" motherhood and even wifehood. Tríona claims that Máirín is so cold, unloving, and career obsessed that Tom escapes to the village pub every night to reconnect with his community and friends. She tells Máirín,

> It's like rememberin' two different men. I remember a sad oul' broken cowp of a man, once your oul' wormin' magic wore away. And him reduced to putting on a pair of shorts and a vest and head to the pub every night. To get away from you. . . . You wore off quick, Máirín, and that's what he used to do. Laugh with his mates. With the normal people round here. With his daughter too. Never seen a man so unhappy, Máirín. So glad to be away from a woman. . . . Women of the town queuing up to dirty his clothes. Thinkin' up ways to make stuff look like sweat. Laughing. Laughing at you. Sitting up here knitting razor blades. (48–49)

The image of Máirín knitting razor blades contrasts a traditional Irish notion of domestic womanhood against a dangerous and lethal weapon. Her exploitation of traditional Irish weaving into a profitable business has become a violent affront to the community around her. Tríona attacks her stepmother with the suggestion that her father's drowning "must have been a pure release . . . that water must have been like a warm fucking blanket compared to the cold clammy dirty oul' air hanging between her fucking thighs" (50). The attack on Máirín's sexuality as a middle-aged woman is also striking. Because she is no longer fertile, Tríona suggests that Tom must not have been attracted to her. Ultimately, Máirín's professional ambition and her disinterest in mothering Tríona are condemned by the community, which still adheres to traditional roles for women and which rejects those who leave their community to find success in the outside world. Máirín's refusal (or inability) to fulfill the traditional gendered role of mother (instead inhabiting the "masculine" role of business owner and breadwinner) recalls Pumpgirl's difficulty in escaping culturally imposed heteronormative gender norms and the punishment that occurs from such transgressions.

While Máirín is condemned for not being motherly or operating under traditional notions of womanhood, Sweeney's mother remains a potent symbol of retribution against women who venture outside of gender norms. Several years earlier, Shirley Sweeney was sleeping with too many married men in town, and the community went to Clodagh, the town matriarch, to seek vengeance. Like Máirín, Clodagh operates directly against classic notions of womanhood: she belongs in a hypermasculine realm of violence and control. During Tom's wake, Clodagh punishes Máirín by revealing to her that Tom was involved in the brutal murder of Shirley Sweeney. Clodagh revels in cruelly describing to Máirín how Tom first seduced and then strangled Shirley: "He used a pair of her oul' tights that were drying on the fire. . . . And when he puts them round her neck wasn't the steam comin' off in puffs and up round him and he couldn't get a grip all right" (83). Clodagh's ease at ordering the killing of Shirley and her delight in recounting it disrupt traditional ideas of femininity. Like Máirín, Clodagh is shown to have no motherly instincts; she jokes about the letters that she and the town continue to send Sweeney after his mother's "disappearance": "Dear son, I am sorry, awful sorry. I took one look at your ugly wee face and done a runner" (84). The town conspired to cover up the murder and tells Sweeney that his mother simply left with a lover and is roaming around Europe, perpetuating the narrative that she is bad because she prioritized sex over motherhood.

Over the years, community members on vacation in Europe sent post-cards to Sweeney from his "mother." At the end of the play, when Sweeney decides to leave town and search for her, Clodagh tries to dissuade him, viciously telling him his whorish mother never loved him: "Máirín's husband knew your mammy . . . Shirley was the fellahs' fave" (95–96). Clodagh's orchestration of Shirley's murder, her indifference to Sweeney's pain at losing a mother, and her pleasure in revealing Tom's murderous past to Máirín bespeaks of a pathological pleasure for violence and cruelty.

The similarities between Clodagh's role as a powerful matriarch policing her community and that of a paramilitary leader regulating his town are extremely troubling and important. The play seems to suggest that the line between civilian and soldier has been blurred even in peacetime. It appears that the violence and trauma of the Troubles has permanently altered the town, to the point where several people have become just as sadistic and cruel as its worse paramilitary members. Clodagh is a brutal, monstrous woman: she has an affair with Tom, she orders the execution of Shirley Sweeney, she bullies and manipulates everyone in the community, and she threatens the life of young Sweeney.

However, it is also suggested that Clodagh is not a naturally cruel and violent individual, but is a product, like the rest of the town, of decades, if not centuries, of violent sectarian conflict. Clodagh is certainly aware that the Troubles have had a traumatic psychological effect on her and the rest of the town: "Whatever the ones in a town's been up to, they're just all trying to scratch on, Máirín. Trying to survive these times and maybe have a bit of craic. With weddings and drinking and fights and feuds. And sometimes bad things get done. Sometimes bad things get done. Jesus we had thirty years of bad things being done. Terrible, shockin' things done, if you take yourself back. There comes a time when you have to turn a blind eye" (65–66). Clodagh explains away Shirley's murder as simply an extension of the Troubles. Shirley's death was just another "terrible, shockin'" thing from the past that blends in with all the other traumas that the town went through, and, at some point, one must simply "turn a blind eye" and forget the past. Clodagh wants Máirín to believe that Shirley's death is just one more dark secret from the Troubles to bury and keep hidden. However, the play illustrates how the past always has a way of bleeding into the present, not only with secrets revealed but also with lingering psychological and emotional scarring. The Troubles and its violent secrets and dark past lingers just under the surface of this community, lying in abeyance, always threatening to rise up and poison the progress of peace. The play suggests that in trying to suppress and reject its violent past, the community only succeeds in perpetuating that historical violence.

An ever-present and pervasive trope in contemporary Northern Irish drama is the power of the traumatic past to haunt and destroy the present. In *Strandline* as well as in each of the post-Agreement plays examined here, the "cultural trauma" of the Troubles is positioned as an inescapable and destructive force, polluting the present and preventing the North from becoming a peaceful state. In their seminal book *Cultural Trauma and Collective Identity*, the scholars Jeffery Alexander, Ron Eyerman, Bernhard Giesen, Neil Smelser, and Piotr Sztompka argue that "cultural trauma occurs when members of a collectivity feel they have been subjected to a horrendous event that leaves indelible marks upon group consciousness, marking their memories forever and changing their identity in fundamental and irrevocable ways."[30] Whereas physical or psychological trauma affects individuals, cultural trauma is defined by a fracturing of group identity. Smelser gives a formal definition of cultural trauma as "a memory accepted and publically given credence by a relevant membership group and evoking an event or situation which is (a) laden with negative effect, (b) represented as indelible, and (c) regarded as threatening a society's existence or violating one or more of its fundamental cultural presuppositions."[31]

The collective narratives that develop around the traumatic event, the subsequent telling, retelling, and cultural positioning of the experience, permanently alter the group's understanding of itself. In Irish history, the Great Famine (1845–52), Partition (1921), the Civil War (1922–23), the collapse of the Celtic Tiger (2008), the Troubles, and the ongoing Northern peace process would be among those events counted as cultural traumas, as each of them have caused dramatic and permanent revisions of group identity.

A key element of cultural trauma is that it can be passed along as a community memory from generation to generation, a phenomenon that has deep resonance in the North. This inherited mental outlook is reflected both in the cyclical nature of violence in *Strandline* and in the community's adherence to a Troubles mentality decades into the peace process. Likewise, in other plays, such as Lucy Caldwell's *Leaves* (2007) and Lisa McGee's *Girls and Dolls* (2006), young people who came of age during peacetime are unable to escape the pervasive influence of the Troubles, causing them to act out with violence toward themselves and others. Whereas women playwrights of the 1980s and 1990s saw history as a way to better understand and reframe the conflict, post-Agreement playwrights tend to view the past as poisonous to the progression of peace. Old prejudices, reflexive assumptions, and fear are absorbed and reconstituted in the present day. At the same time, contemporary writers contend that a continued refusal to confront dark secrets of the past only serves to exacerbate the lingering impact of the Troubles in the present.

Significantly, cultural trauma is shaped by the members of the community who narrate and reimagine such events, chiefly the society's artists. Jeffery Alexander emphasizes that both real and imagined histories are important in the formation of cultural trauma: "Imagination informs trauma construction just as much as when the reference is to something that has actually occurred as to something that has not."[32] Imagination, historical remembrance, and generational storytelling thus deeply influence the formulation of cultural trauma. Although the common history of a collective "may have its origins in direct experience, its memory is mediated through narratives that are modified with the passage of time and filtered through cultural artifacts and other materializations that represent the past in the present."[33] Thus playwrights, musicians, novelists, filmmakers, and producers of cultural value (*even* if they did not directly experience the offending event) play an especially important role in the collective, historical understanding of that trauma and the subsequent revision of group identity. This means that a new generation of artists who have grown up during peacetime will have a significant impact on the way that Northern society continues to think and speak about the Troubles and how it views itself as the region moves further into peacetime.

In *Strandline*, the normalization of Troubles violence and a warfare mentality continues to define the identities of its residents. This is demonstrated when Máirín assures Clodagh that she will not be revealing the town's secrets. Although Máirín knows the right thing would be to inform the police about Shirley Sweeney's murder, she reflexively falls back into old habits: "Speaking out would be the brave thing. The right thing. The big thing . . . [but] I'm good at keeping secrets too. Born till it, I am. 'Whatever you say, say nothin'" (66). Here Máirín references an infamous saying of the Troubles: Whatever you say, say nothing. This mantra reflected an atmosphere in which silence was the only safe option during a period when the state and the police were often at odds with the Catholic community. The play suggests that the culture of secrets and silence arising from the Troubles is still an insidious and ongoing issue during the peace process. Instead of confronting and uncovering the terrible events of the past, communities bury their secrets and push them underground lest they cause further damage in the present. However, the play demonstrates how the secrets of the Troubles, no matter how hard they are hidden or repressed, will always find a way to surface, delivering new and further harm to a new generation. In play after post-Agreement play, this adherence to a Troubles mentality and outlook sits uncomfortably during peacetime, causing further fracture to group identity.

In *Pumpgirl* and *Strandline*, children often receive the brunt of Troubles trauma. As Spallen says, "The most difficult thing to be in this world and the most dangerous thing to be is a woman or a child. I have a lot of children in peril."[34] Although children like Sweeney (as well as Sinead's children in *Pumpgirl*) are the first generation to be born into the peace process and to have no living memory of the Troubles, they all inherit the community memory and trauma of that violence and are directly affected by it: Sweeney's mother is killed, and his own life is threatened, whereas Sinead's children lose their father to suicide and are almost killed by Pumpgirl. In addition to a lingering Troubles legacy haunting the North, the effects of peacetime on the next generation are positioned as unstable. In *Strandline*, the town feels that Sweeney's generation has become weak and needy because, as Clodagh says, "That's what happens . . . when you don't grow up in a war." Eileen believes the "benefit of a bit of conflict would have done you no harm at all" (96). While this is a very humorous moment in the play, the women of the town argue that the Troubles made them strong, independent, and aggressive, able to fight their own battles and fend for themselves. According to Clodagh and Eileen, the peacetime generation lacks these skills. However, Spallen seems to be arguing that it is not the peacetime generation that lacks character but the Troubles generation that has been unable to adapt to peacetime. Members of the older generation are still perpetuating the violent cycles of the past, unable to change the psychology, habits, and survival skills that they developed during the height of the conflict. The Troubles may technically be over, Spallen's plays assert, but the conflict still defines the way that many people view the world.

Reviews from the 2009 Fishamble production in Dublin were mixed but encouraging. The *Times* (London) found that the play "works well on several levels, combining complex thriller, treatise on identity and brooding character study. The setting, an isolated rural seaside community on the border between Northern Ireland and the Republic, is superbly sketched out via Spallen's blackly comic use of vernacular. Despite the wide open spaces of Sabine Dargent's superb set, the director, Jim Culleton, guides proceedings with an air of clammy claustrophobia, building tension as the storm outside comes to mirror the conflict within the house."[35] Other reviewers remarked that Spallen mixed too many complex themes into the play, muddying a clear thesis and making it difficult to sort through the play's competing demands for attention. *The Guardian* complained about the play's lack of clear focus: "Spallen's gift for explosive dialogue is reinforced here. This time she works larger themes into the women's verbal jousting, so many, in fact, that it is not always clear what the main focus is. Post-peace-process politics, the environment, inequality, class envy, the role of the artist: all of these are tossed around, leaving the impression of a whirlpool of ideas, and a writer with big ambitions."[36] The *Irish Times* agreed, "Spallen weaves so many strands into the fabric of the play—property, economy, mythology, environment, banditry, artistry—that it is a challenge to tie them together, to resolve a play thick with detail in a twist of heavy menace: part State of the Nation, part Wicker Man. . . . Between a fastidious plot and a wide scope of allusions, it may be hard to take in everything during one sitting. Yet that owes something to the high tide of Spallen's ideas: awash with style and verve, wit and intellect, provoking further thoughts when those waves roll out."[37] Despite some weaknesses of the script, all the reviewers agreed that the play's themes were astute and illuminating, revealing a hidden side of the post-Agreement North that is rarely talked about or shown on the theatrical stage.

Spallen's work explores the complex and ever-shifting landscape of Northern Irish culture and the lingering effects that the sectarian conflict has had on the emotional and psychological development of Northern citizens. Spallen remains an important and defiant voice that refuses to gloss over vital issues that dominate contemporary Northern society. Although this commitment to examining the darker sides of Northern culture has historically made it difficult for her work to be produced on the island, recent achievements such as her appointment as Lyric's writer-in-residence and productions with Fishamble and Tinderbox suggest a movement toward embracing her and incorporating more inclusive and diverse representations of Northern life on the Irish stage.

7

The Protestant Urban Underclass

Stacey Gregg and Rosemary Jenkinson

Stacey Gregg and Rosemary Jenkinson write about life in urban Belfast. Both playwrights examine working-class Protestant culture and its struggle to adapt from an entrenched wartime mentality to a peacetime Belfast replete with new industry, immigrants, and changing city infrastructure. Their plays underscore the disenfranchisement many people feel within the changing economic, ethnic, and cultural landscape of a post-Agreement North. Despite the switch from rural to urban life, many of the themes in their work are similar to Spallen's. All three playwrights explore increasing class divisions, sexuality, gender politics, and the effects of the peace process on Northern citizens. Gregg and Jenkinson have also struggled to be recognized by the Irish theatre sector, having achieved greater success in the United States and England. Gregg's propensity to write in an antirealist style, and Jenkinson's controversial images of Protestant culture, have made each woman's plays challenging to Irish theatres, especially in the North.

Gregg grew up in Dundonald, an area of east Belfast known for its staunchly conservative loyalist culture. Like many working-class Protestants, her father and brother were employed in the civil service. Gregg spent her youth reflecting her father's loyalist politics, although she never held deep personal beliefs about them. Greg has said that until leaving Belfast for the University of Cambridge, "I was just parroting back what my dad said with great conviction. That is quite a journey for anyone from here to go out and realize that not everybody thinks the way you do or the way that you have been told you should."[1] Growing up within a culture that shunned the arts, Gregg was the first in her family to go to college and the first to explore an artistic career.

Artistic careers were frowned on in loyalist Belfast not only for practical and economic reasons but also for unique cultural ones. In reaction to a perceived flamboyance and emotionality associated with the Catholic Church, Northern Protestant culture has historically worked hard to define itself in direct opposition to these characteristics, embracing a somber and serious conservatism. Correspondingly, it has viewed artistic or theatrical enterprises with suspicion. As Gregg described, "Anything that smelled remotely of equal rights or artsy was gay or Catholic."[2] The arts were thus considered by many within the Protestant community as the lesser domain of Catholics, and something in which good Protestants would not engage.

This discomfort with artistic expression has led to the commonly held view that there are few Protestant artists from the North and that Catholics have been more effective in using the arts to promote their story of the conflict.[3] In a 2000 interview with the *Guardian*, Gary Mitchell, who is from a unionist background, explained the general mindset of the culture: "Protestants don't write plays, you see. You must be a Catholic or a Catholic sympathizer, or a homosexual to do that. No one in our community does that because playwriting is a silly, pretend thing."[4] Despite this persistent stereotype, many Protestants have had prominent roles within the theatre and the arts in general, including the Charabanc women, Marie Jones, Stewart Parker, Gary Mitchell, and others.

Gregg offers another possible theory for the strong association of the arts with the Catholic community. Historically, the majority of housing in the North was reserved for Protestants, who lived in larger homes spread out over wider areas. In contrast, Catholic housing tended to be crowded; large families lived in small homes that were physically close together. This crowded Catholic structure tended to encourage community gatherings, whether it be church services on Sunday, the Gaelic Athletic Association, political rallies, or Irish Fèis.

Class divisions were also less severe in the Catholic communities than in Protestant ones. Whereas there were very few middle- and upper-class Northern Catholic families during the Troubles, the Protestant community was deeply stratified into the extremely poor, the working and middle class, and the upper class. Playwrights such as Gary Mitchell have addressed the stratified nature of this class system in which the loyalist working-class community was expected to fight for and defend Northern territory while rich Protestants lived outside of the war zones in the wealthy suburbs. These powerful, Protestant business owners arguably benefitted from the sectarian divisions politically and economically without having to engage directly in the violence or endanger their own families. The Catholic community, however, was primarily poor and working class and thus typically had fewer of the same internal class divisions and resentments. Gregg theorizes that this flatter class structure plus the physical intimacy of the Catholic community may have allowed the arts to spread more easily, creating a richer tradition for and greater acceptance of artistic expression.

Gregg initially was interested in pursuing visual arts and had intended to study drawing, sculpture, and painting in college. However, when she was accepted into Cambridge to study literature (a high honor in any circumstance but amplified by the fact that she was the first to attend college in her family), she immediately accepted. Despite a difficult cultural transition to the highly privileged environment of Cambridge, Gregg was introduced for the first time to the classical canon of theatre as well as to theatre history. Unimpressed with the classical plays that the university was producing, she directed several experimental shows at Cambridge: "My exposure to theatre was really piecemeal. I was really attracted to [Steven] Berkoff, [Edward] Bond, and more expressionist European stuff, and it didn't occur to me that wasn't going on because I didn't see what was going on because I never went to theatre. I just assumed that was theatre."[5] She was unaware that her attraction to avant-garde theatre was not necessarily reflective of contemporary Irish or British theatre practices. Now, as then, she does not take much inspiration from Irish theatre. She looks primarily toward the visual performance of German expressionism and the experimental theatre traditions of 1960s America. Without a connection to the past, Gregg feels liberated to try new forms and styles, thus bringing fresh outside influences to Northern theatre.

Like Spallen, Gregg has often felt like an outsider: "Growing up in a ways, feeling that you're slightly different, slightly on the edge, like as though you are watching the way you are supposed to do things has had an impact."[6] She channeled this persistent feeling of alienation into her writing. She integrates both Protestant and Catholic characters in her work, showing compassion and understanding for multiple points of view. Indeed, one of Gregg's greatest strengths as a writer is her ability to show the best and worst sides of individuals without condemnation or judgment. Gregg finds humanity in all of her characters whether it be a racist Catholic cab driver who is afraid of losing his job to an immigrant or a Protestant expat returning to Belfast with deep ambiguity toward what he views as the city's closed-minded and parochial culture.

Gregg wrote her first play, *Ismene* (2006), after she graduated from college. Similar to the Field Day and DubbelJoint models of resetting European classics within contemporary Northern Ireland, *Ismene* is based on the law-abiding sister in Sophocles's *Antigone* and reset in Troubles Belfast. As in the Greek original, the play revolves around a sister's response to her brother's death. Gregg's version was inspired by the true story of the McCartney sisters: five Catholic women who fought for justice after their brother was killed by the IRA in 2005. The play explores how *Antigone*'s themes of mourning, violence, and revenge resonate deeply within the Troubled North. *Ismene*, which was produced by a student group at Cambridge, won her a literary agent. However, Gregg then spent several years writing experimental works that failed to get produced by any professional theatres. She speculates that her anti-illusionistic aesthetic and highly poetic language confused audiences, which were accustomed to more realistic, dialogue-based Irish playwriting: "It has been tough. The stuff I write has often not been naturalist and the predominant taste in theatre is so naturalist particularly in London."[7] She received her first opportunities in Ireland through commissions for a few short plays and collaborative pieces produced at smaller theatres such as such as *The Grand Tour* (Rough Magic SEEDS program, 2007) and *Bruised* (Tinderbox, 2008; collaboration). She has also written collaborative pieces with the London-based Bush Theatre (*50 Ways to Leave Your Lover*, 2008) and Paines Plough (*Come to Where I'm From*, 2012).

Since the early 2000s, many Northern theatres have encouraged collaborative writing, with a disproportionate number of women being involved in joint projects. This shift occurred primarily owing to restricted funding as well as a new mandate from the Belfast/Good Friday Agreement that the North be more inclusive with all of its citizens. The Northern Irish Arts Council, in order to fund more groups and projects, encouraged theatres to split their limited funding among as many artists as possible. Theatres then often demonstrated "diversity" and "inclusivity" by grouping together women writers, emerging writers, or ethnic minority writers into collaborative projects to demonstrate that they are working with and supporting unrepresented members of the community. Gregg recalls, "It felt like tick off 'emerging writer' or 'women writers' box, and what better way to do that is than make one play and use six of them all at once? And I don't really believe it gives the best results." She finds that collaborative projects can often result in less successful theatre when writers are assigned to work together rather than collaborating naturally: "I am not convinced, unless it is an organic collaboration and you have sat in the pub with someone for several months and say come on, let's do this, I am not convinced what you get out of that."[8] Charlotte Headrick and John Countryman identify collaborative theatre projects as an important reason for the continued lack of productions by women playwrights in Ireland.[9] When disparate writers are asked to collaborate in a nonorganic fashion, productions tend to be less successful, critics have a hard time interpreting the work, and presses shy away from publication.

Gregg's first full-length play, *Shibboleath* (2009), was a joint commission between the Abbey Theatre (where Gregg had participated in a development workshop in 2008) and the German-based Goethe

Institute. Gregg wrote *Shibboleath* in both German and English as part of the "2009 after the Fall" project, a pan-European initiative to commemorate the twentieth anniversary of the fall of the Berlin Wall. The play takes its title from the Hebrew word meaning an often-outdated cultural custom that distinguishes a particular social group. The term is often used in reference to coded language that clearly identifies membership within a specific sect. *Shibboleath* is about the paradoxical increase in the number of so-called peace walls that have been erected in Belfast since 1998. Despite declarations of peace and the signing of the Belfast/Good Friday Agreement, there were nine walls erected in 1998 alone within areas of Belfast where Catholic and Protestant communities joined in order to separate and "protect" the residents. There are now over forty. The play explores the contradiction that Belfast remains deeply segregated with separate schools and community facilities for Catholic and Protestant neighborhoods almost two decades post-Agreement.

An exchange between Darren, a young boy, and his father, Alan, who is building a new peace wall, captures the essence of the play's message:

DARREN: What's a peace wall do when there's no war?
ALAN: I dunno, suppose people like the idea of them. They paint them up dead nice now, with murals about all the peace we're havin. And they bring the tourists.[10]

The walls are a fundamental paradox: painted with murals about the peace process, they claim to maintain harmony while in reality they continue to segregate the community and perpetuate sectarian divisions. The walls have become a natural and expected part of the physical landscape of Belfast, and the community, like Alan, has become unable to recognize that the walls exacerbate tensions rather than quell them. Furthermore, tourists expect the peace walls to be an integral part of the Belfast experience, signaling how the economics of Troubles tourism has inadvertently prolonged divisions. Darren, however, having grown up in peacetime, has not witnessed the violence that led to the erection of the walls. It takes his questioning of their purpose for his father to think more deeply about the role of the walls. Darren is part of a new generation that often questions accepted practices. For example, he also wishes to attend the "integrated" school that educates Protestant and Catholic children together, despite his parent's wishes.

The play also addresses how Belfast has changed dramatically with the immigration of Eastern Europeans and Africans into the city, generating new class and ethnic prejudices. As the workers slowly build the peace wall, they reflect on how the physical landscape has changed since the height of the conflict. Belfast has transformed from a bombed-out war zone into a cosmopolitan city. As one worker remarks, "Development: hotels, spas, Nandos, boutiques. Few years ago ya couldn't get yourself a latte in Belfast City. Now look." Although prosperity and development has come to Belfast, economic gain remains in the hands of the same politicians and upper-class citizens who benefited from the violence during the Troubles. One worker remembers, "When politicians were incitin' us fodder to fight while they sat back and shook their heads, pursed their lips, washed their lily white hands." Throughout the play, politicians are shown to be ineffectual, selfish, and cowardly, unable to stand up for what is right even in peacetime. Furthermore, Gregg argues, the peacetime economic development in the North has benefitted only the same privileged few who also received financial gain from the Troubles.

The peace wall is played by an actor who sings and speaks to the audience. The "brickies," who are building the wall, move in and out of naturalistic dialogue to include rhythmic verse and chant. They also narrate the sounds of building the wall: "Crack!," "Flop!," "Smack!," "Whack!" Gregg also made certain lines in the dialogue optional for the ensemble to articulate. Therefore, a character will start a thought or sentence but it will be finished by one or more other characters. In doing so, the audience is never able to comfortably settle into standard Irish social realism. The anti-illusionistic techniques require the audience to look at the play's issues in a new light and to question accepted practices such as the paradoxical nature of the peace walls and who is really benefitting from peacetime economic development.

Despite its initial support of the work, the Abbey declined to stage the play in 2009, granting it only a one-night read-through on the Peacock stage. Out of frustration that theatres were not responding to her more experimental work, Gregg decided to write a more commercial and traditional piece as a last attempt to fully break into the professional theatre scene. She wrote *Perve* (2011) and *Lagan* (2011) at the same time; however, the two plays cannot be more different. Gregg describes *Perve* as a "paint by numbers social realist" play while *Lagan* is a stream of consciousness monologue play that eschews any realistic narrative structure. Gregg reflects: "Compared to the stuff I usually do, [*Perve* is] very compact and it's very sparse, and that's part of the aesthetic. I had written all these mad plays with like twelve people and singing walls and people taking limbs off. And then I wrote this one play [*Perve*] that was a bit kind of easy and it got immediately picked up [by the Abbey]."[11] The Abbey's immediate embrace of Gregg's first social-realist play confirmed her suspicion that theatres were weary of engaging with her more challenging experimental work. Gregg thus went from an unknown playwright in 2010 to landing one of the most competitive and coveted platforms in all of Irish theatre in 2011.

Perve, set in a middle-class suburb in the present day, is Gregg's most recognized and widely produced play. Although the dialect locates the play in Ireland, no stage directions specify a location or country. Indeed, the play's setting purposefully has a generic quality to it, extending its production life, leading to several regional stagings in Australia and Canada.

The play revolves around the fallout from a school bullying incident involving sixteen-year-old Sarah. A few girls Photoshop her head onto a naked body and text it to the entire student population. Gethin, her twenty-three-year-old brother, is an aspiring documentary filmmaker still living at home. A neighbor has been accused of being a child molester, and the town has collectively shunned and harassed him. Gethin is not convinced that the neighbor is guilty and believes that cultural hysteria surrounding child molestation has created an environment wherein innocent people can easily be accused of crimes. He decides to prove his point by conducting an experiment. Gethin convinces Sarah to spread a false rumor at her high school that he is a child molester. His plan is to use his video camera to document the hysteria and false accusations that follow in order to show how rumors and suspicions can destroy innocent lives.

Perve is plot driven, centering on the dangers of social media and technology, school bullying, and media and community hysteria regarding sexual molestation. The strength of the play comes from its timely relevance regarding the intersection between sex, teens, and technology. It also taps into the cultural fallout from the Catholic priest sex abuse scandal that has rocked Ireland for the past two decades. As rumors swirl that Gethin has molested children, the police start to uncover the young man's past, stirring up circumstantial evidence of guilt that Gethin had failed to anticipate. During high school, his best friend, Nick, showed Gethin a picture of Nick's naked girlfriend; Gethin texted the picture to friends, spreading it throughout the school. The police also find porn on Gethin's computer along with naked pictures he had taken of himself in order to track his progress lifting weights. Slowly the police build a case based on circumstantial evidence that convinces them of Gethin's guilt. When he tries to show the police the computer files he has compiled along the way to prove his innocence, he discovers that Nick has erased them from his hard drive in revenge for distributing the naked photo years ago. His friend's angry vengeance is not fully explained, however, until the end of the play when it is revealed that Nick was sexually abused as a child by Gethin's uncle. The play insinuates that Gethin's mother suspected the abuse but did nothing to stop it. The play ends with Nick agreeing to argue Gethin's innocence to the police; however, it is unclear whether things have spun so far out of control that Gethin is beyond redemption. The play is a parable about the dangers that may happen when naïve teens recklessly mix technology and sex, and it speaks to the power of rumor and innuendo to destroy lives.

The reaction to the Abbey's production was shaped significantly by the Ryan Report, which was released in 2009. The 2,600-page report was the result of a nine-year inquiry into the sex abuse scandal within the Catholic Church. It found that abuse had been endemic within church-run schools and orphanages for decades, and it thrust child sexual abuse into the media glare and severely weakening church authority in Ireland. Although Gregg did not write *Perve* with Ireland specifically in mind, Irish audiences and reviewers naturally viewed the play as a commentary on the shocking revelations of long-term child abuse. Gregg recalled, "I didn't write it to go on in Ireland. When it was picked up to go on in Ireland, I thought, this could be interesting because Ireland had just come through the Ryan Report and was in a real state of crisis."[12]

Whereas Gregg intended to emphasize the dangerous intersection between sex and technology and how group hysteria can warp such issues, audiences and critics repeatedly honed in on the sex abuse aspect of the play. *The Guardian* wrote, "While the premise is intriguing in the abstract, it doesn't delve deeply enough into the difficult subjects it raises. Revelations of childhood abuse that have been buried in memory are thrown away almost as soon as they surface, leading to a rushed ending that is unsatisfactorily chirpy, beating a hasty retreat from painful reality."[13] The *Guardian* piece proved Gregg right in her prediction that many critics would miss the central concerns of *Perve*: "I knew that people would call it a pedophile play. . . . The most widespread response to *Perve* was there is not enough pedophilia. . . . Whereas I felt I was writing about something a bit different."[14] Similar to *The Guardian*, *The Irish Times* criticized the play for talking around the sexual abuse rather than confronting it directly, deeming it an "abstract on sexual and social perversity that is afraid to get itself dirty."[15] Cultural and historical specificity may have led some critics to focus on the sex abuse aspects of the play rather than the playwright's intended topics, but Gregg is certainly not a writer who is afraid to get herself dirty. Nevertheless, Irish theatres, including the Abbey, declined to stage her more hard-hitting and controversial work.

Lagan, which deals with similar themes as *Shibboleth*, was Gregg's response to the popularity of Irish monologue plays. However, she tried to push and stretch the form, "to push beyond a lot of that great tradition of Irish monologue direct-address plays" in an attempt "to make something really vital that was absolutely in the moment, absolutely of now."[16] In this same year that the Abbey produced *Perve*, the independent British theatre companies Oval House Theatre and Root Theatre Company produced *Lagan*, creating a contrasting display of two radically different works of theatre by the same playwright: one in Ireland's national theatre, known for privileging social-realist and text-based plays, and the other in an off-West End theatre, known for its championing of fringe and experimental theatre.

Lagan has what Gregg considers to be a cumulative effect through its stream-of-consciousness monologue; the voices, emotions, and characters build up over the course of the play, creating what she calls a "density of experience." Gregg's goal was to heighten and condense all the sounds, images, and emotions of present-day Northern Ireland so the audience could view the intense changes that the North was currently experiencing with a more critical eye. Gregg explained, "I wanted to immerse people in Northern Irishness, family, all those claustrophobic things going on."[17] Stream-of-conscious writing in Ireland has a long historical tradition in theatre, poetry, and literature with James Joyce and Samuel Beckett, and more recently, Mark O'Rowe (*Terminus*, 2007) and Eimear McBride (*A Girl Is a Half-Formed Thing*, 2013). Gregg joins this group of challenging writers embracing a mode of writing that requires the audience to actively listen and synthesize intersecting emotions, images, sounds, and ideas.

Thus, in stark contrast to the straightforward plot and realistic dialogue of *Perve*, *Lagan* is an ensemble play that mixes overlapping, sometimes disjointed dialogue with often cryptic monologues. Whereas *Perve* uses casual colloquial speech, *Lagan* is characterized by poetic and lyrical language that is dominated by symbolism and metaphor. The play follows nine individuals in Belfast as they flow into and out of each other's lives. Ian, an aspiring writer, reluctantly returns home from London after many years away. His mother, Anne, has summoned him to Belfast where he is to accompany his seventeen-year-old sister, Aoife, back to London for an abortion. Aoife has had an affair with the middle-aged Terry, who is the abusive father of Fiona. Fiona is stuck in a dead-end job as a checkout girl, and after many years of physical abuse at the hands of her father, she self-harms, cutting her body with razors. She falls in love with Emmett, the only surviving son of Joan. Joan is the ghost of a Catholic woman who haunts the stage, reliving the moment that a bomb took the life of her son, Ryan. Joan is stuck in the purgatory of Belfast, unable to reach her son in heaven and unable to emotionally support her living son. The Taximan is a working-class Catholic, enraged that his job and city are being taken over by immigrants. His children, Tracey and Phil, struggle to make sense of a Northern Ireland that is inundated with a modern, highly sexualized consumer culture yet fails to provide its young people with any positive options for the future.

The play does not have a linear narrative structure like *Perve*. Time moves slowly and then speeds up, there are scenes with the living and the dead, characters narrate their own stage directions, and some characters comment on the scene like a Greek chorus. The play alternates between naturalistic dialogue and overlapping, poetic monologues; the two forms flow into each other, slowly revealing inner thoughts and feelings of characters. The name of the play refers to the River Lagan that runs through Belfast. As *The Telegraph* wrote, the characters "are all connected—either unknowingly or knowingly—and they flow in and out of each others' lives as the Lagan river flows through Belfast."[18] Thus the free-flowing river serves as a metaphor both for the stream-of-conscious language that flows out of the mouths of the characters and for the movement of the characters who travel in and out of one another's lives.

Lagan uses several different theatrical techniques that constantly prevent the play from descending into realism. It evokes Brechtian influences when the actors speak their own stage directions, talk in the third person, and break from dialogue with another actor to express an internal monologue directly to the audience. The actors also speak special effect noises such as the beeping of the check-out scanner when Fiona is ringing up groceries at the local store. Gregg views the theatre as an overtly constructed art form. Theatre is at its best, she argues, not when it tries to reflect real life, but when it embraces its theatrical and fabricated nature, emphasizing its constructs and conventions. In addition to Brechtian devices, Gregg also includes a Greek chorus made up of an ensemble of characters who comment on the action occurring on stage. Beckett's influence is also evoked with the character of Joan, who walks back and forth in a deep groove on the stage, created by years of pacing. The repetitive, senseless action of pacing and how it has come to define her life recalls the similarly stylized repetition in many of Beckett's plays, including *Footfalls* (1975).

Like *Shibboleth, Lagan* captures the many diverse and competing voices, perspectives, and experiences that contemporary Belfast now encapsulates. Two decades into the peace process, this "new" Belfast has transformed physically, politically, economically, and ethnically; however, many of the same problems, prejudices, and cycles of violence remain. Transformed from a rundown war zone, Belfast is now a modern European city with fancy restaurants, coffee shops, shiny new shopping malls, and luxury apartments. However, with the modernization of the city there is new crime and violence as well as an influx of immigrants who are changing the city's color, language, and culture.

In *Lagan*, the character Taximan represents one Catholic working-class perspective. He has seen the peace process and economic development bring an influx of new immigrants into the city, and he is nervous, worried that "no one sticks up for the white workin' man" (8). He is angry that the land his community fought so long and hard for is now being populated by outsiders who, as he sees it, do not understand the complex culture or history of the North. He sees his interests becoming subsumed by the peace process, immigration, and political reform. As the Taximan feels his job opportunities slipping away within the increasingly crowded economy, he lashes out at any ethnicity that can be blamed for changing the economic and ethnic landscape: "If we just had to worry about the odd Chink runnin a takeaway that'd be dead-on . . . but y'know these Romanians or whatever, everywhere now. . . . You never used to get blacks over here . . . Poles is on construction . . . jobs is short, halfa Belfast's at the taxi-in now to get by" (9). Taximan, however, is astute enough to realize that the new immigrant populations are not his biggest obstacles, "but this fucken 'Peace process'—loada tax-dodgin bastards up at Stormont, two, three incomes and claimin expenses for birdie baths and ponies and whathaveye. We're busy down here getting annoyed at the immi-grants and slabberin over scraps when we should be askin who's got it all in the first place. Young ones with halfa brain still taking off 'England." (9). Like *Shibboleth*, *Lagan* argues that the politicians who are supposed to be guiding Northern Ireland into a new era of peace are corrupt. The working classes were consumed by fighting during the Troubles, allowing the elite to maintain an economic and political stronghold on the region, and this cycle is repeating itself during the peace process. The Protestant and Catholic working classes are again being overwhelmed by competition for jobs, while politicians and the rich are left to rule the state and enact legislation that continues to favor the elite and repress the lower classes. In addition, the North's future remains so bleak that young people are still leaving in droves, creating a "brain drain" that saps hope for a resilient future. Peace and reconciliation, Gregg contends, are being conducted in Stormont and elite political arenas instead of within communities. Alarmingly, regular citizens in *Lagan* remain unconnected to and uninvolved in the peace process in any essential manner.

In addition to the dramatically changing landscape of Belfast, an important issue in *Lagan* is whether the North can ever escape its past or whether it will continue to be haunted by the cultural trauma of the Troubles and the generational cycles of poverty, violence, and prejudice that have been born from centuries of conflict. This struggle between the past and the future is best exemplified through the char-acter of Joan who, the stage directions state, is "between worlds." A ghost, stuck in an anguished limbo, weighed down by grief and regret, she is unable to accept her own death or that of her son, Ryan. Joan recalls how she spent her life haunted by an IRA bomb that took the life of her son. She was killed several years later when she went to the local mall and became disoriented as she relived the nightmare of her son's death. She wandered off into a construction site and was accidently crushed by falling scaffolding. The manner of her death is significant. Her son was killed by Troubles violence, and she was killed by the overbuilding and overconsumption of the peace process, argu-ably another kind of (cultural) destruction. Thus Joan haunts Belfast and the stage; she is a symbol of those whose lives were destroyed by sectarian violence, unable to accept the past and unable to move forward. *Lagan* thus positions the North as a location that is haunted by its history, stuck in its own purgatory, and unable to fully move forward into a more positive future. This situation is similar to Spallen's *Strandline*, Lisa McGee's *Girls and Dolls* (2006), and many other post-Agreement plays that show how past violence and a community memory of conflict and prejudice, passed down through generations, have taken over the present, arresting society in its wake.

Despite current-day pressures to embrace the North's new identity as progressive and peaceful, *Lagan* is primarily a portrait of those, like Joan, who have been silenced and marginalized within the peace process. Gregg believes that those who were sidelined during the Troubles, particularly the working classes, are the same groups that today are disconnected from the peace:

> In terms of Northern Ireland and the feeling I was trying to get at is that there is a lot going on in that we are still a very closed people and it almost feels like you are talking about two different places. There is the place that is rushed on, and it's peacetime and there has been investment and it's been developed and it's great. And then there are the people who are still bleeding and who still have wounds and it is becoming less and less acceptable or popular to talk about that. We've reached a point where people are celebrating [the modernization and peace that has come to Belfast], but it is often at the expense of acknowledging people who are being left behind. And I don't say that with any sense of melodrama. I think that people who were most impoverished and most affected by the Troubles are still those same people, and they don't really have much of a voice and they did during the Troubles and they don't now and that must be very confusing, and I speak of this from experience, given my background.[19]

Joan is a prime example of a marginalized person still entrenched in the trauma of the past and unable to keep up with the rapid pace of change the region has recently experienced.

This division between people intent on leaving the Troubles behind and building a new modern Northern Ireland and those who are still stuck in the trauma of the past is further exemplified through the character of Ian. Like Máirín in Spallen's *Strandline*, Ian is perceived by his community to be elitist because he now dresses and sounds like a Londoner. He wears cardigans, his hair is longer, and he has adopted a foreign culture and accent. Friends and neighbors perceive him to be a snob, and even his mother is embarrassed by the changes in him. When the Taximan picks Ian up from the train station, he is angered by the young man's arrogant rejection of Belfast: "Pick up some posh twat can't wait to fuck him out on his ear, gabblin on about the ferry and how he should write a book, doesn't like it here et cetera" (8). Gregg shows that those who have left the North to forge futures elsewhere are generally looked on with suspicion by their communities once they return. This theme is exhibited in countless women's writings, including Charabanc's *Gold in the Streets* (1986), Anne Devlin's *After Easter* (1994), Morna Regan's *Midden* (2001), and Spallen's *Strandline* (2009). Ultimately, Ian and Joan are at the heart of the play, symbolizing the North's constant struggle between the past and the future. Joan is a woman trapped in the past, whereas Ian has fled the North in order to secure a more positive future in England.

Sexuality in relation to the changing face of Belfast is also explored in *Lagan*. Aoife is pregnant with the baby of a much older man, a successful banker who is known in the neighborhood for watching porn and being a "first-class wanker" (33). Aoife's pregnancy has shocked and shamed her mother, Anne, who views her daughter as a whore for getting pregnant. In contrast to her "slutty" daughter, Anne revers her son, Ian, whom she sees as smart, successful, and masculine: "Children are so soft these days, soft as boiled eggs, not like her own strapping Ian, all twelve stone of him, making his fry with capable man-hands, breaking eggs and cursing, not even pausing to fish out the shell. Girls are different. Loose. Cats. Whores" (20). However, the play also subtly suggests that Ian may not be who Anne assumes he is. In one scene, when Anne declares that Ian is single only because he has failed to find the right woman, the rest of the cast *"fidgets, looks off"* (19). Although Anne is unaware, the rest of the characters seem to be cognizant, on some level, that Ian may be gay. Furthermore, Anne may be ready to privately admonish Aoife's sexuality, but she is equally unwilling to address the subject directly with her daughter, preferring to pretend as though Aoife's pregnancy is not happening.

Aoife is not the only woman who is attacked for being sexually active. Fiona sleeps with Emmet, who initially becomes repulsed when he realizes that he is not her first sexual partner: "She's an animal to him. He revulses. Slag. His hands stop. Curl into themselves. Worse, he turns away from her. . . . He was powerful. He's annoyed. He was not her first, clearly, far from it" (38–39). These lines are made more powerful by the fact that Fiona and Emmet say them together in unison. This joint dialogue transforms the lines: Fiona narrates Emmet's reaction with great despair while Emmet simultaneously verbalizes his innermost private thoughts.

Love, sex, and violence merge together in disturbing ways. Fiona equates sex with romantic stories of love that will allow her and Emmet to escape the trauma and misery of Belfast.

> FIONA: Jack and Rose
> Baby and Patrick Swayze
> Shrek and Princess Fiona
> Emmet and Fiona, y'know?
> Stories. Escape. The 'Troubles'—myths and legends as real as
> Finn MacCool, the tooth fairy. I've been searchin. (41)

Fiona has been searching for her own great love story that will transport her away from the realities of her depressing life in Belfast: an absentee father and philanderer and a dead-end job. Despite her desire to escape, Fiona feels that her genetic fate will trap her in a cycle of misery, abuse, and violence. She reflects that at the "bottom of everything is cruelty . . . being Terry's daughter taught me this. Can't hate Terry totally, fucker that he's been, cos I am him, in different skin. It's in me" (41). Interestingly, Sinead in Spallen's *Pumpgirl* also remarks that she is genetically predisposed to being with abusive men. Both

Sinead and Fiona thus see their lives as being controlled by a Northern fatalism, unable to be changed by personal action.[20] Terry also beats his daughter, and Fiona's body is covered in scars from where she cuts herself. She knows paternal and familial affection only as violence, something that she replicates on herself in punishment. For Fiona, sex and love are translated into an escapist fairytale. In contrast, Aoife's sexual escapades have entrapped her in an unwanted and illegitimate pregnancy.

Likewise, youths' understanding of sex and sexuality seems to have become perverted. Tracey, who is eight, has been exposed to sexually explicit and violent films and knows more about "sexting" than someone of her age should. Similarly, her brother, Phil, who is desperately in love with Aoife, is so frustrated and bored by his life that he tells his love interest, "wish something, y'know, would just like, happen, to me . . . like being raped, or something" (49). Philip is so desperate to be seen, to feel important, to have attention paid to him that he naïvely and immaturely insinuates that a violent sexual attack would at least give him sympathy from his family and community. Between sexting, desiring rape, and becoming pregnant at seventeen, young people in Belfast are disconnected with the realities and consequences of sex, a theme that is also at the heart of *Perve*.

Lagan is, in part, a play about a lost generation of damaged young people: Emmet has lost his mother (Joan) and brother (Ryan), Aoife is pregnant at seventeen, Fiona self-harms and is beaten by her father. Ian, who has escaped to England, is the only young person with a full life. He has ambitions to be a great writer and has the ability to look at Northern life and culture with the fresh eyes of someone who has been away. Although Ian is internally conflicted, he is arguably the most emotionally and psychologically healthy of the group, the health achieved by his time away from Belfast. And though this is a generation that has come of age during peacetime, the lingering effects of the past seem to have damaged young people and stunted their emotional and psychological growth.

The complex tension between the past and the future, which is central to many recent women's plays, including *Lagan*, is captured again at the end with a very simple exchange between Ian, who left Belfast for a better life, and Aoife, who stayed behind. Ian left the North so he could have greater freedoms (perhaps sexual in nature), pursue his dream of becoming a writer, and escape the traps of the North. He views his pregnant sister as someone without much future and asks her, "How could you stay here?" Aoife, who believes she has a duty to fight for a better Northern Ireland, sees her brother as abandoning his home, his country, and his family. She replies, simply, "How could you leave?" (54). These deceptively simple questions are profoundly loaded with complex issues and assumptions about the past and future of the North: Is the new North capable of escaping its past history, healing its people, and moving toward a more positive future? Can young people forge better lives with greater educational and job opportunities in the North, or is escape to London and Dublin still the only option for the young? Do citizens have an obligation to stay and improve the community or should the best and brightest continue to seek their fortunes elsewhere? Is the North doomed to repeat its past or can the future be better? These questions are complex because, as Duncan Morrow explains, the trauma of the Troubles is shared both on an individual level and a societal one: "Forgiveness [is] so burning in Northern Ireland . . . [because] so many of the injuries are understood as the grief not only of individuals but of whole communities. . . . The decision to forgive . . . becomes of importance to everyone—because without it the political stability of the whole system is endangered."[21] Thus the personal exchange between brother and sister and their ability to potentially bridge this difficult divide become symbolic of the larger struggle that the North as a whole is addressing. If individuals can work out these issues, Gregg suggests, perhaps there is hope for the future of the state.

The end of *Lagan* is optimistic yet ambiguous about whether the future will be bright. Ian decides to stay in Belfast, although it is unclear for how long, and Anne makes a small step toward reconnecting with her daughter post-abortion. The play concludes with a small, ordinary moment of mother and daughter sitting together outside in

the sun. Their tentative exchange of small talk marks a possible recon-
nection for them and the hope that they will be able to move beyond
the trauma of the abortion to focus on a positive future for Aoife.
Gregg recalls that she "wanted to land on a note of ambivalence and
hope . . . of possible redemption or direction in choices. And I felt
those two characters [the mother and daughter] were particularly rep-
resentative of people I know, of Belfast and Northern Ireland, and that
issue [of abortion] is one that we don't talk about and is a hot topic."[22]
This last image of mother and daughter in the sun, quietly sharing
each other's company, is the final moment of the play and suggests
the divide between generations may be able to be bridged or at least
negotiated without the breakdown of the family structure. There is
hope and possible healing for this family, and there is also a renewed,
if tentative, commitment to the North and to building their futures in
Belfast in a positive way.

In Root Theatre and Oval House's fall 2011 production of *Lagan*,
four actors played all the roles, switching from character to character
simply through a change in voice and physicality. The production was
fast-paced, forcing the audience to focus and listen to the extremely
wordy monologues while picking out the plot hidden within the dense
speeches. Gregg says that she wanted the audience to feel rather than
think. She did not mind if they missed some of the dialogue because
of the rapid pace; instead, she wanted them to experience an emotional impact. However, critics found this to be very challenging for
the audience. Although *The Telegraph* praised Gregg, calling her a
playwright "with a fiercely distinctive voice," and lauded the poetic
stream-of-conscious writing, it also complained that "the pace of the
dialogue doesn't stop and in avoiding silences, Gregg leaves the audience behind."[23] In addition, the *Guardian* underscored the theme
of the arrested past when it described *Lagan:* "Set in post-Troubles
Belfast, a town 'pock-marked with stale fairytales,' it conjures a place
where ghosts still lurk in the shopping centres that were once blown
to smithereens, and attitudes towards sex and sexuality are stuck in
the 1950s." The review went on to praise the play, remarking that the

"snaking structure is clever as the glancing connections between the characters are stealthily revealed, and there is no doubt that Gregg can really write, as she proved in *Perve*."[24]

Just as Abbie Spallen's critical recognition abroad allowed her new opportunities at home, Gregg's success with the Abbey Theatre and Oval House has increasingly brought her work to the attention of Northern theatres. Tinderbox commissioned a new play, *Huzzies*, about the formation of a rock band, which premiered at the 2012 Queens Festival in Belfast. The play integrated original music by Katie Richardson and mixed the experience of theatrical performance with that of seeing a live rock concert in an attempt to lure audience from Belfast's strong music scene into theatre. Northern Irish Opera commissioned a short piece entitled *Jackie's Taxi*, which Gregg co-wrote with the composer Ed Bennett. Like *Lagan* and *Shibboleth*, the operetta explored how Belfast has changed during the peace process, and it premiered along with four other short operas at the Metropolitan Arts Centre (MAC) in July 2012. That same year, Gregg wrote *Override*, commissioned for the Watford Palace Theatre, located on the outskirts of London. Foreign theatres have continued to be supportive of her work. The National Theatre (London) commissioned a new play called *I'm Spilling My Heart Out Here* (2013) as part of their New Connections Festival that pairs emerging playwrights with youth theatre groups and performs new works all over the country. Arts Emerson in Boston staged Global Arts Corps' *Hold Your Tongue, Hold Your Dead* (2014), written by Gregg. This collaborative project explored the intersecting lives of two Protestant and Catholic families who struggle to find meaning, connection, and peace in the post-Agreement North. In addition to its premiere at the Abbey, *Perve* was performed at the Cúirt Festival in Galway in 2012, Montreal's Licerne Theatre in 2012, and Brisbane's Centenery Theatre Group in 2013. Both *Perve* and *Lagan* have been published by Nick Hern Books, ensuring their wider distribution, integration into academic study, and further productions outside of Ireland and the United Kingdom. And, in 2015, the Abbey finally staged *Shibboleth* on its Peacock stage as part of the Dublin Theatre Festival. Gregg's increasing visibility at home and abroad, it is hoped, will encourage more Irish theatres to stage her challenging work and to expand the Irish dramatic canon to include more experimental work.

Like Gregg, Rosemary Jenkinson left east Belfast to attend university in England. Jenkinson is a playwright and short-story writer whose work encompasses many of the themes that other women such as Spallen and Gregg are incorporating into their writing today: gendered violence, youth in peril, class struggles, disillusionment with the peace process, and the effects of lingering Troubles violence. However, Jenkinson's drama tends to concentrate on the male experience. Her work is often darkly comedic and violent and is characterized by a gritty and uncompromising look at Belfast's social ills. Many of Jenkinson's plays are set in her hometown of loyalist east Belfast, and she specializes in young disaffected men who banter in a fast-paced, working-class Belfast dialect. In much of her work, Jenkinson critiques contemporary culture, arguing, like Gregg, that the peace process has left behind a marginalized underclass of poor Protestants. Her plays suggest that without steady jobs or a clear sectarian mission to give structure and meaning to their lives, many young men are floundering, and thus contributing to a post-Agreement Belfast that is increasingly plagued by drug and alcohol abuse, crime, and violence.

Jenkinson returned to Belfast in 2002 out of nostalgia for her country and because she felt disconnected from her roots. Being away for sixteen years gave Jenkinson a fresh perspective and renewed interest in her community: "When you've been away, you see Belfast so much clearer, what it is now, all that makes it more vibrant."[25] Jenkinson had been writing short stories for years; however, she had not worked in theatre until Tinderbox did a short workshop of her first play, *Chocolate Madonna,* in 2002. Lynn Parker of the Dublin-based theatre company Rough Magic saw the workshop and invited her to participate in her company's Seeds II Project in 2004. Jenkinson was subsequently commissioned by the company to write a play; *The Bonefire* (2006) was the result of this effort. The play was produced at the Dublin Theatre Festival, where it won the Stewart Parker BBC Radio Award. Jenkinson attributes Lynn Parker's connection with the North[26] as being instrumental in starting her career: "being a Northern Irish female . . . she was interested in getting those voices out. There was a definite connection there that helped me, and she understood it. Otherwise, I would never have been produced in Dublin."[27] Since then, Jenkinson's plays have been produced by Northern companies such as Ransom (*The Winners*, 2008), Tinderbox (*Bruised*, 2008; collaboration), and the Lyric (*White Star of the North*, 2012; *Love or Money*, 2016). However, the majority of her work, like her female peers, has been produced abroad in London, New York, and Washington, DC.

Like Spallen and Gregg, Jenkinson has generally found foreign theatre companies to be "a lot more receptive" toward women playwrights. "I think it's harder here [in the North] for some reason to get plays on. Of course, in Northern Ireland, we have the least amount of funding in the UK and a lot less than down south in the Republic . . . the opportunities here are not great." Like Spallen and Gregg, Jenkinson has also been frustrated by the trend of Northern theatres to ignore their own playwrights while foreign theatres embrace Irish work: "It is just so ironic that I've had more plays produced in the United States than in Ireland. And my first play was produced in Dublin, so I didn't start [in the North]. . . . You didn't feel any [support in the North]."[28] American theatre companies have been the strongest and most consistent supporters of Jenkinson's work. The Washington, DC, Keegan Theatre Company produced *Stella Morgan* in 2010, *Basra Boy* in 2011, *Cuchullain* in 2012, and *A Midsummer Night's Riot* in 2014. Solas Nua, also in DC, produced *Johnny Meister and the Stitch* in 2010. In addition, *The Lemon Tree* was performed by Origin Theatre Company during the New York-based 1st Irish Festival in 2009.

Like Gregg, Jenkinson first started to be produced in the North when she participated in collaborative and development opportunities at local theatres. She helped write *Bruised* for Tinderbox in 2008 and was also part of Paines Plough's *Come to Where I'm From* project in 2010, for which playwrights wrote and performed monologues about their hometowns. In 2011, she wrote *1 in 5*, a one-act play that was performed in conjunction with plays by three other female playwrights (Marina Carr, Nicola McCartney, and Morna Regan) for Kabosh's poverty project. Like Gregg, Jenkinson has found that collaborative writing projects have limited benefits for their participants. She argues that more women than men are asked to participate because women are expected to share and collaborate more than men: "Theatres are trying to look like they are encouraging women playwrights but what you end up being able to write is a quarter of a play rather than a full play." Jenkinson also points out that a writer's individual voice and creativity will rarely be heard in these projects: "You are never going to stand out because everyone submerges under everyone else." Women are thus expected to adapt their voices and "work well with others," whereas men continue to receive individual space and time to stage their own unique voices. Jenkinson argues that theatres "are trying to look like they are supporting women's writing but it's not really helping. It would probably be better to give one single play to one woman."[29] Women's participation in joint projects may have other unforeseen consequences as well. Critics and publishers tend to respond more positively to single-authored plays. Collaborative works tend to engender mediocre reviews (or no reviews at all), and few are ever published.

The Bonefire (2006) is Jenkinson's first full-length play, and it is also one of her most violent and controversial works to date. The play is set in the working-class Annadale Embankment, a loyalist stronghold within the predominantly nationalist south Belfast. The community has gathered to celebrate the coming annual July 12 parades where loyalists process through Catholic enclaves. The July 12 parades celebrate the 1690 Battle of the Boyne when the Protestant king, William of Orange, defeated the Catholic King, James II, and took over the English throne. Today, these parades are a public display of Protestant claim on Northern territory and a symbol of a staunch unionist commitment to remaining connected to the United Kingdom. The processions are notorious for inciting riots, protests, and violence; marching season (April through August) continues to be one of the most violent and dangerous times in the North.

The Bonefire is set directly in the middle of this highly volatile and inflammatory time of year. Adult Protestant siblings, Tommy and LeAnne, live in the Annadale Embankment and are preparing for a celebratory bonfire. Their festivities are interrupted when two secret IRA members, Jane and Davey, infiltrate the Annandale community by pretending to be loyalists. Jane and Davey intend to set off a bomb in retribution for the loyalist parades. Tommy discovers the plot but LeAnne, who has fallen in love with Davey, convinces the IRA man to switch allegiances to the loyalist Ulster Defense Association (UDA) in order to save himself from imminent death. Davey defects from the IRA and kills his former comrade, Jane, in order to prove his new loyalty to the UDA. LeAnne ends up stabbing her brother, who dies; and the play ends with Davey, a newly minted UDA member, moving in with LeAnne and setting up a new life. The very dark humor of the play combined with the ease with which Davey switches loyalties undermines the fanaticism of paramilitary culture and posits sectarian ideology as hollow.

Tommy and LeAnne, part of a Protestant minority within a largely Catholic neighborhood, spend their days entrenched, on the offensive, and aggressively defining their Protestantism as anything that is the opposite of Catholicism. For example, Tommy flies an Israeli flag over his house after seeing a Catholic family raise a Palestinian flag. A parallel by Northern Catholics who equate English colonization of the North with Israeli occupation of Palestine has long been drawn. However, Tommy does not seem to understand these complex historical and political parallels. He hoists his own Israeli flag only as a symbol of defining himself as resolutely not Catholic. Tommy lives in a world consumed by reacting to republican threats, both real and imagined. When Davey visits Tommy's home while bleeding, Tommy insinuates that Catholics attacked Davey. The mundane truth is that a Protestant neighbor cut Davey by accident. However, Tommy finds that it is much more exciting to fulfill expectations of sectarian violence, thus reinforcing and perpetuating the narrative of sectarian division that the community still clings to for its identity. Making up sensational stories about sectarian clashes in order to gain respect within the community immediately positions the conflict as a potentially false and hollow concept within the play. The absurdity and senselessness of the Troubles is further shown through Tommy's repeated desire to be injured in paramilitary clashes in order to collect financial compensation by government funds set up for victims. A primary reason for Tommy's involvement in the UDA is thus not out of a deep desire to defend Protestant territory and culture or to maintain the union between Britain and Northern Ireland; instead, it is financially motivated.

Loyalty and sense of purpose within the conflict are again undermined by Jenkinson when Davey casually switches from IRA to UDA membership. Davey officially defects from the IRA, joins the UDA, and proves commitment to his newest affiliation by shooting his former IRA colleague, Jane, in the head at point-blank range. By showing that Davey's loyalty is one of convenience, Jenkinson controversially suggests that sectarian affiliation is often arbitrary and lacks a strong belief system. Instead, the conflict has become an exciting, violent adventure that young men and women use to fill their lives with purpose and mission.

Devotion to the loyalist cause is further destabilized in the play through the character of LeAnne. She reveals that she almost joined the Catholic Women's League because they liked her baked goods. Furthermore, because she is smitten with Davey, LeAnne and Tommy are both willing to overlook the fact that Davey was an IRA member who planned to blow them up. Senseless devotion to the conflict seems to go back generations, and the Troubles has broken down the family structure. Tommy and LeAnne's father was in the UVF. He took his own life, but tried to make it look like the IRA killed him in order to spare his family the embarrassment. This pattern of reclassifying self-inflicted or accidental violence as sectarian clashes suggests that the violence between the two communities is often self-perpetuating. *The Bonefire* posits the conflict as a largely empty set of false and imagined beliefs, while tempering this controversial position by showing the very real, gritty, and gruesome violence that continually stems from the factional war.

Jenkinson also suggests that empty loyalist ideology has fundamentally broken down the family structure. Tommy and LeAnne's father and mother both committed suicide. Tommy now takes after his parents, attempting suicide several times a year. When Davey apologizes for getting blood on the floor after accidently being cut by a neighborhood boy, LeAnne responds, "Never worry your head about it. Tommy's spilt loads of his own, cutting his wrist and that."[30]

These darkly comedic references to suicide also reflect a disturbing increase in suicide that the North has recently experienced. Counterintuitively, the suicide rate in the North has almost doubled since the signing of the Agreement. The group most affected by this trend is made up of those who were children during the worst years of the Troubles, roughly 1969–78. Researchers have attributed the increase in suicide to social and psychological factors, including "the growth in social isolation, poor mental health arising from the experience of conflict, and the greater political stability of the past decade." Mike Tomlinson of Queens University, Belfast, has argued: "The transition to peace means that cultures of externalized aggression are no longer socially approved or politically acceptable. Violence and aggression have become more internalized instead."[31] Like Spallen, who shows how Troubles violence has become disturbingly ingrained within the post-Agreement North, Jenkinson emphasizes this same issue in many of her plays. In *The Bonefire*, she illustrates how sectarian violence has become internalized through the legacy of suicide in Tommy's family, through the sexual violence that is perpetrated on the women and children in that same community, and through the internal war between the UVF and the UDA. Rather than fighting against the Catholics, the Protestant community has turned their aggression and fear internally on themselves.

Suicide and intracommunity violence feature prominently in contemporary Northern writing. In Spallen's *Pumpgirl*, Hammy kills himself out of desperation from the lack of jobs and opportunities, Gregg's *Hold Your Tongue, Hold Your Dead* addresses the rising suicide rate since the Belfast/Good Friday Agreement, and Lucy Caldwell's *Leaves* (2007) centers around the return of a young woman to her home in

Belfast after attempting suicide while at college in London. In Spall-en's *Pumpgirl* and *Strandline* the Catholic community has turned vio-lence inward on its own women, Jaki McCarrick's *Leopoldville* (2010) centers around a group of young men who torture and kill a local tavern owner, and Lisa McGee's *Girls and Dolls* (2006) follows two young girls who lure a neighbor's young child to her death. This post-Agreement focus on intracommunity violence is in stark contrast to Troubles plays, which show violence as coming from an outside enemy source. As Tomlinson notes, external aggression is no longer socially acceptable within the peace process narrative, and it appears as though anger, frustration, and fear has thus been internalized within the indi-vidual Catholic and Protestant communities.

Tomlinson has also researched the recent increase in alcohol con-sumption and illegal and prescription drug use. He argues that some Northerners use drugs and alcohol in order to cope with the trauma of the past: "We seem to have adjusted to peace by means of mass medi-cation with anti-depressants, alcohol and non-prescription drugs, the consumption of which has risen dramatically in the period of peace."[32] In her characteristically sardonic manner, Jenkinson addresses this issue in *The Bonefire* with Jane arguing that the nation's reliance on drugs has dulled the peoples' innate desire to riot and kill: "Know what your trouble is, Davey, it's you on the drugs. Drugs aren't natu-ral. Sure, don't they suppress your desire to kill Prods? Keeping our youngsters up at all-night raves when they should be out rioting at the Short Strand?" (44–45). Here Jenkinson mocks the stereotype that Northerners are naturally inclined toward conflict. Jane absurdly argues that the North is now drugged up with antidepressant and antianxiety medication, which has dulled its desire for violence. Jane thus controversially insinuates that the lull in the fighting in a post-Agreement North may be due to a nation using drugs and alcohol to dull their senses rather than a real historical move toward peace.

Jenkinson is careful to discredit this atavistic Irish stereotype, never allowing the audience to sit comfortably with the idea. The ste-reotype of Northerners as innately violent is mocked toward the end of the play when Davey's status as an IRA double agent is discussed.

Defending her love, LeAnne tells her brother, "He's not all bad, Tommy. It's his background" (65). Her, LeAnne suggests that it was Tommy's environment and upbringing during the Troubles that made him violent and fickle, not his innate character. However, Tommy replies: "Don't give me that old excuse. Like, am I a product of my environment? Is it a lifestyle choice? Have I watched too many movies?" LeAnne replies coldly, "No, you're just a mad f**king bastard" (66). In this exchange, LeAnne argues that Tommy is simply a born sociopath, whereas Davey may be a product of the sectarian conflict. Whereas the JustUs Community Theatre Company wanted to present the environmental and historical reasons that drove otherwise peaceful Catholics to extreme violence, *The Bonefire* simultaneously highlights and undermines the stereotype that Northerners are innately violent. This reference to Tommy as a "mad bastard" also calls to mind Martin McDonagh's *The Lieutenant of Inishmore* (2001), in which "Mad Padraic" is a psychotic killer who feels no remorse at torturing or killing those who get in his way, including his own family. This parallel is further reinforced when it is revealed at the end of the play that Tommy planned and participated in a gang rape of his sister. Like McDonagh's "Mad Padraic" who intends to murder his father without hesitation, Tommy rapes his sister with his fellow UDA members and feels no remorse.

There are further parallels between Jenkinson's writing and that of Martin McDonagh. Like McDonagh, who shocked audiences with his casual jokes about Bloody Sunday and IRA violence in *The Lieutenant of Inishmore*, Jenkinson uses dark, controversial humor to satirize some of the most venerated figures and events of the Troubles. When Davey complains that he always has to work for the IRA and never gets to have any fun, Jenkinson uses a famous quotation from hunger striker Bobby Sands in an irreverently mocking fashion:

DAVEY: Why is it we never get to have fun?
JANE: Didn't Bobby Sands say, "Our revenge will be the laughter of our children."
DAVEY: I don't see why it has to skip a generation. (46)

Sands's famous speech is often quoted as a symbol of Catholic strength and perseverance in the face of Protestant oppression. Here Jenkinson transforms it into a casual, comedic complaint. Later in the play, Jenkinson references the mid-nineteenth-century famine as a descriptor for Jane's slender figure. When LeAnne and Tommy find out that Jane is an IRA member, the siblings reflect that they should have realized that she was Catholic based on "the big bap of ginger hair on her . . . [and her] great shape. . . . Cavorting around like an Irish Famine victim" (65).

The excessive and absurd comedic violence at the end of the play further recall a McDonagh aesthetic. Tommy is stabbed by LeAnne (out of revenge for the gang rape) but survives. While he is being carried off to the hospital, bloody and injured, the UDA member Warren shoots Tommy in the kneecap. Warren was sent to punish Tommy for being late in repaying money he borrowed from the UDA. Though Warren meant only to injure him as punishment, the gunshot combined with the knife wound ends up killing Tommy. The excessive and gratuitous nature of the violence is comical, as are its unintended consequences, which surprise and befuddle LeAnne, Davey, and Warren.

Like Spallen and Gregg, Jenkinson repeatedly exposes how the sectarian conflict has broken down healthy family bonds and subjected women and children to sexual assault. Sex is continually linked with violence, and, like Clodagh in Spallen's *Strandline*, Jenkinson positions women as both the perpetrators and victims of that violence. The play suggests that LeAnne may have raped Davey while he was passed out from drinking. Tommy accuses LeAnne: "He was forced! Yes! You forced him, ya stupid hoor!" (27). LeAnne's sexuality is also constantly under attack in the play; men are simultaneously attracted and repelled by her soft, flabby, overweight body. Warren lobs the most vicious attack on LeAnne, telling her brother Tommy, "If Hitler were alive today, he'd sterilize her. Fucked-up genes. Interbred" (60).

Sex and sectarian violence again intermingle when, at the end of the play, Davey hands Tommy a gun and tells him to shoot Jane in the head to prove his loyalty to the UDA. When Davey blanches at the demand, Tommy responds, "I know, it's mad. I thought I'd be pumping one into her myself tonight, but not like this" (76). The gun is thus likened to the penis and shooting a woman in the head is compared to penetration. Ancient misogynistic superstitions about women are also conjured. When the neighborhood gathers to burn Jane on the bonfire, there is speculation that women take longer to burn than men because they are "watery bastards . . . crying and peeing all the time. Leaking out of both ends they do" (74).

Catholic women's sexuality is also singled out as a prize for Protestant men. Tommy had an affair with a Catholic woman and may have had an illegitimate child with her. Catholic women, according to Tommy, like the danger of sleeping with a Protestant; they like to be "colonized" and "conquered" (34), just as the English colonized Ireland. Tommy is shunned for sleeping with a Catholic woman because, although he has no relationship with his child, he has done a disservice to the community by increasing the population of the Catholic resistance. The UDA member Warren berates Tommy "for breeding baby Taigs over in Carryduff to come and burn us out" (63).[33]

The extent that the sectarian conflict and paramilitary culture has destroyed the community and created a distorted relationship between sex and violence is demonstrated most directly when Tommy tells Jane that "the UDA does have its good side. For instance, there are no rapes round here. No pedophiles or nothing. Although, in saying that, the children are that sexually advanced, you don't need to abuse them behind closed doors. Or in a hedge. They'd force it on you themselves given half a chance" (34). Tommy's contention that there are no rapes, of course, directly contradicts what both he and the UDA did to his sister years before. In addition, Tommy insinuates that children in the community are viewed as sexually mature and aggressive, forcing sexual relationships on unsuspecting adults. The community thus accepts sexual relationships between adults and children as normal. Indeed, later in the play, Warren freely admits that he prefers to have sex with those who are "under the age of consent" (81).

LeAnne's gang rape by her brother and the UDA, however, is the most shocking of the assaults on women's bodies. When Tommy declares at the end of the play that his sister enjoyed the rape—"she groaned at all the right bits"—LeAnne stabs him, casually declaring, "It's all right, I'll cry later" (82). This is a portrait of a deeply disturbed family that uses physical and sexual violence casually and routinely in their everyday lives, suggesting that they have become desensitized to the violence they have consistently lived with. The gang rape of LeAnne on July 11, several years previously, also suggests that the UDA's excited anticipation for July 12 spilled over into the misplaced violence of raping their own women. This idea that fervor over anticipated sectarian clashes often becomes internalized within individual communities is demonstrated again later in the play when LeAnne recounts a story about the last July 12 when a brother ran his sister over with his car and then beat her to death with a flagpole. LeAnne says that the police attributed the murder "to him being in a pure lather from the thrill of the day" (37).

Furthermore, the men of *The Bonefire* act out a perverse and extreme misinterpretation of masculinity inspired by the murals, flags, and fetishized stories that celebrate a mythologized history of Protestant power and idealism. Cormac O'Brien writes that Jenkinson's male characters "aspire to a culturally constructed fantasy of loyalist manhood that is . . . not only harmful and limiting, but also toxic and fatal." He goes on to state that "often fatal paradigms of masculinity cling to a self-glorified past while simultaneously troubling the present."[34] Because the loyalist community finds itself marginalized in the post-Agreement North, this historical memory of former power makes the present-day estrangement even more difficult. In peacetime, loyalist identity and purpose have been subsumed by the new goals of the peace process, and in response, the men of *The Bonefire* have resorted to an extreme hypermasculinity in an attempt to re-create and draw out a misinterpreted mythology of past Protestant power. As O'Brien points out, "within the play's world, the men understand their behavior to be appropriate to their gender, social, and geographic positioning. . . . Thus the performance of masculinity becomes the relentless pursuit of a fantastical and asymptotic ideal, constructed wholly by subsuming and performing what the subject sees in the masculine public world, rather than by engaging in self-reflection or drawing from the inner-self."[35] The post-Agreement plays analyzed in this book are filled with emasculated, disenfranchised men who have been unable to adapt to peacetime.

This fracture of traditional identity structures in the post-Agreement North is one that is echoed in many contemporary plays. Over the course of centuries, trauma becomes, as Ron Eyerman writes in the context of the formation of African American identity, "a social condition, a lived experience, producing a distinctive way of life, a culture, a community, and finally an identity."[36] The Catholic community reconstituted the Troubles (as well as the larger colonization of Ireland) as the primary maker of its identity. The sectarian conflict, "not as an institution or an experience but as a point of origin in a common past,"[37] formed an all-consuming origin story in the formation of contemporary Northern identity.

However, in the wake of the Troubles, these identities have started to splinter; this "tear in the social fabric"[38] within the Protestant and Catholic communities can be seen in countless post-Agreement plays where characters labor to find new identities and purpose within the tenuous and poorly defined peace. Male characters struggle to reconcile themselves to the fact that their societal roles during the Troubles are no longer productive or valued during peacetime. The men in the plays of Abbie Spallen, Stacey Gregg, and Rosemary Jenkinson are all adrift. Unemployed, emasculated, and disoriented by the changing economic, ethnic, and social landscape of the North, they lash out against women, ethnic minorities, and children. Women in these plays cautiously test the new peace by venturing out professionally, personally, and sexually only to be brutally punished and returned to the conventional domestic sphere. In addition, the collective identities of the Catholic and Protestant communities as well as that of Northern Ireland as a whole are debated, revised, and challenged in these plays. As Ron Eyerman writes, "A traumatic tear [in group identity] evokes the need to 'narrate new foundations,' which includes reinterpreting the past as a means toward reconciling present/future needs."[39] As peace-process playwrights look back at the Troubles, they have begun to reinterpret and recast that history and experience in order to help explain present-day challenges. A new sense of Northern identity, of Catholic identity, and of Protestant identity is being sought. Northern women playwrights are playing an important role in sifting through competing and shifting identities as well as helping to reshape a new historical understanding of the Troubles "as a means toward reconciling present/future needs." In *Bonefire*, *Basra Boy*, *Johnny Meister and the Stitch*, and other plays, Jenkinson positions the post-Agreement Protestant male as struggling to navigate a peace-process North that has displaced the identity structures formulated during the Troubles. In doing so, she argues that this population must be supported and integrated into a collective post-Agreement identity in order for a true peace to be established.

Despite Martin McDonagh's *The Lieutenant of Inishmore*, which debuted in Ireland in 2003 as part of the Dublin Theatre Festival, Dublin seemed to be entirely unprepared for the dark, violent humor of *The Bonefire*. Dublin critics complained that the violent humor was too shocking and that Jenkinson's depiction of loyalist culture was too disturbing to view humorously. John McKeown of London's *Daily Mail* wrote, "[Implausible events] unfold to the point of riotous nightmare, made more horrible by the knowledge that these annual drug-fuelled bacchanals are actually still celebrated. The most disturbing point is when Tommy and Warren mock Jane, who is face down on the pavement, business suit torn and spattered with blood, having been gang-raped. Under such a barrage, any deeper import the play has is wiped out. We can't feel anything for the characters."[40]

Jenkinson's use of dark humor to critique loyalist culture sat uncomfortably with many critics, who repeatedly expressed discomfort at the violent images on stage that were supposed to be subversively comedic. Karen Fricker wrote in the *Guardian*, "Jenkinson's play is meant to be a comedy, but how it was ever supposed to work on stage is hard to fathom. The internal life of the loyalist community is still so unknown as to be exotic to many Irish people, yet Jenkinson assumes a complicit audience who can laugh with wry recognition at people who are described as pig-ignorant, incestuous, lawless rapists."[41] As Fricker notes, loyalist culture is rarely shown on the Irish stage; Gary Mitchell remains the primary theatrical scribe of unionist life. Perhaps because Dublin critics and audiences so rarely see loyalism dramatized, witnessing such brutal and psychopathic depictions of an unfamiliar culture was both shocking and unnerving. Audiences may have felt it was politically incorrect for them to laugh at that already marginalized community's expense.

Understandably, there were many elements to the play that upset audiences and reviewers: the negative portrayal of loyalist culture, the casual gang rape of LeAnne, and the irreverent references to important historic events and people in Irish history. Although McDonagh had initially received a mixed critical reception in Ireland, this eventually grew into begrudging admiration for his work. Jenkinson, however, seems to have been punished for writing such a play. Indeed, scathing critical attacks of *The Bonefire* have discouraged her from writing as controversial depictions of loyalist life in subsequent plays. Jenkinson believes the harsh criticism was, in part, due to the fact that southern audiences do not react well to representations of sectarianism, especially loyalist culture, which remain largely unexamined.[42]

Furthermore, Jenkinson views Northern theatre as much more direct and political than the theatre of the Republic, which often makes critics uncomfortable: "We write a lot more directly and head-on than someone from the south in general. They are more conservative. . . . Northerners are rougher and more in your face than southern people."[43] This translates, Jenkinson argues, into Northern theatre being grittier and blunter than its southern counterpart.

In contrast to *The Bonefire*, Jenkinson's later monologue plays, *Johnny Meister and the Stitch* (2008), *Basra Boy* (2011), *Cuchullain* (2012), and *A Midsummer Night's Riot* (2014) focus entirely on young, urban working-class males. *Basra Boy* follows two working-class east Belfast teens, Speedy and Stig, who have fallen prey to drugs, violence, and crime owing to boredom and lack of jobs. Their parents are absent figures, and Speedy's mother is more concerned with her revolving set of boyfriends than her son. Both young men are members of the East Sons of Ulster flute band, and it is the only authority they recognize and the only institution that gives purpose and structure to their lives.

The Protestant marching band tradition historically has been vilified for its propensity to march through Catholic enclaves, engendering violence and protests. However, the flute band is positioned in the play as the only form of positive structure that Speedy and Stig have. Jenkinson controversially suggests that in the absence of positive government or societal structures—such as education, jobs, social services, or strong family support—the marching bands play an important societal role by giving meaning and pride to young men who otherwise feel alienated as members of the working-class unionist culture. Before joining the band, Speedy and Stig had little sense of direction or identity and filled their time with petty crime and alcohol.

While remnants of the Troubles affect the lives of these young men, another distant war rumbles in the background. When Stig leaves the marching band and joins the British military stationed in Iraq, the low-grade localized war that is still being fought in the North is contrasted with the large-scale destruction of war affecting the entire Middle East and the town of Basra, where Stig is stationed.

The wars in Iraq and Afghanistan and the lingering war in Belfast begin to merge toward the end of the play. During a parade celebrating the return of Northern soldiers from Iraq, Speedy is beaten by another member of the flute band. While Speedy is pummeled in Belfast, sounds from the war in Afghanistan (helicopters, call to prayers, armored vehicles, dogs barking, explosions) intermix with the sounds of the parade and the beating. The play flashes to Stig in Afghanistan, who is losing his leg in an explosion at the exact same moment that Speedy is beaten within an inch of his life thousands of miles away in Belfast. Although both young men chose very different paths, both end up physically and emotionally wounded by war. Speedy does not understand why the cycles of violence in the North continue: "Thought to meself, how can cities as beautiful as this give birth to bombers. And it's not our fault. From the playground to the battlefield. The marchin, the diggin, from the Somme to the bomb to the Troubles, we been reared for the slaughter for centuries."[44] Speedy believes that violence is so inbred and reflexive in the people of the North that it has become a natural part of their existence; it is part of their history, their legacy, and their duty to their ancestors to continue the fight. Speedy's understanding of the sectarian conflict as an inevitable and natural cycle is a view held by some in the North, and this mind-set has been identified by Seamus Heaney and other scholars as one of the most difficult obstacles to stopping cycles of violence.

The play then cuts to several months later with Speedy fully recovered from the beating. He is now a dole office clerk, having given up drugs and alcohol. Stig has returned home from the war; however, he has been emotionally and psychologically damaged and stays indoors. The play ends with a plea from Speedy, beseeching his old friend to rejoin the world. In a reversal of his previous ideology that Northern violence is inevitable and inbred over generations, Speedy promises Stig that he does not need to fall back into the reflexive patterns of sectarian warfare:

> The blood is up, it's never gonna go and I don't want it to go, I want to live with it and we're not the sons of Ulster, Stig, we never were, and all we have to defend is ourselves, we are free of it now, the Boyne is dead, it's just me and you.
> The blood is up.
> The blood is up with love, that's all.
> The blinds fly open.[45]

Speedy tells Stig that they bear no responsibility for the imagined besieged state of Ulster. They can doff off the obligation of hundreds of years of history, including the infamous Battle of the Boyne. Speedy tries to convince Stig that they are responsible only for themselves now; they are free of the history that has shackled and forced them to repeat cycles of violence and the ensuing poverty that it inevitably brings.

Although most of the play is uniformly pessimistic about the options and future for its young people, the play surprisingly ends on a positive note with the image of Stig opening the blinds of his window in response to his friend's pleas. Although, as Speedy says, the violence will never fully cease, he and Stig are independent autonomous individuals who need not be slaves to cycles of warfare. As Stig opens his window, it is, perhaps, a sign that he is ready to reenter the world and create for himself a more positive future. Basra Boy played at the west Belfast festival, Féile an Phobail, in August 2012, demonstrating the diversity of competing viewpoints that the historically nationalist festival now includes regularly in its lineup.

Jenkinson's *Come to Where I'm From* (2010) for Paines Plough (London) is perhaps her most direct critique of post-Agreement Belfast. The monologue is sarcastic, sharp, and witty, painting a bleak picture of a city that has failed to make much progress socially or economically two decades into the peace process. Jenkinson acerbically sums up the North as "the land of poets, scholars and petrol bombers," suggesting that "all tourists really come for is the Titanic and the Troubles—that's all we're really famed for, people dying en masse."[46] Jenkinson presents current-day Belfast as a community struggling to move forward, mired in social and political ills such as poverty, crime, violence, racism, rampant unemployment, and drugs that have been born from decades of sectarian warfare.

In one of the most pessimistic parts of the monologue, Jenkinson posits that the current peace is a temporary respite in a society locked in an endless cycle of conflict: "And let's face it, we all know this peace is just a wee rest. Another ten years down the line, they'll all be digging up their weapons with JCB's, scrabbling out in the yard for their handguns." One of the main problems that Jenkinson identifies is the North's desperate desire to move on from the Troubles at the expense of proper self-reflection and healing. She says, "This is the period after war, the period of collective amnesia and blindness. We've become a nation of holocaust-deniers, we can't even look at ourselves." For Jenkinson, this refusal to examine the past, this obsession with moving forward, and this denial of past traumas and injustices have created a stunted society, one that repeats entrenched historical cycles without self-reflection. Despite Jenkinson's unrelenting and unflinching examination of current-day Belfast, she ends her monologue clarifying her love-hate relationship with the city: "I'm slagging off Belfast because that's what we do. It's all part of an inverted covert subversive love we have for ourselves. Pretend to hate what you love, it's all part of our dual-nationality, dual-personality bipolarism, our two tribes locked in a loving embrace to the death." Like her plays, Jenkinson's monologue is unapologetic, harsh, darkly humorous, and includes unpopular and uncomfortable portrayals of the city and its people. However, she often tempers her dark views of the North with her deep affection for its people and culture, including moments of optimism as she often does in much of her dramatic work.

Like her female contemporaries, pessimism toward the peace process and distrust of politicians are central to Jenkinson's work. In *The Bonefire*, the only reference to the peace process or repairing cross-community relations is a sarcastic comment when LeAnne picks up Jane's extremely heavy briefcase and asks, "What's she got in here? The peace process?" (31). This description of peace and reconciliation as heavy, unwieldy, and burdensome is illustrative of how Jenkinson positions peace in each of her plays. The fact that the peace process is also locked away in a private suitcase suggests that the process remains the secretive workings of politicians and that the average citizen feels removed from it. Like Gregg and Spallen, Jenkinson suggests that the peace process is being worked out in private by elite government officials rather than on the ground with everyday citizens. In addition, drugs, alcohol, lack of education, and unemployment are repeatedly shown to be destructive influences in Jenkinson's work, as they are in the plays of Spallen and Gregg. The physically present but emotionally absent and sexually promiscuous mother also recurs in Jenkinson's plays. Fathers, on the other hand, are rarely seen and are often not even mentioned, as though their absence is to be expected or implicitly accepted, whereas maternal neglect is viewed as a more egregious infraction.[47]

Ultimately, Spallen, Gregg, and Jenkinson argue that Troubles violence and continuing sectarian prejudice remain central and damaging aspects of Northern society. Their plays address the breakdown of the family structure, sexual violence toward women, and a lingering Troubles violence that continues to haunt citizens of the North. Each playwright also identifies lack of support from domestic theatres, the marginalization of Northern theatre within Irish drama, and few opportunities for women playwrights as the primary obstacles that have prevented women writers from gaining greater inclusion within the Irish dramatic canon. Despite these difficulties, Spallen, Gregg, and Jenkinson remain vital cultural critics within Irish theatre, giving voice to those who rarely have a presence on the theatrical or political stage. In doing so, they continue an important tradition within women's playwriting of highlighting and empowering the silenced and hidden underclasses of the North.

8

Experimental Theatre and Queer Dramaturgy

Shannon Yee

In recent years, several Northern Irish theatres have embraced experimental and nontraditional theatre techniques, moving away from conventional text-based plays rooted in social realism. Kabosh Theatre Company now specializes in site-specific theatre and installation, Big Telly Theatre Company and Tinderbox Theatre Company have both produced site-specific shows since 2000, and Prime Cut Productions and Skinnybone Theatre produced successful immersive theatre projects in 2012 and 2013, respectively.[1] There is a growing sense among Northern theatre practitioners that social realism, long embraced in Ireland, can no longer adequately express the fractured identities, complex political status, economic upheaval, and uncertainty about the future that embodies the post-Agreement North.

Much of the theatre produced during the Troubles used social realism to promote realistic and truthful experiences of living within sectarian conflict. These plays tended to have clear and focused stories that reflected the urgency and specificity of Northerners' individual and collective experiences. In contrast, theatre of the post-Agreement

Sections of this chapter were previously published as "Blurring Boundaries and Collapsing Genres with Shannon Yee: Immersive Theatre, Pastiche, and Radical Openness in Northern Ireland," in *Radical Contemporary Theatre Practices by Women in Ireland*, ed. Miriam Haughton and Maria Kurdi (Dublin: Carysfort Press, 2015), 135–50.

North tends to reflect the confusion, ambivalence, and ambiguity that have come with peacetime. This uncertainty has been reflected in complex experimental play structures that often include the blurring of genres, nontraditional theatre techniques, and audience interaction.

Since 2000, a wide variety of experimental theatre projects have been performed in the North. Tinderbox Theatre performed a site-specific piece called *Convictions* (2000) at the Crumlin Road Courthouse in Belfast; audience members were led through different rooms of the historic building while scenes addressed shifting notions of what constitutes justice, punishment, and passing judgment in the post-Agreement North. In 2010, Kabosh staged an interactive theatre piece called *The West Awakes* (2010), which took audience members on a walking tour of west Belfast, playing off the popularity of political tours given to tourists by former Republican prisoners. This production challenged the role of the media in shaping the conflict and in privileging certain narratives of the Troubles. Kabosh also produced *1 in 5* in 2011, which was staged in the Limavady workhouse for the poor in Derry/Londonderry. This production explored the ongoing issue of poverty by staging contemporary scenes within the site-specific framework of the Limavady workhouse (known for enforcing brutal work and living conditions between 1842 and 1932). In addition to challenging spectators to experience theatre in a new way, each of these productions addressed complex debates in contemporary Northern society in a manner that promoted complexity and defied a singular interpretation. Rather than telling one specific story or trying to engender a particular emotional or intellectual response, experimental post-Agreement theatre tends to encourage ambiguity in spectators' experiences and highly individualistic interpretations of the performances. Adding to this growing trend of interactive and experimental theatre practices is the artist Shannon Yee.[2]

Yee is a Belfast-based practitioner whose work collapses traditional theatrical boundaries and blurs genres, mixing multimedia, music, dance and movement, sound technology, installation art, and experimental theatre traditions. As a biracial, queer, Chinese-American immigrant playwright with an acquired brain injury, she may epitomize in a single body a new range of diversity and change that has come to the North in the past two decades: "My multiple identities are something that feature a lot in my work—that concept of *other*. I always see myself as political, and the personal as political, and writing as my expression connected to that. I am a woman writer, I am an immigrant writer, I am a queer writer, I am a biracial writer. I am all of that and I am proud of that because it makes me who I am."[3] Yee uses her multiple minority identities to tackle difficult and taboo subjects in nontraditional ways. Her artistic work pushes the boundaries of theatrical form and structure while also advocating for those on the margins of Northern society such as the Lesbian Gay Bisexual Transgender (LGBT) community and those with disabilities. One of her most complex and politicized works combines two taboo subjects in the North (homosexuality and the Troubles) into a unique genre-bending, immersive theatre experience entitled *Trouble* (2013 and 2015). Another of Yee's performance pieces, *Reassembled, Slightly Askew* (2012 and 2015),[4] uses installation and advanced binaural technology to address the sensitive subjects of disability and brain trauma. In 2008, Yee contracted a rare brain infection that left her with mild impairments such as noise sensitivity and the occasional inability to verbalize her thoughts. Both *Trouble* and *Reassembled, Slightly Askew* defy conventional theatrical form, pulling from different artistic traditions and technologies to create pastiche artworks that also directly advocate for those on the margins. With her unique blend of artistic technique and influences, Yee creates individualized and interactive performances for her audience members that place the spectator at the center of the theatrical experience and engender compassion, empathy, and understanding for those who identify outside of traditional identity politics in the North.

Yee received her BA in theatre at Smith College in Massachusetts[5] and trained at the National Theatre Institute at the Eugene O'Neill Theatre Center in Connecticut before moving to Belfast in 2004 to marry her partner, Gráinne Close. Yee and Close were wed in the United Kingdom's first civil partnership ceremony. Although Northern Ireland was the last place in the United Kingdom to decriminalize homosexuality in 1982, it was also the site of the first civil partnership when Yee and Close were legally joined in 2005. A BBC television documentary charted this journey, making Yee and Close well known within the Northern queer community.[6] Yee chose to live in Belfast because she felt that she could have a significant impact on the arts scene, which was experiencing a period of growth and development: "I felt something bubbling under the surface from a creative point of view. It is a do-it-yourself kind of atmosphere here. If there is something you would like to do, it is small enough, manageable enough that you can find people who love to be creative and do something."[7] Yee also found that Belfast had less cultural noise and competition to break through than Dublin or Galway, which had more developed theatre sectors. Easier access to government officials was another important benefit of living in the small Belfast community. Yee's art often involves political issues (healthcare reform, disability challenges, and queer activism), and she will frequently invite local politicians to her events in the hope that her art might affect people on the policy-making level. While being in the North has helped Yee generate innovative and creative art pieces, the relative homogeneity of the region and lack of professional ethnic actors have also restricted her ability to write more aggressively about immigrant and ethnic minority experiences: "I can't get my work done here because there are no actors of color, ethnic minority actors who are local. I managed to get one piece up that was part of the Art of Regeneration Program for Young Audiences in 2007, and the important thing to me was that the Polish characters were played by Polish actors. The feedback from the young audiences was that seeing Polish actors was their favorite part."[8]

As a foreigner and immigrant, an ethnic minority, a proud and visible queer activist, and a person with recent brain trauma, these multiple identities put Yee firmly outside of the status quo and on the margins of mainstream conservative Northern culture. However, they also have given her a freedom and neutrality in some situations. Yee's outsider status has allowed her to be seen as a neutral party who does not carry the history or prejudices of the sectarian conflict with her or the assumption that she is working with a specific agenda. In most other locations, Yee's identity would be highly politicized, but in the North, where everything is political, her status has paradoxically depoliticized her in certain important ways. As a result, Yee has been allowed intimate access to painful parts of Northern history that tend to be off-limits for people born there. Thus to be a foreigner in the North has advantages and disadvantages: that person is excluded not only from ownership over particular histories, politics, and cultural traditions but also from assumptions that she carries sectarian sympathies.

Yee has found it extremely useful in her artistic work to be seen as a neutral party. In 2004 and 2005, she ran a program called Creative I: Celebrating Our Diversity through Arts in Banbridge, Northern Ireland. This was a free, arts-based summer program for children from low-income or ethnic minority backgrounds as well as those with physical or learning disabilities. The participants were made up of Catholics, Protestants, and immigrant children. Yee believes she was hired for this project specifically because her foreign and biracial status allowed her to engage cross-community and ethnically diverse groups toward productive goals.

Her outsider status would help her again when she received funding from the Northern Arts Council to create a new artistic project entitled *Trouble*. Yee first received funding in 2010 from the Arts Council of Northern Ireland to develop a theatre project, which would eventually become *Trouble*. Yee views the project as an important documentation of a history that has not been taught to the current generation of young men and women who are growing up with the privileges achieved by the queer activists who came before them. Yee reflects, "You get to this generation of young people today who are proudly walking down the street hand in hand which is amazing but they have no idea who Jeff Dudgeon is. That is what I find tragic and that is part of the reason why I am doing this. You have this new generation who fortunately has no idea what it was like to grow up during the Troubles. . . . But when it comes to the privileges they have . . . there is a certain amount of education that needs to be conveyed."[9]

Yee traveled around the North and collected the stories of queer rights advocates who were active during the Troubles. Yee feels that her status as an ostensibly neutral outsider and also as someone who has experienced being different all her life leant her the credibility to gain Arts Council funding and also to gain the trust of the men and women whom she interviewed. In addition, her very visible and public status as the first couple to achieve legal civic partnership in the United Kingdom also allowed members of the queer community to open up to her. The project charts how the first generation of Northern gay activists in the 1960s and 1970s fought for and achieved important milestones in the fight for equal rights. The achievements and infrastructure that this first generation realized created a solid foundation for a second generation of prominent activists during the early 1990s. The last decade of the twentieth century was the first time a cohesive queer community developed and chose to stay in the North rather than leave (most often for London). In her blog, Yee describes the project as:

> A biographical, immersive, verbatim, interview-based play that explores the experiences of a generation of individuals from the LGBT community that realized their sexuality while growing up during the Troubles in Northern Ireland. The play interweaves individuals' personal stories of cultural identity, sexuality and coming out, religion, feminism, sectarianism, racism, conversion therapy, paramilitaries, politics, the normalization of violence and the effects of the Troubles on the psyche with important historical moments including the Hunger Strikes, the rise of the social LGBT scene and activism, the IRA ceasefire and Good Friday Agreement, the murder of Darren Bradshaw in the Parliament Bar, and the police raids on gay men which led to the European Court case that decriminalized homosexuality in NI.[10]

Yee is one of the first people in the North to address the intersections between queer identity and the Troubles, and this is the first time the Arts Council has funded such an effort.

Queer theatre in the North has slowly become more visible in recent years. TheatreofPlucK, the North's first publically funded queer theatre company, has performed several shows addressing queer issues such as *Automatic Bastard* (2006/7), *We Always Treat Women Too Well* (2008), *Bison* (2009/10), *D.R.A.G: Divided, Radical And Gorgeous* (2011/12), and *Lesbyterian MissConceptions* (2012/13). Sole Purpose Productions, based out of Derry/Londonderry, recently performed *Pits and Perverts* as part of the 2013 Derry/Londonderry City of Culture celebrations. The play follows a young gay man who leaves Derry/Londonderry at the height of the Troubles to forge a freer life in London and becomes involved in the gay community's support of the Welsh Miner's strike of 1984–85. In addition, the celebrated playwright Frank McGuinness is noted for his queer dramaturgy, and playwrights such as Martin Lynch (*Crack Up*, 1983), Robert Glendinning (*Mumbo Jumbo*, 1986), Tim Loane (*Caught Red Handed*, 2002), Jaki McCarrick (*Belfast Girls*, 2012), and Stacey Gregg (*Lagan*, 2011; *Scorch*, 2015) have included in their work characters struggling with issues of sexuality and gender identity.

Yee is furthering this growing dialogue about queer culture and art with *Trouble*, which she developed with Anna Newell (artistic director of Replay Theatre Company in Belfast) and Niall Rea (set designer and founder of TheatreofPlucK). Newell is known for her site-specific and immersive theatre projects that incorporate music, dance, installation art, and technology. Rea has an astute design aesthetic and has also produced artistic work exploring the intersections between sexual identity politics and sectarian divisions in the North.[11] Together, the three theatre practitioners designed a dynamic, immersive experience that blended technology, art installation, music, dance, and verbatim theatre into a performance that allows each audience member to contribute his or her own experiences, memories, emotions, and ideas about queer identity and the Troubles.

In a culture that tends to talk in euphemisms and coded language, or prefers silence altogether, the directness and honesty of those Yee interviewed for the production is striking, especially given the culture of secrecy and shame that has historically surrounded queer identity in the North. The following are excerpts from three interviews she conducted and reflect the range of perspectives, memories, and opinions that circulated during the Troubles:

> I was 15 when The Troubles came in . . . at at at an age y'know what do you do y'know do you defend your country or or or or, er, or what you do, y'know. And again. None of my family, none of my friends, my school friends, knew about my sexuality. You daren't—a told them cuz they wouldn't be your friends for much longer cuz it was a "no-no." They might've been experiencing the same but I didn't know about them neither. There weren't any groups where we could go where you can sit and talk about why you were feeling what you were feeling, y'know . . . there were seven of us, my mother had enough to be getting on with. You did feel very lonely and isolated.

> I got called a "fenian bitch" by a guy in a uniform with a gun cuz I didn't say hello. (*pause*) Walking through Ballymurphy on my own I had a series of 6 paratroopers who simulated a rape with their voices and it was horrible because I was caught in between them and I didn't want to show them they had any impact on me. I didn't feel safe. But it wasn't because I was lesbian. You had to hide where you were from, you had to hide where you were going to, where you were coming back from. You had to make sure you called a cab company that would go to the area you wanted to go to. (*pause*) Even when I say this, I can still feel the fear.

> I was about 16 at the time, and I went to a phone box on Agnes Street because I'd seen it in the Belfast *Telegraph* that Cara-friend gays and lesbians and that was the first I'd said to myself, I'm a lesbian, that's what's wrong with me. (*laughing*) Know what I mean? So I rang them and they says come over to number four University Street and this was just a meeting place for people. And I met these two and I said I wanted to meet more people like me. I wanted to go to the disco. So they said all right, how about this Friday night? And I'm always late. Always late. And one of them had gone ahead

thinking I wasn't going to turn up. But I went in. I took the step and it was the best step I ever took. Because once I got in there it just felt like I was home. It didn't matter the place was packed with Catholics and Protestants or Jews or whatever. It was just, I felt, "this is marvelous."[12]

The dialogue in *Trouble* is composed from the original interviews that Yee conducted and was initially inspired by the verbatim theatre and docudrama style of the American playwrights Anna Deavere Smith and Eve Ensler. Verbatim theatre, which is a subset of docudrama, started in the United Kingdom during the 1970s.[13] It typically uses taped recordings of interviews and speeches, which are then transcribed and used as the primary (or only) source of dialogue in the performance. Performers of verbatim theatre often try to replicate the natural vernacular speech of the original recordings as closely as they can, replicating breaths, stutters, dialects, and emotion. Furthermore, verbatim drama is often a form of political theatre or social activism, using the stage to publically voice the stories and experiences of an oppressed group. It became increasingly popular during the 1990s, buoyed by two of the best-known verbatim practitioners in the United States: Smith and Ensler. Smith produced two of her most famous pieces, *Twilight: Los Angeles* and *Fires in the Mirror*, in the early 1990s; both plays addressed issues of race, identity, and prejudice in America. Ensler is best known for the *Vagina Monologues* (1996), which explores women's sexuality, relationship to their bodies, and pressure to conform to social norms. Smith and Ensler interviewed and recorded conversations with ordinary people and then transcribed (word-for-word) and edited the stories into a compelling series of monologues that comprise their plays.

In the North, this purest form of verbatim theatre has rarely been presented. This is perhaps in part due to the fatigue felt toward the pervasiveness of the monologue play in Ireland. However, a few theatre companies have recently begun to experiment with verbatim techniques. Replay Theatre, which is dedicated to youth audiences, performed *Bulletproof* in 2010; this production used interviews with teens living with mental health issues as the basis for its dialogue.[14] In addition, the writer and director Kevin O'Connor created a production in 2012 entitled *Troubled Conversations*, which based its dialogue on interviews with ex-provisional IRA volunteers and victims of sectarian violence.[15] Inspired by the strong verbatim tradition in the United States, Yee decided to use verbatim theatre techniques and combine them with more recent innovations in site-specific and immersive theatre. Immersive theatre, which has become extremely popular in London and New York in the last ten years, grew out of the American theatre practitioner Richard Schechner's environmental theatre movement of the 1960s. Environmental theatre worked to erase the traditional boundaries between audience and performer and encouraged interaction between actors, audience members, and the performance space. Similarly, immersive theatre, which did not emerge in its current form until 2000, encourages audiences to interact with the performance using all five senses. Typically, audience members move through the performance space, exploring their surroundings at will, such as rummaging through the set dressings, opening up drawers, reading letters or books, or unlocking secret boxes. The experience also involves interacting with the performers, often drinking and eating food that is offered, and sometimes smelling scents related to the performance. The goal of the immersive theatre experience is to transform the audience member into an active participant in the show and to break the traditional rules of theatre that require spectators to stay passively and quietly in their seats. Site-specific theatre, which started in the 1970s, was also a natural outgrowth of the environmental theatre movement and is defined by performance in nontraditional theatre spaces (such as a public restroom, a forest, or a historic building).

The influences of verbatim, immersive, and site-specific performance traditions were clearly at work in the 2013 production of *Trouble*. During the summer of 2013, Yee launched an invitation-only workshop version of the production, which was performed at the Metropolitan Arts Centre (MAC) in Belfast. Individuals were led into the performance space one by one and allowed to wander through several interlinking rooms at their own pace, allowing each audience member a unique and personal experience of the project. Spectators also used flashlights to make their way through the darkened rooms, each of which had a different theme and reflected the different stories told to Yee during her interviews.

In the first room, audience members listened to Yee's recorded voice as she talked about the origins of the project, her interview process, and the artistic decisions she contemplated in making *Trouble* an immersive theatre experience. In doing so, Yee highlighted her role as the author of the project and made visible the process and goals behind interviewing and constructing the stories of gay identity during the Troubles. Interspersed throughout the other rooms were Yee's recorded observations about the people she had interviewed. Thus the audience members heard a brief description about what the interviewees looked like, how they sounded, their gestures, and their emotions before then hearing an excerpt from the original interview voiced by an actor. Yee's descriptions allowed audience members to imagine a more comprehensive picture of the person whose story they were about to hear while still maintaining the anonymity of the interviewees.

In one room, videos of actors' eyes and lips were projected onto the walls as audio recordings of the interviewees' stories were played. The room addressed the complex, fractured, and hybrid identities that lesbians struggled with during the height of the Troubles. Interviewees' stories described how feminist, sectarian, and lesbian agendas often clashed, preventing Protestant and Catholic women from forming a cohesive community of support and advocacy. The following excerpt that was voiced by an actor for audience members reflects these ideas and also underscores how Yee embraced verbatim theatre traditions by having actors re-create the interviewees' speech patterns and mannerisms in order to replicate the original interviews as closely as possible:

> We were talking about it in the women's movement. It was usually a fairly lively debate. Because Republican women and the women's movement wasn't as blended as it could've been. It should've been a blended thing but I think it was. . . .
>
> (*pause; "let me try again"*)

There was radical feminism and there was socialist feminism and then there was like, the Republican women and women prisoners and somehow these groups were. . . .

(*pause; "let me try again"*)

We were such a small country we had to join together, but it was as if there were areas where there was unease, where it was threatening. Problematic. I don't know why. There were different agendas. Different ideas for the step forward. Different ideas for political change. Different priorities. Women in prison, abortion, lesbian rights—I feel those things are all valid and yet, I could never seem to. . . .

(*pause; "let me try again"*)

Arguments and rows would break out. I couldn't see how any of those issues were different. It's as if one issue was given attention then another section would think, what about ours? It's like there wasn't room to co-exist.[16]

The room captured how fractured and divisive the lesbian community often was during the Troubles and also emphasized the complex multiplicity of oppressive forces such as sexism, homophobia, religion, nationality, and colonialism, which often created division rather than cohesion for women in the North.

In the middle of another room, two female actors performed meeting each other for the first time at an alternative Belfast nightclub during the 1980s. Audio recordings of actors reciting excerpts from interviews were played over loudspeakers. The monologues described the LGBT social scene during the Troubles along with the unspoken rule that sectarian identity was checked at the door when one entered an alternative club. Audience members heard stories that recounted how queer identity often overpowered sectarian identity: "The gay scene seemed neutral on the surface anyway . . . well, they were there to get a shag and get off so they weren't gonna start . . . if they were thinking 'Oh, you're Catholic' or 'Oh, you're Protestant' that was put aside for the sake of . . . a night's fun. I never heard anything sectarian or felt anything sectarianism in the gay scene. I never had a care for who anybody was, or where they were from. I was just in Belfast to find lesbians. I didn't care if they were Catholic or Protestant."[17]

Another monologue described how Belfast City Centre was abandoned at night during the Troubles, which allowed the gay community to socialize at night without much intervention: "Whenever the Troubles were at their height, the only bars that were open in Belfast City Centre were the gay bars. The Crow's Nest, the Parliament, Delaney's. The only people that didn't give a shit about the Troubles were the gays—we got out there and we partied and we had a good time. Because the city centre was a no-go area, the city centre was the gays' domain at night, there was nobody else about. You didn't have to worry about people seeing you. I guess we were pioneers in a way."[18]

In another room, set in the gay club scene, a disco ball swirled while a lone man sang romantic ballads from the 1980s pop charts. The room evoked the loneliness and isolation of being gay during the Troubles even when present in a busy alternative nightclub. Another room offered a one-on-one experience between actor and spectator. One audience member at a time was allowed to enter a small room where a single actor in his underwear delivered a monologue about Darren Bradshaw. Bradshaw was a Royal Ulster Constabulary (RUC) officer who was killed in the Parliament Bar in Belfast (a well-known gay bar) by the Irish National Liberation Army in 1997.[19] As the actor recited the monologue, he slowly got dressed in his uniform, finally revealing to the audience member that he is an RUC officer. The monologue explored the repercussions of Bradshaw's killing throughout the gay community and how it ultimately brought Protestant and Catholic men together to support civil and human rights. When the monologue was over, the RUC officer fingerprinted the audience member and gave her a copy of her fingerprints and an excerpt of the interview about Bradshaw before ushering her out of the room.

Another room was filled with small lockers, some of which held notebooks representing the interviews and stories that Yee had collected in her research. Each notebook included where the interviewee was born, some biographical details, and also contained a selection from the interview. Audience members could read the excerpts or go to one of the lockers that had speakers inside and listen to an actor performing an excerpt from the interview. At one particular locker, the audience's gaze was directed out a window and into an alleyway, creating an important moment of site-specific theatre. As they listened to the narrative on the locker's speaker, they heard the story of a closeted gay man who recounted to Yee how he watched one day with envy as another man casually bought a newspaper called the *Gay Times* at the local book store. Listening to the story, the audience member gazed out the window into the alley, imagining the encounter. The spectator was thus transformed into the role of the closeted gay man watching with desire and envy as he saw another man feel confident and proud enough to do the seemingly simple task of buying a newspaper without shame or fear.

Audience members also walked by a room they could not enter but where they could hear a shower running. This room evoked the difficult experience for young gay students of having to shower publicly with their classmates after sports class, an issue that arose several times in Yee's interviews. As audience members walked by, they constructed the meaning of the room individually based on their own personal experiences. Thus the sound of the shower running might evoke deeply personal resonances for one audience member, whereas it might not affect another at all.

Most of the rooms at the MAC workshop worked in this manner. Each room evoked ideas, memories, associations, and emotions rather than telling a straight narrative of LGBT experiences during the Troubles. Audience members were invited to construct meaning and impact by adding their own personal memories and feelings to the immersive experience of the show. In doing so, everyone's experience of *Trouble* was profoundly different and deeply personal. *Trouble* was also unique in that its structure allowed the multiplicity of different reactions, ideas, and emotions that Yee heard in her interviews to overlap, intersect, and meld together. The result was that one narrative, perspective, or character was never allowed to dominate the experience.

In the fall of 2015, a newly revised version of Trouble was performed as part of *Outburst* and then transferred to Belfast City Hall as a video archive installation. The *Irish Times* called the piece "chilling and challenging" and *Exeunt Magazine* described it as "a provocative performance installation."[20] The new version centered around a twelve-foot-high transparent cube with multiple competing video screens wired to each side. Audience members were led into the blackened auditorium and positioned around the cube. Some screens filled with images of the Troubles while other screens showed actors recounting the emotional stories of those Yee interviewed. The filmed monologues were performed by several high-profile Northern actors including Marie Jones, Carol Moore, and Ian McElhinney. As audiences rotated around the cube, different stories were projected on each side, creating a cacophony of completing sounds and stories, so that no single voice could dominate the whole. The critic Chris McCormack likened it to "a rush of repressed histories released at once, threatening an overload."[21]

A single actor, again playing Darren Bradshaw, sat motionless inside the cube unclothed. After a half hour of videotaped monologues, the inside of the cube lit up and Bradshaw slowly started to dress in his RUC uniform while recounting the story leading up to his death. After finishing his monologue, the darkened auditorium burst into music, and the lights of a disco ball beckoned the audience to gather around several young actresses dancing to club music. Bradshaw joined the dance floor, energizing the audience with a sense of joy and free abandon before a dark hooded figure entered the circle and shot him pointblank in the head. The music abruptly stopped, the lights came up, and the audience was ushered out in the lobby amidst feelings of horror, confusion, and grief.

The mixture of thoughtful political and personal analysis of the videotaped monologues combined with the joy and emotional relief of the nightclub dancing was starkly contrasted with the horror and immediacy of the assassination, shocking and heightening the audiences' senses and emotions. The performance challenged spectators to leave the complacency that comes with historical distance and to reexperience the visceral immediacy of violence levied against gay people, connecting the past to the present historical moment. Pertinently, the transfer of *Trouble* to Belfast City Hall that December coincided with the High Court's hearing on a case that Yee and Close brought, challenging the law barring same-sex couples from marrying in the North. The performance was thus a powerful counterpoint to the direct political action that Yee was taking on behalf of marriage equality in the North, again linking her to the history of Northern women's political activism through the stage.

Yee's work on *Trouble* is difficult to quantify or categorize. It is ultimately an experimental pastiche that pulls from a variety of different art forms, including immersive and site-specific theatre, verbatim theatre and docudrama, installation art, dance, text-based drama, and sound and projection technology. Yee describes the project variously as a "quasi-historical archive that's part verbatim theatre," a "living history," and an archive of memory and emotion.[22] Another useful way of characterizing Yee's work is as a form of pastiche theatre.

The American queer theatre artist Taylor Mac has used the term "pastiche" to describe his own form of theatre, which, like Yee, pulls from a variety of different theatrical and artistic traditions. Mac uses influences from musical theatre, camp, drag, disco, glam rock, Japanese Noh drama, vaudeville, puppetry, dance, installation art, film, and popular culture.[23] In doing so, Mac mixes high and low art forms to create a new cohesive performance that draws from many diverse sources but ultimately creates a unified performance tradition that is complete and whole rather than fractured or divisive (as postmodern theatre tends to be). Mac rejects all forms of social realism, as he believes it reinforces heteronormative traditions. In a public speech entitled "I Believe: A Theatre Manifesto by Taylor Mac," which the artist performed at the 2013 Under the Radar Festival "From Where I Stand Symposium" in New York City, Mac proclaimed, "I believe homophobia, racism, and sexism—in the theatre—often manifests itself through the championing of 'Realism' and 'Quiet' plays."[24] Similarly, theatre artists in the post-Agreement North have been using experimental theatre techniques in part to break with the past and to challenge traditional narratives of history, identity, and territory. *Trouble* and *Reassembled, Slightly Askew* both borrow from multiple influences, creating unique pastiche artworks that take inspiration from technology, media, science, music, audio and sound, storytelling, dance and movement, and theatre. In doing so, they prevent audience members from reflexively interpreting their art through a sectarian lens and challenge spectators to shed their preconceptions and absorb the experience through new, unbiased senses. However, unlike post-modern theatre, which tends to create discord, fracture, and disharmony when pulling from multiple artistic, cultural, and technological sources, Yee's performance pieces tend to encourage compassion, empathy, and cohesion even while acknowledging difference.

Although the taboo subject matter of *Trouble* arguably puts it on the margins, the core of the project is in line with more mainstream goals that the Northern government is currently championing with peace and reconciliation. Although the peace process in the North is often narrowly understood to be an effort to create cooperation and peace between Catholics and Protestants, the broader goal is arguably to promote compassion and understanding for those who are different and to find strength in diversity. In line with this ambition, Yee's theatre fosters compassion, empathy, and understanding for differences, and she uses nontraditional forms, structures, and techniques to get these ideas across to her audience members. Yee's larger project could perhaps be characterized as promoting cultural pluralism and hybrid identities. Whereas the North has long enforced essentialist identity politics on its citizens by encouraging a singular identity in line with sectarian affiliation, Yee's artistic work encourages audiences to embrace the multiple identities that come from their gender, religion, profession, and politics, and illustrates how Northern culture can be strengthened by hybrid identity.

Trouble is not Yee's first foray into pushing the visibility of queer identity beyond the comfortable boundaries of Northern culture. In 2007 Yee, along with Niall Gillespie, Patrick Sanders, Michele Devlin, and Ruth McCarthy, founded Outburst, a queer arts festival. The annual event is Ireland's only multidisciplinary, ten-day arts festival, and it showcases theatre, dance, film, visual art, music, storytelling, readings, stand-up comedy, academic lectures, and writing and performing workshops. For Yee and the other founders, Outburst was yet another expression of embracing and enriching one's outsider status. McCarthy reflects, "Growing up and feeling different in all sorts of ways really informs your view on the world and how you express yourself culturally. Often it's that outsider perspective in whatever form that can critically cast an eye on society. And we always try and capture that essence in the programme."[25] Through *Trouble* and Outburst, Yee has had a significant impact on the public space of Belfast, promoting an open, proud, and positive image of the queer community through the arts.

In addition to her multidisciplinary work with *Trouble* and Outburst, Yee has also produced a complex performance piece based on the severe illness she contracted that left her with permanent brain trauma. In 2008, a sinus infection turned into a subdural empyema, a rare brain infection that required multiple operations and months in the Acute Neurology Ward at Royal Victoria Hospital in Belfast. She turned this harrowing experience into a performance piece entitled *Reassembled, Slightly Askew,* which debuted at the 2012 summer Pick n' Mix Festival in Belfast. She designed the piece in conjunction with the Sonic Arts Research Centre at Queens University, which uses 3D-sound and binaural technology. Binaural technology reproduces recorded sound in a manner that is similar to the way that humans naturally hear (with sound coming from above, behind, and below a person); this is in contrast to stereophonic sound that artificially splits sound into right and left speakers to re-create sonic directionality. The effect of a binaural recording is a much more realistic and intimate experience that re-creates the sensation of live, unrecorded sound. Yee has had to manage physical and cognitive fatigue and hyperacuity as a result of her brain surgeries, and she wanted to create a performance that would give her audience a sense of the aural experience that she had on a daily basis.

Interwoven with the sound sensations, Yee created a fragmented narrative of her time and recovery in the hospital in an attempt to transport the audience inside her head. In the performance piece, audience members entered a room where they lay down on a hospital bed.

An actress dressed as a nurse put an eye mask and earphones on the participant, creating darkness and sensory withdrawal. The nurse then asked questions such as: "Have you or someone you know personally or professionally experienced any of the following: brain tumor, concussion, Multiple Sclerosis, Parkinson's disease. . . ." Through earphones, each person listened to a series of sounds that took the listener on an aural experience of Yee's diagnosis of brain trauma through the process of her recovery. Yee calls the piece a "choreography of sound and dramatic narrative."[26] *Reassembled, Slightly Askew* is part art installation, part radio drama, and part visceral auditory experience. A review from *Culture Northern Ireland* asserted: "It is a deeply affecting recreation of the process whereby Yee's brain was disassembled then put back together, 'slightly askew.' A wrap-around soundscape, combined with drama, music and vivid word pictures, marks the first phase of an internal nightmare."[27] Although *Reassembled, Slightly Askew* and *Trouble* are very truthful and realistic in their content, each of their dramatic forms is very interdisciplinary and experimental, and both projects speak to the hybridity of Yee's work and to her identity as an artist. Yee reflects: "There is a move in entertainment generally towards a blurring of the boundaries. There is this weird blurring of definitions and from that there is a lot of hybridization happening. I think *Reassembled* is certainly [hybrid] because it's not a radio drama, although you listen to it, it's not specifically only sonic arts because there is a dramatic narrative and through-line, and hopefully it's not just biomedical content."[28]

Like *Trouble, Reassembled, Slightly Askew* is based on real-life experiences, and it does not tell or narrate what happened to the audience member but rather places the spectator at the center of the performance, effectively moving the audience from voyeurs to participants. Each person is asked to experience another's emotional and mental journey and encouraged to find compassion and empathy for the stories they are experiencing. Yee believes that the audience's experience of entering into her brain, thoughts, and emotions has the potential to transform a clinical understanding of brain trauma into a better physical and emotional appreciation of a patient's experiences. This has the potential to transform doctors' care, enhance family empathy, and create better support for the recovery process.

Usually a very private person, Yee states that she was willing to expose her personal struggles and private medical history "for those reasons of trying to bring awareness of brain injury and what that experience is like. . . . [*Reassembled, Slightly Askew*] is the closest thing to getting inside [not only] what was specific to my experience but also [gaining a better understanding about related issues such as] fatigue, noise sensitivity, and cognitive overwhelm."[29] In exposing such a profoundly personal experience, Yee is practicing what Taylor Mac would describe as radical openness. Mac believes that the more truthful, exposed, honest, and emotional a performance is, the more the audience will connect to their own humanity. In the mission statement posted on his website, Mac explains: "I believe the more personal risk I take in the work, the more the audience will relate and see the whole of their humanity reflected back at them. So, through art, I try to be as masculine, feminine, ugly, beautiful, intelligent, base, chaotic, graceful, joyful, sorrowful, perfect and flawed as I am in real life."[30] Mac regularly practices radical openness by performing biographical shows, including one based on his difficult relationship with his father (*The Young Ladies Of*, 2008) and by laying himself bare physically and emotionally in all his performances.

Yee also seems to be practicing a form of radical openness in her own work and life. In 2005, Yee and Close allowed filmmakers to document the first civil union in the United Kingdom when they were wed at Belfast City Hall, and they have again allowed the same filmmakers to document their court case for marriage equality. *Trouble* also engages a form of radical openness by asking Northerners to share stories of their sexuality and by revealing a history of queer activism that until now has largely been overlooked in the North. Although the interviewees are not named in the performance, their stories are deeply personal and honest and are recounted word-for-word in the manner they were originally told. Furthermore, *Reassembled, Slightly Askew* is not simply a form of autobiographical theatre but an intimate look at Yee's private medical history, the inner workings of her traumatized brain, and her emotional and cognitive journey in coming close to death. The North has historically privileged personal privacy as both a cultural preference and a survival mechanism within sectarian conflict. Yee's works, therefore, have perhaps even greater impact and meaning, as they are brave examples of a radically open and honest form of artistic communication.

As an immigrant with multiple minority identities, Yee has proven to be vitally important in diversifying and regenerating a more inclusive arts sector in the North. Her bravery at tackling taboo or marginalized subject matter, the innovative forms and immersive experience of her performances, the honesty and truthfulness of her work, and her emphasis on engendering better understanding, commonality, compassion, and empathy for those on the margins of Northern culture make her work radical, innovative, and vitally important. In addition, putting the audience (rather than the actor or text) at the center of her work and encouraging each spectator to construct his or her own narrative empowers Yee's audiences and connects them to difficult subject matter in an intimate and effective way. Although her multiple minorities identities may put Yee on the margins of Northern culture, she proves that it is a fruitful place to be as an artist, and she demonstrates that the most pioneering and inspiring creative work can often come from being an outsider looking in.

Conclusion
Making Strides

As Northern Ireland has struggled to transition from conflict to peace over the past century, theatre has captured and reflected the political, social, and cultural changes that the state has experienced. Throughout this period, women used theatre as a tool to advocate for social and political change, and since the 1980s, theatre has played a particularly important role in documenting how women's social and political status has changed with the transition of the state.

During the first half of the twentieth century, women used their feminist, socialist, and nationalist impulses to act, direct, establish theatre companies, and write plays that critiqued the state. Under increasing state censorship, this theatre challenged restrictive gender roles, and women inserted their voices and bodies into a national dialogue on the future of the state. Alice Milligan's widely influential *tableaux vivants* injected drama directly into the active politics of the Irish nationalist cause and advocated for women's rights, Patricia O'Connor used the stage to engage the public in a dialogue about the state educational system and restrictive professional opportunities for women, and Mary O'Malley founded and developed the prestigious Lyric Theatre. Women also played a significant role in establishing infrastructure for the later development of an indigenous Northern drama. They helped found several professional and amateur theatre companies in Belfast, such as the Ulster Group Theatre, the Belfast Arts Theatre, and the Little Theatre.

These initial contributions became fully realized during the 1980s when women theatre practitioners came to the forefront. During this time, Charabanc broke from normative representations of women on stage to present complex, empowered, and vocal female characters. Its plays were inspired by feminist and socialist ideologies, and the company used cross-community and cross-border touring as a way to bridge sectarian divisions and infuse women's voices into the political process in the North. Charabanc's work was welcomed throughout the island, and the company helped to provide the foundations for today's independent theatre sector. Its success led Marie Jones and Pam Brighton to found DubbelJoint and to continue the cross-border touring model while also expanding the form and subject matter of its work. DubbelJoint's support of the JustUs Community Theatre Company allowed an additional group of politicized women to use the stage as a way to promote an alternative experience of the Troubles: that of nationalist women. The contributions of these companies were complemented by the successes of Anne Devlin, Christina Reid, and Jennifer Johnston, who increasingly had their work produced at major theatres during the 1980s and 1990s.

Today, women theatre practitioners are similarly engaged in sorting through the complex and shifting grounds of the peace process with a special view as to how women are being affected. Abbie Spallen, Stacey Gregg, Jaki McCarrick, Lisa McGee, Lucy Caldwell, and others are exploring women's political, social, gender, and economic roles within the peace process.

Northern women playwrights also have a strong history of challenging the text-based, social-realist tradition of Irish theatre. Alice Milligan's *tableaux vivants* and Mary O'Malley's passion for symbolist theatre were some of the early forms that Northern women used to express their creative voices. The collaborative devised work of the Charabanc and JustUs theatre companies used women's personal stories from the local community to formulate authentic plays that directly reflected the voices and experiences of their communities. Both companies pulled from socialist, feminist, Brechtian, and Living Newspaper traditions to create organic ensemble plays with rough, minimalist aesthetics. The post-Agreement theatre of Stacey Gregg, Shannon Yee, Zoe Seaton, and others has pushed the boundaries of dramatic form, collapsing genres and embracing international influences to create unique interactive and experimental performances. Northern women have often used minimalist or experimental approaches out of necessity: funding constraints or the need to tour productions easily and economically. However, this history of experimental theatre techniques can also be viewed as embodying women's marginalization within Northern culture and Irish theatre. Sidelined as female, as Northerners, and as theatre-makers, some women have embraced forms and structures that reflect that sense of alienation. The fragmented and genre-bending forms of experimental theatre may also better mirror the deep political and societal instability that the state has experienced. In the North, visual art, music, theatre, and film have often been branded as sectarian by critics and audiences alike, in an attempt to fit the otherwise complex and messy forms of art into the neat categories demanded by the conflict. This is, perhaps, why some artists have started to proactively defy categories, blurring theatrical forms and pushing the boundaries of what theatre is in an almost defiant attempt to avoid categorization.

Throughout the history of Northern drama, certain themes recur in women's writing. The changing economic, political, ethnic, and structural landscape of the North is critiqued. Violence is used as a weapon against women, restrictive gender norms limit women's opportunities, children are repeatedly in peril, women rail against the confines of motherhood, and poverty is positioned as a central impediment toward women's freedom. A dedication to those who are disenfranchised and without voice has also been at the heart of women's writing since the formation of the state.

Some themes in women's work, however, have changed significantly. In contrast to the strength that women found in female bonding during the Troubles, post-Agreement plays are marked by an alienation from other women and a general lack of support from the wider community. Whereas the plays of Charabanc and JustUs show how community strength is forged through women's relationships, in the plays of Spallen, Gregg, McCarrick, McGee, and others, female bonding is no longer positioned as an alternative to male violence. Troubles drama tends to show emboldened, politicized women who find hope and support in their families and communities. In contrast, post-Agreement plays are defined by isolated female characters who are trapped in outdated gender roles. In these plays, the family unit has fragmented; young people are lost in a haze of alcohol, sex, and drugs; children are in danger; sex is linked to violence; and the future is bleak and uncertain.

Furthermore, the characters of post-Agreement theatre—such as Fiona in Gregg's *Lagan* and Sinead in Spallen's *Pumpgirl*—see their lives as predetermined by a Northern fatalism, unable to be changed by personal action. This is in direct contrast to Troubles plays by women, which argue that individual agency and community activism can effect positive change. In post-Agreement theatre, a deep cynicism pervades current-day analysis of the peace process, characterizing the construction of peace as something that politicians do in private and that is disconnected from real people's lives.

Cynicism is further demonstrated in contemporary women's writing through the power of history (colonization, partition, civil rights abuses, and the Troubles) to impede progress. "The assumption," as Tom Maguire describes, "that a pathological fixation with history is the cause of the current conflict, rooting the society firmly in the past,"[1] is expressed in the works of Spallen, Gregg, McGee, Caldwell, Jenkinson, and many other contemporary writers. This significant cultural trauma and fracture of group identity are at the core of post-Agreement dramatic writing by women.

Whereas Charabanc and JustUs exposed history in order to show their audiences the opportunity for change, today's writing suggests that the conflict has a stranglehold over the North, effectively inhibiting growth and stability. The Troubles may technically be over, the playwrights assert, but the conflict still defines the way that many citizens view the North. This tonal change from the optimism and empowerment of the 1980s to disenfranchisement and distrust within women's writing during the peace process is significant and disorienting.

Whereas the official peace process narrative fostered by the Northern Irish government promotes images of the North as a stable, peaceful, optimistic, and transparent society, post-Agreement drama speaks to a different experience and understanding of the North's current status. The failed promises of "a shared future," "stable political structures," and the "equality of opportunity . . . and reconciliation,"[2] litter the scripts of post-Agreement drama.

Women during the 1980s and 1990s struggled to produce their plays and fund their writing; nevertheless, they received broad respect and acknowledgement for playing an important role in Irish theatre. Since this period, however, Northern women playwrights and theatre practitioners have suffered significant setbacks. Not only does their work continue to be underfunded and underproduced, but they also have lost the island-wide recognition for their contributions that their predecessors enjoyed. Significant budget cuts combined with growing disinterest in producing political or controversial work has meant that women are finding it very challenging for their art to be produced in the North. In February 2007, Pam Brighton spoke of the extremely limited range of narratives that the media portray about the conflict: "There are only two stories the BBC wants now . . . 'my life as a bomber' or 'Belfast is like everywhere else.'"[3] Opposing this trend, Tim Miles writes that the plays of Gary Mitchell present "a counter-narrative to the hegemonic movement towards peace and 'normalization' in Northern Ireland" and "resist what [Mitchell] calls 'the peace process narrative,' an ideological construct that presents peace in binary extremes of success or failure."[4] Just as certain narratives were shaped, controlled, and privileged during the Troubles, the peace process has likewise developed its own restrictive narratives that tend to swing to simplistic extremes without reflecting the complicated nuances of transitional periods. Art that shows Northern culture and the peace process in complex, ambiguous ways tends to receive less support.[5] As the journalist Malachai O'Doherty wrote in 2003, "There is pressure to direct arts and community funding towards those who best represent the elements of the predominant political model."[6] This observation could help explain why women

246 | Political Acts
246 | Political Acts

playwrights, who often interweave storylines that counter normative representations of conflict and peace, have received less funding and fewer productions.

Another reason for the recent lack of challenging theatre productions could stem from the historical uneasiness that the North has with politically charged theatre. Throughout much of its history, politically engaged drama has been shunned, censored, and seen as culturally taboo. More recently, "Troubles fatigue" and a focus on the progress of peace have prevented more theatre productions from directly engaging with issues of the conflict. Shannon Yee speculates,

> Northern Irish theatre is the theatre of a minority experience—not many people have experienced the Troubles. Just like in the States we have had the African American minority experience, the GBLT minority experience, the women minority experience. And that seems to have a natural trajectory of the kinds of plays that get done. [They have an] initial visibility, validating the minority experience. That seems to be the first chapter. Then there tends to be that post-period where people are sick of hearing of those stories. And [troubles fatigue] is what is happening here now. And that might explain why there haven't been so many women playwrights produced.[7]

Yee posits that the initial desire to explore women's experiences of the conflict during the 1980s has been replaced with a broader societal disinterest in anything conflict-related. After spending decades fighting and negotiating, there is exhaustion to the point of apathy in seeing old issues represented in a new light; a wish to move forward has usurped any desire to analyze the past. Plays that overtly address the Troubles either as a past or present trauma or that highlight controversial sociopolitical issues are arguably less well received by audiences who wish to look forward rather than backward. Furthermore, a common criticism is that political drama, agit-prop performance, or theatre with a sectarian viewpoint is incendiary, biased, and not as "artistic" as drama that shows cross-community perspectives or centers around peace, further discouraging challenging or controversial productions. However, the history of women's participation in Northern theatre defies the notion that artistry and cultural value can only derive from evenhanded, bipartisan work. It demonstrates how controversial and sectarian drama can have both artistic and cultural value in presenting minority perspectives and experiences.

A lack of provocative or overtly political theatre productions in recent years may also reflect a new conservatism that has come with peacetime. Few if any recent Northern plays have resulted in the same kind of controversy, calls for funding withdrawal, or heated debates that the edgy productions of the 1980s and 1990s inspired. During the fragile years of peace, society may call for a more moderate approach from its citizens in order to maintain the delicate status quo and not descend into chaos. War is the time for revolution and for challenging cultural norms; peace, on the other hand, is the time for collective support, fragile acceptance, and reinforcing mainstream standards, even to the detriment of those on the margins. Many contemporary female playwrights express frustration with this institutionalized conservatism and see their plays as a challenge to this norm, asking people to look beyond the surface of the post-Agreement North.

Further reasons for the lack of support of women theatre practitioners may come from the continued cultural dismissal of women's voices as less important. As Rosemary Jenkinson has said, women's work appears to have "a short shelf life" in the North, and their contributions are often forgotten or not acknowledged at all. Tom Maguire argues that women's accomplishments are often treated as exceptions to the rule rather than as evidence of real lasting change. Loren Kruger "has argued against seeing the advancement of individual women within the existing institutions of theatre as a sign of liberation, since such institutions might 'absorb individual female success without in any way threatening the legitimacy of the masculinist and capitalist definitions of that success.' While the provision of roles for women on the stage and within the industry is important, she cautions also that the staging of dramatic texts by women can be accommodated as 'trademarks of a new commodity, 'plays by women.'"[8] Thus, the staging of plays by Devlin, Reid, and others during the 1980s was arguably accommodated by the mainstream without threatening it.

The community-based and devised works of Charabanc and Just-Us, in particular, were easier to celebrate since they did not threaten the mainstream professional theatre. The low operating costs and barebones aesthetics bore no resemblance to the productions put on by the Lyric or those imported from London. The more polished plays of Devlin, Jones, and Reid, which were staged at the Lyric, were largely treated as anomalous exceptions to otherwise male-dominated seasons.

In addition to marginalizing women's accomplishments as isolated anomalies, knowledge of and appreciation for the strength and influence of women's contributions throughout Northern Irish history seems to have been lost. Despite a strong legacy of women theatre practitioners such as Milligan, O'Connor, O'Malley, Devlin, Reid, Jones, and others, few of the writers interviewed for this research felt a connection to the theatre of the past or saw the advances of the 1980s and 1990s as being influential in their own work. This suggests that there is a larger cultural dismissal of women's writing in the North that contemporary women themselves have unconsciously absorbed. In addition, women's discomfort with highlighting gender issues in their work and being classified as a "woman writer" has helped to perpetuate this cycle of marginalization. As long as women see their gender as a potential detractor from their work, these issues will persist.

Women in the Republic have helped to combat erroneous notions that there are few women playwrights by joining together and celebrating their work. In 1992 and 1993, Glass House Productions produced "There Are No Irish Women Playwrights," which staged neglected works of Lady Gregory[9] and Teresa Deevey, along with plays by Marina Carr and others. More recently, during the 2010 and 2011 seasons, Aideen Howard, the literary director for the Abbey Theatre from 2006 to 2015, programmed four plays written by women (Carmel Winters, Elaine Murphy, Stacey Gregg, and Marina Carr) and developed staged readings and limited workshop runs of four other women's works. In 2005, before Howard arrived at the Abbey, only 17 percent of unsolicited submissions came from women; in 2012, women submitted 40 percent of the scripts the Abbey received.[10]

ion 249

Howard speculates that once women saw the Abbey producing more female playwrights, they were encouraged to submit their work. For years, Marina Carr was the only contemporary, internationally recognized woman playwright. The status of several women writers from the Republic has since risen dramatically, including that of Stella Fehilly, Carmel Winters, Nancy Harris, Ursula Rani Sarma, Elaine Murphy, Geraldine Aron, and Deirdre Kinahan.

The marginalization of women in Irish theatre, however, remains an important issue island-wide. Despite the Abbey's staging of four women's works between 2010 and 2011, it is important to note that the plays were produced on the Peacock Stage. The Peacock is the smaller black-box theatre, which is significantly less prestigious than the main stage. Furthermore, the increased visibility of women's work between 2010 and 2011 was in stark contrast to the Abbey's centenary season (2004), which failed to stage a single female playwright. Moreover, when the Abbey Theatre announced that its 2016 season, commemorating the 1916 Easter Rising, included only a single female playwright, it was met with massive uproar from the public, academics, and theatre practitioners. The Abbey's glaring omission inspired extensive media attention and a national conversation over the continued exclusion of women in Irish theatre. It also, significantly, gave rise to the feminist theatre advocacy group #WakingTheFeminists (an ironic play on the title of the Abbey's 2016 program, "Waking the Nation"). Since the firestorm at the Abbey, #WakingTheFeminists has become a grassroots organization advocating gender equality in the Irish theatre sector and has started conversations with the boards and directors of the Abbey, Gate Theatre, Druid Theatre Company, Rough Magic Theatre Company, Dublin Theatre Festival, Dublin Fringe Festival, and Project Arts Centre.

In contrast to the increasing demands within the Republic that Irish theatre be more inclusive of women, Northern theatres and playwrights alike continue to dismiss similar projects. As Tom McGuire writes, "Initiatives which have created opportunities for women in Northern Ireland's theatre, however, have often rejected an overt espousal of feminist politics and in many instances the participants have remained adamant that their work should not be ghettoized as 'women's theatre.'"[11] The Republic, however, has demonstrated that using a gendered lens to examine women's work does not have to be restrictive or marginalizing. In fact, promoting women's contributions encourages other women to write and submit their work and helps to combat persistent notions that there are few women playwrights on the island. Emphasizing women's accomplishments is especially important in the North, where a militarized masculinity has been the status quo and where the contributions of Brian Friel, Stewart Parker, Owen McCafferty, Gary Mitchell, and the Field Day Theatre Company dominate most discussions of Northern drama. Despite the significant contributions of women practitioners to the development of Northern Irish drama, women continue to be underproduced and underrepresented. Northern women's discomfort with stressing gender issues in their work and being classified as a "woman writer" has helped to perpetuate this cycle of marginalization.

Finally, the global financial crisis begun in 2007, and the subsequent consequences to arts funding, has heavily impacted theatre in the North. Funding cuts in 2015, in particular, were devastating, threatening the survival of many of Belfast's most established and well-known independent theatres. Tinderbox Theatre and Kabosh both received 44 percent funding cuts from the Arts Council; the Belfast Festival, which has run annually for over fifty years, lost its primary source of funding from Queens University; and established groups such as the Lyric, the Grand Opera House, and the MAC are dealing with significant staff and budget reductions. With reduced resources and staff, there are fewer opportunities to provide development workshops, writing classes, commissions, and internships that encourage and develop new talent and can target underrepresented groups such as women.

Despite the challenges in getting productions mounted and the tonal pessimism that pervades Northern drama by women, there is also hope in contemporary women's writing and signs of progress for women practitioners. Stacey Gregg's *Lagan* ends with the family unit reunited, a mother and daughter reconnecting, and the absent son remaining in Belfast to forge a brighter future. Rosemary Jenkinson's *Basra Boy* demonstrates how the current generation can break free from the historical cycle of sectarian violence. Despite the vicious attacks they experience on their ocean voyage, the women in Jaki McCarrick's *Belfast Girls* disembark in Australia optimistically determined to forge a better life. In addition, women's contributions are adding a new level of diversity to Northern theatre by experimenting with new forms and genres, addressing taboo subjects, and infusing foreign influences to help innovate theatre and push cultural boundaries. Shannon Yee is one of the first artists to address the intersection between sexual identity and the Troubles, combining two taboo subjects into a powerful performance piece. Zoe Seaton's Big Telly theatre company has experimented with various forms of physical theatre, even staging an underwater production, *The Little Mermaid* (2005), in community swimming pools. Stacey Gregg continually pushes the traditional boundaries of dialogue-based Irish theatre to infuse visual and symbolist influences in her plays.

Women remain a central, if unrecognized, influence within the Northern theatre sector today, and the range of women's playwriting and participation reflect that strength. Bernie McGill wrote the musical *The Haunting of Helena Blunden* (2010) for Big Telly, a ghost story that reveals dark secrets from the early twentieth century. Brenda Murphy, who cowrote *Binlids*, *Forced Upon Us*, and *Working Class Heroes* for the JustUs Theatre Company, is still writing, most recently the international hit *A Night with George* (2011). This one-woman comedy explores the inner life of a prisoner's wife whose husband leaves her for another woman after being released from jail. The production toured the North and south of Ireland, the United Kingdom, and the United States. Jaki McCarrick's *The Mushroom Pickers* premiered at the Southwark Playhouse (London) in 2006 and ran in New York in 2009. Her play, *Leopoldville* (2010), staged at the Tristan Bates Theatre in London, is based on a horrific true-life murder that was committed in her hometown of Dundalk by a group of young men during the early 1990s. *Belfast Girls* (2012) examines the history of forced deportation of poor women and unwed mothers to Australia during the Great Famine. The play explores the sectarian prejudices of the late nineteenth century and also includes a lesbian relationship. Lisa McGee's *Girls and Dolls* was produced at Tinderbox in 2006 and addresses how violence from the past can never be escaped and will continue to haunt and inform the present. Lucy Caldwell's *Guardians* (2009), *Leaves* (2007), *Notes to a Future Self* (2011), and the radio play *Girl from Mars* (2008) have been produced in Ireland and the United Kingdom. Her work addresses the lingering effects of the Troubles on young people. Morna Reagan's *Midden* (2001) and *The House-keeper* (2012) were produced by the Rough Magic Theatre Company. *Midden* is about a woman's difficult homecoming back to the North after fifteen years of making her fortune in Philadelphia. The play premiered at the Playhouse in Derry/Londonderry. Nicola McCartney's *The Millies* was produced by Replay Productions in 2003, and *Melmoth the Wanderer* was produced by Big Telly in 2012. She has also written pieces for two collaborative projects: *1 in 5* (2011, Kabosh) and *Convictions* (2000, Tinderbox). Vittoria Cafolla has worked with Kabosh on *Raiders of the Lost Story Arc* (2011) and with Skewiff Theatre Company on *The Waiting Room* (2010). She is also a member of Agent 160, a UK-wide theatre company composed of women playwrights who produce their work in England, Scotland, Wales, and Northern Ireland. Finally, the Field Day Theatre Company selected the journalist and emerging playwright Clare Dwyer Hogg to premiere *Farewell* as part of the Derry/Londonderry City of Culture 2013 celebrations. Dwyer Hogg has the prestige of being not only one of the first playwrights produced by Field Day since the late 1990s but also the first female playwright.

Dozens of more women are acting, directing, producing, and running the administrative duties within Irish theatres. Carol Moore, originally from Charabanc, is directing both film and theatre. Eleanor Methven, also originally of Charabanc, is a successful actress working in both the North and south. Paula McFettridge is the artistic director of Kabosh, which is devoted to site-specific theatre in the North. Lynn Parker, niece of the Northern playwright Stewart Parker, is the artistic director of Dublin-based Rough Magic. The director and producer Rachel O'Riordan has produced several works with her company Ransom Productions, and she established the three-year Write on the Edge workshop (2007–10), which developed emerging Northern playwrights.

Although this book focused primarily on theatre produced in Belfast, which remains the theatrical capital of the North, there are several important theatres in other areas in the North: the Playhouse and the Millennium Forum in Derry/Londonderry, the Ardhowen Theatre in Enniskillen, the Riverside Theatre in Coleraine, and the Burnavon Arts and Cultural Centre in Cookstown (Tyrone). Most of these program a combination of touring productions as well as locally produced theatre, music, and dance performances. Perhaps the most important regional producing theatre is Big Telly, based in Portstewart on the north Antrim coast. The artistic director Zoe Seaton directs and produces devised plays and experimental performances. Derry/Londonderry also has the professional theatre company Sole Purpose Productions, which is run by Patricia Byrne. Sole Purpose, in conjunction with the Rainbow Project (a gay advocacy group), produced *Pits and Perverts* in the fall of 2013 as part of Derry/Londonderry's City of Culture celebrations.

The diversity of work being written, staged, acted, directed, and produced by women in the North today demonstrates the importance of women in establishing a more vibrant and diverse theatre sector. The political science scholar Miriam Anderson optimistically argues that peace processes "offer opportunities for domestic, transnational and international advocacy groups to mobilize and contest various aspects of state-civil society relations. . . . Mobilization occurs, in part, because violent conflict and peace talks produce changes in 'opportunity structure' which create the conditions of 'grievance' and 'optimism' necessary for social movement mobilization."[12] The shift from silence and entrenched attitudes toward identifying and speaking more openly about problems in society has the potential to create new space for women to have their voices heard and the inequality in their daily lives addressed. In addition, by embracing the basic tenants of the Northern Irish peace process—"inclusivity and equable representations"—Anderson argues that women can better advocate for those principals to be applied more fairly to them.[13] The plays analyzed here reflect an opening up of that space and the airing of grievances that the peace process has brought.

The Northern government has signaled that arts and culture will be important tools through which the region will be able to transform its image and reputation within the island and abroad. In its directive entitled "Together: Building a United Community" (2013), the Northern Irish Executive mandates "the continued use of the arts . . . as a means of improving good relations" and acknowledges that the "Department of Culture, Arts, and Leisure has an important role to play in ensuring that good relations principles are mainstreamed."[14] Theatre is playing an increasingly important role in this project, combating the code of silence that has been inherent in the North and finding new ways of addressing past trauma, violence, injustices, and prejudices that have often been taboo subjects. In a society that has Troubles fatigue, theatre is engaging the past and showing how it informs the present-day peace process in a way that politics and government simply have not been successful in doing. Many Northerners, distrustful, fed up, and skeptical of any political rhetoric associated with peace, may find more productive conversations within nontraditional arenas such as art and culture. Women's voices are once again at the forefront of these dramatic conversations, using theatre to advocate for women's rights, to imagine alternative ideas for political and social change, and to commemorate, dramatize, and reconstruct Northern Irish identity as the state transitions away from conflict and toward peace.

NOTES | BIBLIOGRAPHY | INDEX

Notes

Introduction

1. A nationalist political party originally founded in 1905 with the aim of achieving an independent Ireland. A split in the party around 1970 over whether to support the Irish Republican Army's use of force in the North led to Sinn Féin's new identity as the Provisional IRA's political wing and as the nationalist community's political and public voice. Once associated primarily with republicanism, it has become a mainstream political party with strong influences in both the North and Republic.

2. The Belfast Agreement, also known as the Good Friday Agreement, was signed on April 10, 1998 and signaled the official start of the peace process in Northern Ireland. The deal set up a power-sharing executive between nationalists and unionists, secured the release of paramilitary prisoners, and gave Northern citizens the right to vote about the future status of the state's relationship with Britain and the Republic of Ireland.

3. A period of violent sectarian conflict in the North from roughly 1969 to 1998.

4. Northern Ireland Tourist Board, "Perceptions of Derry/Londonderry UK City of Culture 2013," 3, 5.

5. Phelan, "Beyond the Pale," 124.

6. McKeown, "Spreadsheet of Deaths Associated with Violence in Northern Ireland, 1969–2001."

7. McDonnell, *Theatres of the Troubles*, 21.

8. Mulholland, *Northern Ireland*, 76–77.

9. Glossary terms for republicanism and loyalism as listed on the Conflict Archive on the Internet (CAIN): http://cain.ulst.ac.uk/othelem/glossary.htm.

10. The DUP, founded by Ian Paisley, is the larger of the two main Unionist political parties in Northern Ireland.

11. "Integrating Northern Ireland's Education."

12. Niall Glynn, "More Mixed Couples Tying the Knot," BBC News, November 6, 2009, http://news.bbc.co.uk/2/hi/uk_news/northern_ireland/8344480.stm (accessed March 3, 2013).

13. Northern Ireland Office, "Police (Northern Ireland) Act 2000," 5.

14. Police Service of Northern Ireland, "Workforce Composition Figures."

15. Connolly, *Evolution of the Lyric Players Theatre*, 18.

16. Roche, *Contemporary Irish Drama*, 159.

17. Lojek, "Eleanor Methven and Carol Moore," 345, 344.

18. Patrick Lonergan's *Theatre and Globalization*, 2009.

19. Jennifer Johnston (b. 1930) was born in Dublin but wrote extensively about the North through plays, novels, and short stories. Her plays were produced by the Lyric Theatre during the 1980s and early 1990s.

20. Foley, *Girls in the Big Picture*, 40.

21. Kilmurray and McWilliams, "Struggling for Peace."

1. Nation, Conflict, and the Politics of Feminism

1. Only in the past few years have there been serious debates about how to update the language of the Constitution.

2. "Irish Constitution, 1937," 160–62.

3. Valiulis, "Neither Feminist nor Flapper," as quoted in Hayes and Urquhart, *Irish Women's History Reader*, 154.

4. Phelan, "Beyond the Pale," 117.

5. Ashe, "Virgin Mary Connection," 575.

6. Ibid., 576.

7. Ashe, "Gendering Ethno-Nationalist Conflict," 770.

8. Little, "Feminism and the Politics of Difference," 164.

9. Foley, *Girls in the Big Picture*, 26.

10. Sales, *Women Divided*, 202.

11. Little, "Feminism and the Politics of Difference," 164.

12. Ibid.

13. The reasons for this are linked to the development of the civil rights movement within the nationalist community in the 1960s, which politicized many Catholic women as well to restrictions within the unionist communities and the Protestant Church.

14. Rooney, "Women's Equality," 42.

15. Ibid., 43.

16. Ashe, "Virgin Mary Connection," 577.

17. Kilmurray and McWilliams, "Struggling for Peace."

18. Little, "Feminism and the Politics of Difference," 165–66.

19. This tendency is connected to Gayatri Spivak's idea of woman's "double colonization" in her essay "Can the Subaltern Speak?" (1988), which argues that women in colonized or previously colonized nations are subject to two forms of

oppression: from patriarchy as well as from the colonizing force. This is an idea that Irish feminists have embraced, arguing that women in colonial nations have a double bind from which to extract themselves.

20. Crenshaw, "Demarginalizing the Intersection of Race and Sex."

21. Crenshaw, "Mapping the Margins," 1242.

22. McWilliams, "Violence against Women," 89.

23. Ibid., 80–81.

24. The Royal Ulster Constabulary was the name of the Northern Irish police force until it was given the more neutral title of the Police Service of Northern Ireland in 2001.

25. McWilliams, "Violence against Women," 85.

26. Aretxaga, *Shattering Silence*, 77.

27. Bloody Sunday occurred on January 30, 1972 in Derry/Londonderry when the British military opened fire on hundreds of unarmed civil rights marchers. Twenty-six were shot and thirteen died, the entire event captured by news cameras and reporters. The role of the British military in the massacre was covered up until the Saville Inquiry in 2010 finally acknowledged British responsibility.

28. Although Peace People is still in existence as of this writing, Williams left in 1980, and the organization now focuses its efforts internationally.

29. Fearon and McWilliams, "Swimming against the Mainstream," 132.

30. Kilmurray and McWilliams, "Struggling for Peace."

31. Ibid.

32. Connolly, "Feminist Politics and the Peace Process," 146.

33. Simona Sharoni as quoted in Ashe, "Gender and Ethno-Nationalist Politics," 157.

34. Kilmurray and McWilliams, "Struggling for Peace."

35. McDowell, "Commemorating Dead 'Men,'" 350.

36. Bernard Adams, "Mary O'Malley Obituary," *The Independent*, April 29, 2006, http://www.independent.co.uk/news/obituaries/mary-omalley-476063.html (accessed April 12, 2016).

2. Theatre and State Censorship

1. Connolly, *Evolution of the Lyric Players Theatre*, 18.

2. Lojek, "Seeding New Writing," 34.

3. Mannion, *Urban Plays of the Abbey Theatre*, 35.

4. Pilkington, *Theatre and the State*, 169.

5. Connolly, *Evolution of the Lyric Players Theatre*, 30. During the 1960s, increasing sectarian violence and tension was complemented by audience desire for escapist entertainment, making it difficult to stage plays that directly addressed the conflict.

6. Ibid.

7. Roy Connolly reports in *Evolution of the Lyric Players Theatre* that the Grove Theatre was subject to more than fifty bomb scares in 1970 (32).

8. E. Jane Dickson, "Women on the Verge of Falling in Love," *Belfast Telegraph*, March 8, 1997.

9. Connolly, *Evolution of the Lyric Players Theatre*, 29.

10. Pilkington, *Theatre and the State*, 192.

11. Ibid., 187–88.

12. Pádraic Whyte, "Review of *Over the Bridge*," *Irish Theatre Magazine*, April 2, 2010, http://www.irishtheatremagazine.ie/Reviews/Current/Over-the-Bridge (accessed March 7, 2013).

13. Lionel Pilkington notes that the living room is emptied of all domestic furniture and personal effects in order to clear space for the command center of the Defense Committee. The women and child who once occupied the domestic space are entirely ejected and displaced by the men's efforts to transform the home into a masculine political sphere. Pilkington, *Theatre and the State*, 206.

14. Morash, *History of Irish Theatre*, 245, 246.

15. Pilkington, *Theatre and the State*, 209.

16. This production was sponsored by Sinn Féin, signaling early Republican interest in using arts and culture as a form of propaganda. Sinn Féin would continue to use arts and culture as a tool for political reform and as a way of promoting its ideology with the sponsorship of Féile an Phobail, the JustUs Community Theatre Company, and other artistic and cultural groups.

17. Trotter, *Modern Irish Theatre*, 169.

18. Connolly, "Knowing Their Place," 215.

19. Playzone was founded in 1977 by the Northern theatre director Andy Hinds and the Dubliner Frank Brennan.

20. Winter, "That's Not Theatre, Love!," 20.

21. Stage '80 was founded by Michael Poynor.

22. Connolly, *Evolution of the Lyric Players Theatre*, 40.

23. John Boyd, "Postscript," *Threshold* 24 (Spring 1973): 85, as quoted in Connolly, *Evolution of the Lyric Players Theatre*, 13.

24. The controversial July 12 parades honor Protestant King William's victory over Catholic rival King James II in 1690. Protestant groups often march through Catholic enclaves, engendering protests and violence on a yearly basis.

3. Raising the Curtain

1. Scott Boltwood, Research Notes on the Ulster Group Theatre, Emory and Henry College, Virginia, January 2015.

2. Boltwood, "Ulster Group Theatre."

3. "Dramas of Ulster Life," *The Northern Wig and Belfast Post*, October 19, 1940.

4. In *Evolution of the Lyric Players Theatre*, Roy Connolly reports that Interplay gave 254 performances at 99 schools in 1972 before an audience of 69,000 school children (33). Interplay is significant for touring children's theatre and also as a training ground for the celebrated playwright Marie Jones.

5. Originally called Belfast Thespians Repertory Theatre.

6. The play by Christa Winsloe (translated and adapted by Barbara Burnham) presented the tragic story of a young sensitive girl at a German boarding school who is punished by the headmistress after declaring her adoration for one of her schoolteachers.

7. McNulty, *Ulster Literary Theatre and Northern Revival*, 21.

8. *Tableaux vivants* (living pictures) were typically frozen snapshots of dramatic moments, made up of actors and objects representing a larger idea. They were often narrated and underscored with dramatic music.

9. Morris, *Alice Milligan and the Irish Cultural Revival*, 8.

10. Ibid.

11. Ibid., 9.

12. Phelan, "Beyond the Pale," 111.

13. Morris, *Alice Milligan and the Irish Cultural Revival*, 12.

14. Ibid., 8.

15. Morris, "Becoming Irish," 91.

16. Influenced by the American and French Revolutions, the United Irishmen organized an unsuccessful rebellion against British occupation of Ireland during the summer of 1798. The extremely violent rebellion led to deeper resentment and divisions between Protestants and Catholics and also caused the abolishment of the Irish Parliament, increasing British control over the island. The uprising was a popular subject of nationalist poetry, fiction, and drama, with Yeats and Gregory's *Cathleen ni Houlihan* (1902) as the most celebrated theatrical example. The historical significance of the uprising within contemporary sectarian discourse in the North has also inspired Northern playwrights such as Stewart Parker (*Northern Star*, 1984) and Gary Mitchell (*Tearing the Loom*, 1998) to explore the historical repercussions of the uprising within contemporary Northern politics.

17. Morris, "Becoming Irish," 79.

18. Morris, *Alice Milligan and the Irish Cultural Revival*, 22.

19. Morris, "Becoming Irish," 93.

20. Morris, *Alice Milligan and the Irish Cultural Revival*, 20.

21. Ibid., 5.

22. Ibid., 21.

23. Ibid., 22.

24. Ibid.

25. In 1898, Milligan teamed with the unionist Rosamond Praeger to design sets for a nationalist *tableaux* performed in Belfast.

26. Morris, *Alice Milligan and the Irish Cultural Revival*, 23.

27. Phelan, "Beyond the Pale," 112.

28. McNulty, *Ulster Literary Theatre and Northern Revival*, 22.

29. Ibid.

30. O'Connor's given name was Henrietta Norah, and she also published under the name Norah Ingram. Most scholars list 1908 as her year of birth; however, Scott Boltwood has determined that her baptismal certificate lists her birth date as December 4, 1905. Thank you to Scott Boltwood, who contributed valuable archival research on O'Connor.

31. Byrne, "Sam Thompson."

32. Boltwood, "Ulster Group Theatre."

33. *Highly Efficient*, directed by R. H. MacCandless, ran from September 21 to October 24, 1942 and was revived by the Ulster Group Theatre in 1947 for a one-month run.

34. Keyes, *Going Dark*, 73.

35. O'Connor, *Highly Efficient*, 7, 10.

36. Phelan, "Beyond the Pale," 118.

37. Mary opens and reads a letter addressed to Margaret, she helps a friend cheat on a scholarship test, and she helps her fellow students cheat on their mental arithmetic when the school inspector evaluates Margaret's class. This last action calls into question whether Margaret's teaching diploma has been fairly earned.

38. O'Connor, "Choosing Teaching as a Career," 92–93.

39. Byrne, *State of Play*, 34.

40. *Belfast News Letter*, October 13, 1942, as quoted in Byrne, *State of Play*, 35.

41. "The Group Theatre," *The Irish News*, as quoted in Byrne, *State of Play*, 35.

42. "Theatres and Cinemas," *Belfast News Letter*, as quoted in Byrne, *State of Play*, 35.

43. Keyes, *Going Dark*, 73.

44. O'Connor, *Farmer Wants a Wife*, 26–28.

45. Ibid., 27.

46. Phelan, "Beyond the Pale," 123.

47. Ibid., 117.

48. Connolly, *Evolution of the Lyric Players Theatre*, 73.

49. O'Malley, *Never Shake Hands with the Devil*, 315-16.

50. Connolly, *Evolution of the Lyric Players Theatre*, 74.

51. Ibid.

52. O'Malley, *Never Shake Hands with the Devil*, 83.

53. Ibid., 84.

54. Ibid., 316.

55. Connolly, "Knowing Their Place," 211.

56. Ibid., 212.

57. Bernard Adams, "Obituary: Mary O'Malley," *The Independent*, April 29, 2006, http://www.independent.co.uk/news/obituaries/mary-omalley-476063.html (accessed April 12, 2016).

58. "Lyric Players Theatre," *Arts in Ulster* series, broadcast Northern Ireland Home Service, February 10, 1966, radio script in Theatre and Performing Arts Archive, Linen Hall Library, Belfast, Northern Ireland (hereafter LHL), as quoted in Byrne, *The Stage in Ulster from the Eighteenth Century*, 56.

59. Connolly, *Evolution of the Lyric Players Theatre*, 54.

60. O'Malley, *Irish Theatre Letter*, 185.

61. McCready, *Baptism by Fire*, 69.

62. O'Malley, *Irish Theatre Letter*, 182.

63. McCready, *Baptism by Fire*, 116.

64. Connolly, *Evolution of the Lyric Players Theatre*, 50.

65. McCready, *Baptism by Fire*, 58.

66. Adams, "Obituary: Mary O'Malley."

67. O'Malley, *Never Shake Hands with the Devil*, 221.

68. In order to maximize the amount of public funding the Lyric could receive, the trustees recommended amending the Lyric's policy to play the national anthem before the first and last play of each season.

69. McCready, *Baptism by Fire*, 60.

70. Connolly, *Evolution of Lyric Player's Theatre*, 88. The Committee for the Encouragement of Music and Arts (CEMA) was the main public arts funding body in the North between 1942 and 1962.

71. O'Malley, *Never Shake Hands with the Devil*, 239, 240.

72. Connolly, "Knowing Their Place," 212.

73. Connolly, *Evolution of Lyric Players Theatre*, 91.

74. Between its founding in 1951 through its 1996 season, the Lyric produced the following works by women: 1954, *Seadna*, Joy Rudd. 1954, *Falcons in the Snare*, Elizabeth Boyle. 1956, *The Children of Lir*, Joy Rudd. 1958, *Wolf in the Wood*, Dorothy Watters; *The Voice of Shem*, Mary Manning; *The Heart's a Wonder*, Nuala and Mairin O'Farrell. 1961 and 1963, *The Rising of the Moon*, Lady Augusta Gregory. 1967 and 1969, *Smock Alley*, Mairín Charlton. 1970/71 season, *The Heart's a Wonder*, Nuala and Mairín O'Farrell. 1976/77 season, *The Gathering*, Edna O'Brien. 1978/79 season, *Once a Catholic*, Mary O'Malley. 1983, *Tea in a China Cup*,

Christina Reid; *Cider with Rosie*, Laurie Lee. 1985/86 season, *Joyriders*, Christina Reid. 1988/89 season, *The Belle of Belfast City*, Christina Reid. 1994/95 season, *Christmas Eve Can Kill You*, Marie Jones; *Joyriders*, Christina Reid. 1996, *Desert Lullaby*, Jennifer Johnston.

75. Máirín and Nuala O'Farrell were best known for *The Heart's a Wonder*, their musical adaptation of *The Playboy of the Western World*.

76. Connolly, ""Knowing Their Place," 212.

77. Ibid.

78. Connolly, *Evolution of the Lyric Players*, 97.

79. Ibid., 98.

80. Adams, "Obituary: Mary O'Malley."

81. McCready, *Baptism by Fire*, 62.

4. Community Engagement

1. Pronounced *Sharabang*: the name comes from an open-air benched wagon that was used in the early twentieth century for group excursions on weekends or holidays.

2. Eleanor Methven, interview with Fiona Coffey, Dublin, Ireland, June 27, 2012.

3. Ibid.

4. Winter, "That's Not Theatre, Love!" 20; also quoting Kershaw, *Politics of Performance*, 5.

5. Although the Field Day Theatre Company had members from both Protestant and Catholic backgrounds, the company often promoted nationalist-themed work. Charabanc remained purposely nonsectarian. Brenda Winter, a Catholic, left the company in 1983. The remaining actresses were Protestant, but the company always had Catholics in administrative and other contributive roles.

6. Lojek, "Eleanor Methven and Carol Moore," 346.

7. Methven, Interview with Coffey, June 27, 2012.

8. Catherine Foster, "Belfast Troupe Takes Irish Drama Abroad," *Christian Science Monitor*, May 14, 1987, 24.

9. In later years, Charabanc did end up hiring some male actors, but in the majority of plays actresses performed the male roles themselves.

10. Martin, "Charabanc Theatre Company," 91.

11. Methven, interview with Coffey, June 27, 2012.

12. Lojek, "Playing Politics with Charabanc Theatre Company," 99–100.

13. Charabanc, *Four Plays*, xxi.

14. Charabanc and Lynch, *Lay Up Your Ends*, 74.

15. Cerquoni, "Women in Rooms," 163.

16. Although several women political prisoners had joined the previous hunger strike of 1980 and had participated in the no-wash protests from 1980 to 1981, none of them died, and they did not receive public attention for their contributions.

17. Methven, interview with Coffey, June 27, 2012.

18. Martin, "Charabanc Theatre Company," 97.

19. Maguire, *Making Theatre in Northern Ireland*, 163.

20. Foley, *Girls in the Big Picture*, 40–41.

21. Ibid., 40, quoting Lojek, "Playing Politics with Belfast's Charabanc Theatre Company," 95.

22. Lojek, "Troubling Perspectives," 332.

23. Martin, "Charabanc Theatre Company," 95.

24. Ibid., 97.

25. Ibid.

26. DiCenzo, "Charabanc Theatre Company," 183.

27. Lojek, "Charabanc Theatre Company's *Lay Up Your Ends*," 106.

28. Lojek, "Eleanor Methven and Carol Moore," 344.

29. Ibid., 345.

30. Methven, interview with Coffey, June 27, 2012.

31. Henderson and Hadfield, "Nothing Run of the Mill," 27, LHL.

32. This issue would plague the nationalist-leaning DubbelJoint and JustUs theater companies, both of which inspired accusations of slander and sectarianism from unionist critics, audiences, and politicians.

33. Eugene Malony, "The Lynch Scalpel Leaves Them in Stitches," *The Irish News*, May 16, 1983, reproduced in Charabanc and Lynch, *Lay Up Your Ends*, 157.

34. Rosalind Carne, "The Past Put through the Mill," *The Stage Guardian*, July 8, 1983, reproduced in Charabanc and Lynch, *Lay Up Your Ends*, 168, 170.

35. Martin Cropper, "Review of *The Girls in the Big Picture* at the Drill Hall," *The Times* (London), November 18, 1986, LHL.

36. Tinderbox was founded by Tim Loane and Lalor Roddy.

37. DiCenzo, "Charabanc Theatre Company," 184.

38. Lojek, "Eleanor Methven and Carol Moore," 352.

39. *Now You're Talking, Gold in the Streets, The Girls in the Big Picture*, and *Somewhere over the Balcony* were published in a single volume in 2007; *Lay Up Your Ends* was published in 2008; and *The Hamster Wheel* was published in 1995 as part of an anthology entitled *The Crack in the Emerald: New Irish Plays* (David Grant, editor).

40. Wilmer, "Women's Theatre in Ireland," 357.

41. Lojek, "Playing Politics with Charabanc Theatre Company," 93.

42. Victoria White, "Charabanc at the Terminus," *Irish Times*, July 13, 1995, LHL.

43. Harris, "Review of *Somewhere Over the Balcony*," 47, LHL.

44. Lojek, "Eleanor Methven and Carol Moore," 352.

5. Political Drama and Controversy

1. In the late 1990s, Brighton took over primary direction of the company. Brighton and Jones had a falling out after Brighton sued Jones in 2001 for author credit and royalties for *Stones in His Pockets*.

2. Phelan, "The Critical 'Gap of the North,'" 597.

3. In 2014, a more transparent initiative granted a total of €285,000 to ten different groups for cross-border exchange, hoping to spark greater island-wide touring.

4. Sophie Gorman, "Mother of All the Behans," *Irish Independent*, July 7, 1998, LHL.

5. Ibid.

6. Moore, "Black Taxis Play Program," 2003, LHL.

7. Peter Cromer, "Cow Trouble," *What's On*, February 9, 1993, LHL.

8. Ibid.

9. Jones, *Stones in His Pockets and A Night in November*, 108.

10. This theme is also seen in Martin McDonagh's *Cripple of Inishmaan* (1996), which follows the "cripple" Billy Claven, who leaves the rural, parochial island of Inishmaan for Hollywood only to have his romantic visions of fame and fortune in the film industry dashed.

11. Ned Kelly, "*A Mother's Heart*—To the Heart of the Conflict," *An Phoblacht*, February 18, 1999, 15, LHL.

12. Ibid.

13. Toby Harnden, "IRA 'Mata Hari' to Play Mother of Troubles Victim," *Daily Telegraph*, February 22, 1999, LHL.

14. Jane Coyle, "Terminator's All Greased Up," *Sunday Life, Belfast Telegraph*, LHL.

15. Harnden, "IRA 'Mata Hari.'"

16. Ibid.

17. The "no-wash" or "dirty" protests lasted from 1978 to 1981. The protests started in reaction to the cessation of Special Category Status in 1976. Republican prisoners who previously had been awarded special privileges as political prisoners were now treated as criminals and forced to wear prison uniforms rather than their own clothing. The prisoners refused to shower, exit their cells, or use the bathroom. Prisoners smeared their excrement on their cell walls and poured their urine under the doorways. Women from the Armagh Women's Prison smeared their menstrual blood on the walls.

18. John Mullin, "A Terrorist in the Wings," *The Guardian*, February 24, 1999, LHL.

19. Plays written by former republican prisoners include *Des* (Campbell, 2000), *The Laughter of Our Children* (Campbell and McKeown, 2001), *A Cold House* (Campbell and McKeown, 2003), and *Voyage of No Return* (Campbell, 2005).

20. McDonnell, *Theatres of the Troubles*, 170.

21. JustUs Community Theatre Company, "Production Program of *Murphy's Law*," LHL.

22. McDonnell, *Theatres of the Troubles*, 171.

23. Eoin Ó Broin, "A Community's Starring Role," *An Phoblacht*, August 7, 1997, 15, LHL.

24. Mullin, "A Terrorist in the Wings."

25. Internment lasted between August 1971 and December 1975. During this time, the British military and the RUC arrested and detained without trial hundreds of Catholics suspected of being involved in paramilitary activity. Two hunger strikes took place in 1980 and 1981. In 1980, seven prisoners participated in the strike, which lasted fifty-three days and resulted in no deaths. After it became clear that the British government had not met any of the demands of the initial strikers, a second hunger strike started in 1981. Bobby Sands, who was elected a Member of British Parliament while on strike, died along with nine other men.

26. The only theatrical representation of women hunger strikers, *Now and at the Hour of Our Death* (1989), was performed by the British theatre company Trouble and Strife, which was cofounded by the Northern Irish actress Maeve Murphy. The show was performed in Belfast, Dublin, and New York.

27. Begona Aretxaga, *Shattering Silence*, 114–15.

28. Jennifer Johnston, *Twinkletoes*, in Kearney and Headrick, *Irish Women Dramatists, 1908–2001*, 240.

29. The cast included Maura Brown, Bridie McMahon, Sue Ramsey, Jim Doran, Keil Kempton, Christine Poland, Anne Marie Adams, Niamh Flanagan, Brenda Murphy, Margaret Mooney, Mairead Ni Adhmaill, Connor Grimes, Noel McGee, Brid Keenan, John McParkland, Mark O'Shea, and six children.

30. Ó Broin, "A Community's Starring Role," 15, LHL.

31. Hurley, "Ordinary People, Extraordinary Times," LHL.

32. Ó Broin, "A Community's Starring Role," 15, LHL.

33. Webster, "Rattling out the Historical Myths of Republican Belfast," 5, LHL.

34. Gerry Adams, "A Personal Play from Belfast," *Irish Voice*, November 1997, 28, LHL.

35. Brighton, "Directing *Binlids*," 18, LHL.

36. During this four-and-a-half-year period, 1,874 Catholics were arrested. In contrast, 107 Protestants were detained. Melaugh, "Internment—Summary of Main Events."

37. JustUs Theatre Company, *Binlids*, unpublished script, 1997, 11–12, LHL.

38. Aretxaga, "Shattering Silence," 50.

39. The Aberfan disaster occurred in October 1966. A massive landslide caused by poor mining practices killed 116 children and 28 adults in the Welsh mining town of Aberfan.

40. JustUs, *Binlids*, 25. *Fenian* is a derogatory slang word for Irish Catholics and/or nationalists.

41. Brighton, "Directing *Binlids*," 19, LHL.

42. Pam Brighton, Bridie McMahon, and Brenda Murphy, "Interview with Liane Hanson," Weekend Edition Sunday, *National Public Radio*, WNYC, New York, October 18, 1998, as quoted in McDonnell, *Theatres of the Troubles*, 171.

43. Maguire, *Making Theatre in Northern Ireland*, 59.

44. Joseph Hurley, "Ordinary People, Extraordinary Times," *Irish Echo*, October 21–27, 1998.

45. JustUs Theatre Company, "Play Program of *Binlids*," 1997, LHL.

46. Gerry Adams wrote program notes for *Just a Prisoner's Wife* as well.

47. JustUs, "Play Program of *Binlids*," LHL.

48. Brighton, "Directing *Binlids*," 18–19, LHL.

49. Hurley, "Ordinary People, Extraordinary Times," LHL.

50. Adams, "A Personal Play from Belfast," 28, LHL.

51. Adams's promotion of cultural activities include cofounding Féile an Phobail and support of Cultúrlann McAdam Ó Fiaich, an Irish-language arts and cultural center on the Falls Road in west Belfast, which also houses the Irish-language theatre company Aisling Ghéar.

52. Malachi O'Doherty, "Play-Acting of the Wrong Kind for an Audience in West Belfast," *Belfast Telegraph*, August 3, 1999, 10, LHL.

53. David McKittrick, "Why Irish Protestants Are Hungry for a Voice," *The Independent*, October 31, 2008, http://www.independent.co.uk/arts-entertainment/films/features/why-irish-protestants-are-hungry-for-a-voice-979855.html (accessed March 14, 2013).

54. Ó Broin, "A Clear Case of Political Censorship," 22, LHL.

55. Pam Brighton, "Drama's Portrayal of Forgotten Injustices," *Irish News*, August 14, 1997, 8, LHL.

56. Heresford, "Rhetorical Memory, Political Theatre and the Traumatic Present," 104.

57. Ibid., 105.

58. Hurley, "Ordinary People, Extraordinary Times," LHL.

59. "Executive Summary of the Proposed Cross-Cultural Exchange Program," 1998, LHL.

60. Derek Scally, "Shake, Rattle and Roll: Belfast Play Prepares for US Debut," *The Craic*, July 22, 1998, 17, LHL.

61. Webster, "Rattling out the Historical Myths of Republican Belfast," 5, LHL.

62. Maguire, *Making Theatre in Northern Ireland*, 56.

63. Ibid., 57.

64. Toby Harden, "Arts Council Funds Play That Jokes IRA Killings," *Electronic Telegraph*, August 11, 1997, LHL.

65. Ibid.

66. Ibid.

67. JustUs Theatre Company, *Forced Upon Us*, 3, LHL.

68. In 1912, half a million Protestant men and women all over Ireland signed a pledge against Home Rule in Ireland that became known as the Ulster Covenant.

69. B-Specials was a reserve police force in Northern Ireland known for its brutal raids on Catholics during the Troubles.

70. JustUs, *Forced Upon Us*, 45–46.

71. O'Doherty, "Play-Acting of the Wrong Kind," LHL.

72. The term "quango" (quasi nongovernmental organization) is used in Ireland and the United Kingdom to describe a semipublic body funded and often staffed by the government; however, it is not subject to the same level of scrutiny and accountability as official government bodies. Robert McMillen, "Anti-RUC Play Has Funding Removed," *Irish News*, January 23, 1999, 14, LHL.

73. Smyth, "Shots in the Arts," 22, LHL.

74. Ibid.

75. Jennings, "Artists Lobby for Change," 22.

76. Mic Moroney, "Just as a Play," *Irish Times*, July 29, 1999, LHL.

77. The Special European Union Programs Body was established under the Belfast/Good Friday Agreement in part to administer funds to promote cross-community and cross-border peace and reconciliation. Between 1995 and 2013, the Northern Irish government received almost €2 billion from the European Union and other sources to promote peace.

78. O'Doherty, "Double Trouble," 21–22, LHL.

79. Ó Broin, "A Clear Case of Political Censorship," 22, LHL.

80. Padraig MacDabhaid, "Arts Council Censorship," *An Phoblacht*, July 29, 1999, 17, LHL.

81. The word "Royal" in the name implied allegiance to the British crown and the term "Ulster" legitimized the partition of the six counties into a separate state.

82. Although the goal was to have an equal number of Catholics and Protestants in the PSNI, the heavy recruitment and promotion of Catholics ended in 2011. In March 2011, Protestants encompassed roughly 70 percent of the police force and Catholics made up the remaining 30 percent. The PSNI published a workforce

plan in 2015 showing that Catholics account for less than 30 percent of the current applicant pool.

6. Borderlands and the Rural North

1. Abbie Spallen, phone interview with Fiona Coffey, May 22, 2012.

2. Pavel Barter, "That Petrol Emotion," *The Sunday Times* (London), August 24, 2008, 8.

3. Grania McFadden, "The Driver, the Pumpgirl, Her Lover and His Wife," *Belfast Telegraph*, August 29, 2008, http://www.belfasttelegraph.co.uk/entertainment /theatre-arts/the-driver-the-pumpgirl-her-lover-and-his-wife-28445216.html.

4. Tinderbox Theatre was initially interested in producing the play, but it did not have the funding. Northern theatres continue to lose opportunities to stage their best playwrights because of funding issues.

5. Barter, "That Petrol Emotion," 8.

6. Ibid.

7. Spallen, phone interview with Coffey, May 22, 2012.

8. Kiran Acharya, "Abbie Spallen," *Culture Northern Ireland*, September 12, 2010, http://www.culturenorthernireland.org/article/1488/abbie-spallen (accessed March 4, 2013).

9. David Lewis, "Theatre Review: *Pumpgirl*," *Culture Northern Ireland*, October 12, 2010.

10. McFadden, "The Driver, the Pumpgirl, Her Lover and His Wife."

11. Spallen, phone interview with Coffey, May 22, 2012.

12. Lewis, "Theatre Review: *Pumpgirl*."

13. McFadden, "The Driver, the Pumpgirl, Her Lover and His Wife."

14. Barter, "That Petrol Emotion," 8.

15. British and Irish theatres create a distinction between "commissions" and "attachments." A commission is when a theatre pays the playwright to write an original play. An attachment, however, typically involves a commissioned play as well as a larger amount of support, including office space, official affiliation with the company, mentorship, and opportunities for workshops and community outreach.

16. Fintan O'Toole, "Fintan O'Toole's 2015: The Importance of Being Inclusive," *The Irish Times*, December 19, 2015.

17. Spallen, e-mail correspondence with Fiona Coffey, September 10, 2012.

18. The monologue play has been an extremely popular genre in contemporary Irish playwriting. Scholars speculate that this stems from the ancient Irish storytelling tradition and oral culture. Financial and logistical considerations (such as smaller cast size and limited sets) have also popularized the form, making it easier and less expensive to produce and tour. Fintan O'Toole has also identified the success of Brian Friel's *Faith Healer* (1979) as beginning a shift in the popularity of the

monologue play, which, among Irish writers, was previously associated primarily with Samuel Beckett. Contemporary Irish playwrights who have embraced the form include Marie Jones, Owen McCafferty, Jennifer Johnston, Lucy Caldwell, Gary Mitchell, Frank McGuinness, Enda Walsh, Conor McPherson, Mark O'Rowe, and Eugene O'Brien, among many others.

19. Spallen, *Pumpgirl*, 16.

20. Butler, *Gender Trouble*.

21. Butler, "The Body You Want," 85.

22. Butler, "Performative Acts and Gender Constitution," 420.

23. Maguire, *Making Theatre in Northern Ireland*, 105.

24. Lojek, "Not So Sainted," 189–90. Lojek also notes that motherhood is treated very differently in Anne Devlin's *After Easter*, in which motherhood helps Greta reject suicide.

25. Lynne Walker, "Festival Reviews: *Pumpgirl*, Traverse Theatre," *The Independent* (London), August 10, 2006, 20.

26. Caryn James, "From Ireland, Love Songs in the Key of Desperation," *New York Times*, December 5, 2007, 5.

27. Lewis, "Theatre Review: *Pumpgirl*."

28. Spallen, *Strandline*, 10.

29. Justin Bergman, "Memo to Yeats: Ireland Has Changed," *The New York Times*, November 18, 2007, 10.

30. Jeffery Alexander, "Toward a Theory of Cultural Trauma," in Alexander et al., *Cultural Trauma and Collective Identity*, 1.

31. Neil Smelser, "Psychological and Cultural Trauma," in Alexander et al., *Cultural Trauma and Collective Identity*, 44.

32. Alexander "Toward a Theory of Cultural Trauma," 9.

33. Ron Eyerman, "Cultural Trauma: Slavery and the Formation of African American Identity," in Alexander et al., *Cultural Trauma and Collective Identity*, 74.

34. Spallen, phone interview with Coffey, May 22, 2012.

35. Declan Burke, "*Strandline*," *The Sunday Times* (London), November 29, 2009.

36. Helen Meany, "Review: *Strandline*," *The Guardian*, November 23, 2009, https://www.theguardian.com/stage/2009/nov/22/strandline (accessed Sept. 28, 2016).

37. Peter Crawley, "*Strandline*," *The Irish Times*, November 21, 2009, http://www.irishtimes.com/culture/stage/strandline-1.776398 (accessed Sept. 28, 2016).

7. The Protestant Urban Underclass

1. Stacey Gregg, interview with Fiona Coffey, Belfast, Northern Ireland, May 27, 2012.

2. Ibid.

3. David McKittrick, "Why Irish Protestants are Hungry for a Voice," *The Independent*, October 31, 2008.

4. Fiachra Gibbons, "Truth and Nail," *The Guardian*, April 9, 2000, http://www.guardian.co.uk/culture/2000/apr/10/artsfeatures.northernireland (accessed March 14, 2013).

5. Gregg, interview with Coffey, May 27, 2012.

6. Ibid.

7. Andrea Byrne, "Young Playwright in Class of Her Own," *Independent.ie*, May 29, 2011, http://www.independent.ie/incoming/young-playwright-in-class-of-her-own-2660765.html (accessed March 14, 2013).

8. Gregg, interview with Coffey, May 27, 2012.

9. Headrick and Countryman, "Damned If You Do; Damned If You Don't," 61.

10. Stacey Gregg, *Shibboleth*, unpublished manuscript, 2009, no page numbers.

11. Gregg, interview with Coffey, May 27, 2012.

12. Ibid.

13. Helen Meany, "*Perve*—Review," *The Guardian*, June 6, 2011, http://www.guardian.co.uk/stage/2011/jun/06/perve-review (accessed March 14, 2013).

14. Gregg, interview with Coffey, May 27, 2012.

15. Peter Crawley, "This Week We Were . . . ," *The Irish Times*, June 4, 2011, 8.

16. Gregg, interview with Coffey, May 27, 2012.

17. Ibid.

18. Daisy Bowie-Sell, "Stacey Gregg's New Play *Lagan* at the Oval House Is Ambitious and a Little Misguided," *The Telegraph*, November 10, 2011.

19. Gregg, interview with Coffey, May 27, 2012.

20. Interestingly, pessimism and a fatalistic sense of doom are strong characteristics of Troubles cinema. In contrast, post-Agreement films tend to be characterized by a sense of optimism and the belief that individuals can enact significant change. The opposite trend is apparent in Northern theatre written by women, which exhibits greater optimism in its Troubles plays than the doom and pessimism exhibited in its recent peace process plays.

21. Morrow, "Forgiveness and Reconciliation."

22. Gregg, interview with Coffey, May 27, 2012.

23. Bowie-Sell, "Stacey Gregg's New Play *Lagan* at the Oval House."

24. Lyn Gardner, "Review: Theatre: *Lagan* Oval House, London," *The Guardian*, November 2, 2011.

25. Rosemary Jenkinson, phone interview with Fiona Coffey, May 31, 2012.

26. Lynn Parker was born in Belfast and is the niece of the playwright Stewart Parker.

27. Jenkinson, phone interview with Coffey, May 31, 2012.

28. Ibid.

29. Ibid.

30. Jenkinson, *The Bonefire*, 15.

31. "Suicide Rates Soar after Peace Deal," *Belfast Telegraph*, July 26, 2012, http://www.belfasttelegraph.co.uk/news/northern-ireland/suicide-rates-soar-after-peace-deal-28774829.html (accessed March 14, 2013).

32. Ibid.

33. "Taig" is derogatory slang for Irish Catholics and is used primarily in the North.

34. O'Brien, "Following in Caryl Churchill's Footsteps," 396.

35. Ibid., 401.

36. Eyerman, "Cultural Trauma and Collective Identity," 77.

37. Eyerman, *Cultural Trauma*, 16.

38. Eyerman, "Cultural Trauma and Collective Identity," 61.

39. Ibid., 63.

40. John McKeown, "A Good Spark but No Flames in This Belfast Drama," *Daily Mail* (Irish Edition), October 6, 2006.

41. Karen Fricker, "Theatre Review: *The Bonefire*," *The Guardian*, October 4, 2006.

42. Jenkinson, phone interview with Coffey, May 31, 2012.

43. Ibid.

44. Rosemary Jenkinson, *Basra Boy*, unpublished manuscript, 27.

45. Ibid., 28.

46. Rosemary Jenkinson, *Come to Where I'm From*, unpublished manuscript, 2010, no page numbers.

47. *White Star of the North* (2012) features a well-meaning and present father figure.

8. Experimental Theatre and Queer Dramaturgy

1. Prime Cut produced an immersive project called *The Baths* (2012), and Skinnybone Theatre produced *Happy Friday* (2013).

2. Yee's legal last name is Sickles, but she writes creatively under the pen name Yee.

3. Shannon Yee, interview with Fiona Coffey, Belfast, Northern Ireland, June 1, 2012.

4. Previously titled *Recovery*.

5. Yee also received a master's degree in creative writing at Queens University, Belfast.

6. This documentary was first aired on December 19, 2005 on BBC1.

7. Shannon Yee, "Interview with Marie-Louise Muir about *Hatch* and the Belfast Fringe Festival," *BBC Arts Extra*, October 2011.

8. Yee, interview with Coffey, June 1, 2012.

9. In 1981, Jeffrey Dudgeon successfully petitioned the courts to decriminalize homosexual relationships in Northern Ireland. Homosexuality was legalized in the North in 1982, eleven years before the Republic of Ireland. Yee, interview with Coffey, June 1, 2012.

10. Shannon Yee, "Gay & Troubled Synopsis," Shannon Yee Blog, July 22, 2011.

11. TheatreofplucK toured *D.R.A.G.—Divided, Radical, and Gorgeous* around the island in 2012; the play addressed coming of age as a gay man during the Troubles.

12. Shannon Yee, *Trouble*, October 15 draft version, 2016, 15, 19, 26.

13. The British documentary film movement of the 1930s and 1940s, the Living Newspaper Theatre of the Depression-era United States, radio drama, Joan Littlewood's Theatre Workshop of the 1950s and 1960s, and the works of Peter Cheeseman and Charles Parker all influenced the rise of verbatim theatre. For more information see Paget, "Verbatim Theatre."

14. The playwright Gary Owen interviewed dozens of teenagers who struggle with depression, attention deficit hyperactivity disorder, and manic depression, and then built the play around these personal stories.

15. *Troubled Conversations* was performed by four actors in a short, three-night run that toured community centers in Cavan, Derrylin, and Clones. In addition, other playwrights are starting to experiment with other forms of docudrama, such as Owen McCafferty's *Titanic* (2012), which explored the two-month investigation regarding the sinking of the *Titanic*, pulling language from newspapers and court documents. In addition, *Bloody Sunday: Scenes from the Saville Inquiry*, which was produced by the London-based Tricycle Theatre, toured Derry/Londonderry and Dublin in 2005. This play was created by the London-based British journalist and playwright Richard Norton-Taylor, who used language from the Saville Inquiry, court documents, and newspapers to create a docudrama piece that exposed the corruption of the original investigation.

16. Shannon Yee, *Trouble*, MAC workshop version, 2013.

17. Ibid.

18. Ibid.

19. The INLA is a republican paramilitary group that split off from the Irish Republican Army in the early 1970s.

20. Jane Coyle, "Review—Trouble: A Rock and a Hard Place," *Irish Times*, November 10, 2015, http://www.irishtimes.com/culture/stage/review-trouble-a-rock-and-a-hard-place-1.2433351. Chris McCormack, "Still Fighting," *Exeunt Magazine*, November 16, 2015, http://exeuntmagazine.com/reviews/trouble/.

21. McCormack, "Still Fighting."

22. Shannon Yee, Skype interview with Fiona Coffey, October 16, 2013.

23. Edgecomb, "The Ridiculous Performance of Taylor Mac."

24. Mac, "I Believe: A Theatre Manifesto by Taylor Mac."

25. Nawaz, "Outburst Queer Arts Festival 2011," *Culture Northern Ireland*, November 3, 2011, http://www.culturenorthernireland.org/article.aspx?art_id= 4545 (accessed March 19, 2013).

26. Yee, Skype interview with Coffey, October 16, 2013.

27. Jane Coyle, "Theatre Review: Pick 'n' Mix Festival," *Culture Northern Ireland*, June 11, 2012, http://www.culturenorthernireland.org/article/5019/theatre -review-pick-n-mix-festival (accessed March 19, 2013).

28. Yee, Skype interview with Coffey, October 16, 2013.

29. Ibid.

30. Mac, "I Believe: A Theatre Manifesto by Taylor Mac."

Conclusion

1. Maguire, *Making Theatre in Northern Ireland*, 61.

2. Northern Ireland Executive, *Together: Building a United Community*, 2.

3. Miles, "Fighting the Peace," 71.

4. Ibid., 66.

5. However, this is arguably different for Northern cinema, which has recently released several films that show nuanced and ambiguous representations of the peace process, such as *Omagh* (Pete Travis, 2004) and *Five Minutes of Heaven* (Oliver Hirschbiegel, 2009).

6. O'Doherty, "A Bit of Nuisance," 75.

7. Yee, interview with Coffey, June 1, 2012.

8. Maguire, *Making Theatre in Northern Ireland*, 102.

9. The Abbey Theatre has notoriously neglected Lady Gregory's works while constantly staging those of her male contemporaries such as Synge, O'Casey, and others.

10. Aideen Howard, Lecture given at the O'Connell House for the University of Notre Dame's Irish Seminar 2012, Dublin, Ireland, June 20, 2012.

11. Maguire, *Making Theatre in Northern Ireland*, 102.

12. Anderson, "Transnational Feminism and Norm Diffusion in Peace Processes," 15.

13. Ibid.

14. Northern Ireland Executive, *Together: Building a United Community*, 89.

Bibliography

Archives

Theatre and Performing Arts Archive, Linen Hall Library, Belfast, Northern Ireland (LHL).

Unpublished Plays

Cafolla, Vittoria. *The Waiting Room*. 2010. Provided by Author, 2012.

Caldwell, Lucy. *Girl from Mars*. Radio play. 2008. Provided by Author, 2012.

———. *Guardians*. 2009. Provided by Author, 2012.

Gregg, Stacey. *Come to Where I'm From*. 2010. Provided by Author, 2012.

———. *Shibboleth*. 2009. Provided by Author, 2012.

Jenkinson, Rosemary. *Basra Boy*. 2011. Provided by author, 2012.

———. *Come to Where I'm From*. 2010. Provided by Author, 2012.

———. *Cuchullain*. 2012. Provided by Author, 2012.

———. *White Star of the North*. 2012. Provided by Author, 2012

Jones, Marie. *The Government Inspector*. 1993. LHL.

JustUs Theatre Company. *Binlids*. 1997. LHL.

———. *Forced Upon Us*. 1999. LHL.

Kabosh. *1 in 5*. 2011. Provided by Kabosh, 2012.

McCarrick, Jaki. *Belfast Girls*. 2010. Provided by Author, 2012.

———. *Leopoldville*. 2010. Provided by Author, 2012.

McGill, Bernie. *The Haunting of Helena Blunden*. 2010. Provided by Author, 2012.

Regan, Morna. *Slinky*. 2011. Provided by Author, 2012.

Yee, Shannon. *Hatch*. 2011. Provided by Author, 2012.

———. *Reassembled, Slightly Askew*. 2015. Audio Recording. Provided by Author, 2015.

———. *Trouble*, MAC workshop version. 2013. Provided by Author, 2013.

———. *Trouble*, October 15 draft version. 2016. Provided by Author, 2016.

Published Sources

Agenda Northern Ireland. "Integrating Northern Ireland's Education: Models for Change." *Agenda Northern Ireland Magazine*, November 2, 2010. http://www.agendani.com/integrating-education. Accessed March 3, 2013.

Alexander, Jeffrey, Ron Eyerman, Bernard Giesen, Neil J. Smelser, and Piotr Sztompka, eds. *Cultural Trauma and Collective Identity*. Berkeley: Univ. of California Press, 2004.

Anderson, Miriam. "Transnational Feminism and Norm Diffusion in Peace Processes: The Cases of Burundi and Northern Ireland." *Journal of Intervention and Statebuilding* 4, no. 1 (2010): 1–21.

Aretxaga, Begona. *Shattering Silence: Women, Nationalism, and Political Subjectivity in Northern Ireland*. Princeton, NJ: Princeton Univ. Press, 1997.

Ashe, Fidelma. "Gender and Ethno-Nationalist Politics." In *Northern Ireland after the Troubles: A Society in Transition*, edited by Colin Coulter and Michael Murray, 156–74. Manchester: Manchester Univ. Press, 2008.

———. *Gender, Nationalism and Conflict Transformation: New Themes and Old Problems in Northern Ireland*. London: Routledge, 2010.

———. "Gendering Ethno-Nationalist Conflict in Northern Ireland: A Comparative Analysis of Nationalist Women's Political Protests." *Ethnic and Racial Studies* 30, no. 5 (2007): 766–86.

———. "The Virgin Mary Connection: Reflecting on Feminism and Northern Irish Politics." *Critical Review of International Social and Political Philosophy* 9, no. 4 (2006): 573–88.

Blankenship, Mark. "*Pumpgirl*." *Variety Magazine*, December 10, 2007.

Bolger, Dermot, ed. *Druids, Dudes, and Beauty Queens*. Dublin: New Island Press, 2001.

Boltwood, Scott. "Ulster Group Theatre: From Foundation to the Festival of Britain." Public talk given at the Linen Hall Library, Belfast, April 20, 2012. http://www.culturenorthernireland.org/features/performing-arts/ulster-group-theatre-foundation-festival-britain. Accessed Sept. 28, 2016.

Brighton, Pam. "Directing *BinLids*." *Back Stage Magazine*, October 7, 1998.

Butler, Judith. "The Body You Want: Liz Kotz Interviews Judith Butler." *Artforum* 31, no. 3 (1992): 82–89.

———. *Gender Trouble: Feminism and the Subversion of Identity*. New York: Routledge, 1990.

———. "Performative Acts and Gender Constitution: An Essay in Phenomenology and Feminist Theory." In *Feminist Theory Reader*, edited by Carole McCann and Seung-kyung Kim, 462–76. New York: Routledge, 2010.

Byrne, Ophelia. "Sam Thompson." *Culture Northern Ireland*, April 19, 2006. http://www.culturenorthernireland.org/article/748/sam-thompson. Accessed April 12, 2016.

———. *The Stage in Ulster from the Eighteenth Century*. 1997. LHL.

———. *State of Play*. 2001. LHL.

Caldwell, Lucy. *Leaves*. New York: Dramatists Play Services, 2009.

———. *Notes to a Future Self*. London: Faber & Faber, 2011.

Carruthers, Mark, Stephen Douds, and Tim Loone, eds. *Re-imagining Belfast: A Manifesto for the Arts*. Belfast: Cultural Resolution, 2003.

Cerquoni, Enrica. "Women in Rooms: Landscapes of the Missing in Anne Devlin's *Ourselves Alone*." In Sihra, *Women in Irish Drama*, 160–74.

Chambers, Lilian, Ger FitzGibbon, and Eamonn Jordan, eds. *Theatre Talk*. Dublin: Carysfort Press, 2001.

Charabanc. *Four Plays: "Inventing Women's Work"*. Edited by Claudia Harris. Buckinghamshire: Colin Smythe, 2006.

Charabanc, and Martin Lynch. *Lay Up Your Ends: A 25th Anniversary Edition*. Edited by Richard Palmer. Belfast: Lagan Press, 2008.

Clarke, K. "A City Bruised: Belfast's Playwrights Negotiate the Path to Peace." *Theatre* 41, no. 1 (2011): 9–25.

Coffey, Fiona, "Blurring Boundaries and Collapsing Genres with Shannon Yee: Immersive Theatre, Pastiche, and Radical Openness in Northern Ireland." In *Radical Contemporary Theatre Practices by Women in Ireland*, edited by Miriam Haughton and Maria Kurdi, 135–50. Dublin: Carysfort Press, 2015.

———. "Marie Jones and the DubbelJoint Theatre Company: Performance, Practice, and Controversy." In *The Theatre of Marie Jones*, edited by Tom Maguire and Eugene McNulty, 107–21. Dublin: Carysfort Press, 2015.

Condren, Mary. "Gender, Religion, and War." In *Religion and the Politics of Peace and Conflict*, edited by Linda Hogan and Dylan Lee Lehrke, 125–58. Eugene, OR: Wipf & Stock, 2009.

———. "Sacrifice and Political Legitimization: The Production of a Gendered Social Order." *Journal of Women's History* 6–7 (Winter–Spring 1995): 160–89.

Connolly, Linda. "Feminist Politics and the Peace Process." *Capital & Class* 69 (1999): 145–59.

Connolly, Maria. *Massive*. Belfast: Tinderbox Theatre Company, 2002.

Connolly, Roy. *Evolution of the Lyric Players Theatre: Fighting the Waves*. Belfast: Edwin Mellen Press, 2000.

———. "Knowing Their Place: The Ulster Lyric Theatre, the Lyric Theatre, and the Northern Irish Theatre Scene." *Theatre History Studies* 30 (2010): 202–19.

Coyle, Jane. "Terminator's All Greased Up." *Belfast Telegraph*. 1999. LHL.

———. "Theatre Review: Pick 'n' Mix Festival." *Culture Northern Ireland*, June 11, 2012. http://www.culturenorthernireland.org/article/5019/theatre-review-pick-n-mix-festival. Accessed March 19, 2013.

Crenshaw, Kimberlé. "Demarginalizing the Intersection of Race and Sex: A Black Feminist Critique of Antidiscrimination Doctrine, Feminist Theory and Antiracist Politics." In *Feminism and Politics*, edited by Anne Phillips, 314–43. New York: Oxford Univ. Press 1998.

———. "Mapping the Margins: Intersectionality, Identity Politics, and Violence against Women of Color." *Stanford Law Review* 43 (July 1991): 1241–99.

Devlin, Anne. *After Easter*. London: Faber & Faber, 1994.

———. *Ourselves Alone*. New York: Dramatists Play Services, 1986.

DiCenzo, Maria. "Charabanc Theatre Company: Placing Women Center Stage in Northern Ireland." *Theater Journal* 45, no. 2 (1993): 175–84.

DubbelJoint Theatre Company. *PlayographyIreland*. http://www.irishplayography.com/company.aspx?companyid=33. Accessed March 19, 2013.

Edgecomb, Sean. "The Ridiculous Performance of Taylor Mac." *Theatre Journal* 64, no. 4 (2012): 549–63.

"Executive Summary of the Proposed Cross-Cultural Exchange Program." 1998. LHL.

Eyerman, Ron. "Cultural Trauma and Collective Identity." In *Cultural Trauma and Collective Identity*, edited by Jeffrey Alexander, Ron

Eyerman, Bernard Giesen, Neil J. Smelser, and Piotr Sztompka, 60–111. Berkeley: Univ. of California Press.

———. *Cultural Trauma: Slavery and the Formation of African American Identity.* Cambridge: Cambridge Univ. Press, 2001.

Fearon, Kate, and Monica McWilliams. "Swimming against the Mainstream: the Northern Ireland Women's Coalition." In *Gender, Democracy and Inclusion in Northern Ireland,* edited by Carmel Roulston and Celia Davies, 117–40. London: Palgrave, 2000.

Fitzpatrick, Lisa, ed. *Performing Feminisms in Contemporary Ireland.* Dublin: Carysfort Press, 2013.

Foley, Denise. "Review: Inis Nua's *Pumpgirl.*" Irishphiladelphia.com, January 14, 2011. http://irishphiladelphia.com/2011/01/review-inis-nuas-pumpgirl/. Accessed March 14, 2013.

Foley, Imelda. *The Girls in the Big Picture: New Voices from Ulster Theatre.* Belfast: Blackstaff Press, 2003.

———. *Not Another Troubles Play.* Belfast: Arts Council of Northern Ireland, 2011.

Gregg, Stacey. *Lagan.* London: Nick Hern Books, 2012.

———. *Perve.* London: Nick Hern Books, 2011.

Grene, Nicholas. *The Politics of Irish Drama: Plays in Context from Boucicault to Friel.* Cambridge: Cambridge Univ. Press, 1999.

Harrington, John, and Elizabeth Mitchell, eds. *Politics and Performance in Contemporary Northern Ireland.* Amherst: Univ. of Massachusetts Press, 1999.

Harris, Claudia. "Review of *Somewhere Over the Balcony.*" *Theatre Ireland,* no. 13 (1987): 47–48.

Harris, Susan. *Gender and Modern Irish Drama.* Bloomington: Indiana Univ. Press, 2002.

Hayes, Alan, and Diane Urquhart. *The Irish Women's History Reader.* New York: Routledge, 2001.

Headrick, Charlotte, and John Countryman, "Damned If You Do; Damned If You Don't: Competing Feminisms in Irish Theatre." In Fitzpatrick, *Performing Feminisms in Contemporary Ireland,* 59–80.

Henderson, Lynda, and Paul Hadfield. "Nothing Run of the Mill." *Fortnight Magazine,* no. 194 (May 1983): 27.

Heresford, Wendy. "Rhetorical Memory, Political Theatre and the Traumatic Present." *Transformations* 16, no. 2 (2005): 104–17.

"Integrating Northern Ireland's Education: Models for Change." *Agenda Northern Ireland Magazine*, November 2, 2010. http://www.agendani.com/integrating-education. Accessed March 3, 2013.

"Irish Constitution, 1937." https://www.constitution.ie/Documents/Bhunreacht_na_hEireann_web.pdf. Accessed April 21, 2016.

Jenkinson, Rosemary. *The Bonefire*. Kindle Edition. London: Methuen Drama, 2006.

Jennings, Sharon. "Artists Lobby for Change." *Fortnight Magazine*, November 1999.

Johnston, Jennifer. *Selected Short Plays*. Dublin: New Island Press, 2003.

———. *Three Monologues*. Belfast: Lagan Press, 1995.

Jones, Marie. *Stones in His Pockets and A Night in November*. London: Nick Hern Books, 2000.

Jordan, Eamonn, ed. *Theatre Stuff: Critical Essays on Contemporary Irish Theatre*. Dublin: Carysfort Press, 2009.

JustUs Theatre Company. "Production Program of *Binlids*." 1997. LHL.

———. "Production Program of *Murphy's Law*." March 11–16, 2001. LHL.

Kearney, Eileen, and Charlotte Headrick, eds. *Irish Women Dramatists, 1908–2001*. Syracuse, NY: Syracuse Univ. Press, 2014.

Kershaw, Baz. *The Politics of Performance: Radical Theatre as Cultural Intervention*. London: Routledge, 1992.

Keyes, John. *Going Dark: Two Ulster Theatres*. Belfast: Lagan Press, 2001.

Kilmurray, Avila, and Monica McWilliams. "Struggling for Peace: How Women in Northern Ireland Challenged the Status Quo." *Solutions* 2, no. 2 (2011): http://www.thesolutionsjournal.com/node/893. Accessed July 27, 2016.

Kurdi, Maria. *Representations of Gender and Female Subjectivity in Contemporary Irish Drama by Women*. Lewiston, NY: Edwin Mellen Press, 2010.

Lewis, David. "Theatre Review: *Pumpgirl*." *Culture Northern Ireland*, October 12, 2010. http://www.culturenorthernireland.org/article.aspx?art_id=1518. Accessed March 14, 2013.

Liddy, Brenda J. *The Drama of War in the Theatre of Anne Devlin, Marie Jones, and Christina Reid*. Lewiston, NY: Edwin Mellen Press, 2010.

Little, Adrian. "Feminism and the Politics of Difference in Northern Ireland." *Journal of Political Ideologies* 7, no. 2 (2002): 163–77.

Lojek, Helen. "Charabanc Theatre Company's *Lay Up Your Ends*." *New Hibernia Review* 2, no. 3 (1998): 102–16.

———. "Eleanor Methven and Carol Moore (Scanlan) in Conversation with Helen Lojek." In Chambers, FitzGibbon, and Jordan, *Theatre Talk*, 342–54.

———. "Not So Sainted: Mothers on the Contemporary Irish Stage." In *Essays and Scripts on How Mothers Are Portrayed on Stage*, edited by Beth Osnes and Anna Andes, 171–201. London: Edwin Mellon Press, 2010.

———. "Playing Politics with Charabanc Theatre Company." In Harrington and Mitchell, *Politics and Performance in Contemporary Northern Ireland*, 82–102.

———. "Seeding New Writing, Seeking More Analysis: Belfast's Charabanc Theatre Company." *Irish Studies Review* no. 8 (Autumn 1994): 30–34.

———. "Troubling Perspectives: Northern Ireland, the 'Troubles' and Drama." In *A Companion to Modern British and Irish Drama: 1880–2005*, edited by Mary Lockhurst, 329–40. Hoboken, NJ: Wiley-Blackwell, 2010.

Lonergan, Patrick. *Theatre and Globalization: Irish Drama in the Celtic Tiger Era*. London: Palgrave Macmillan, 2009.

Lovendusky, Eugene. "Cast of 'Pumpgirl' Filling the Tank at MTC." Broadwayworld.com, December 3, 2007. http://www.broadwayworld.com/article/Cast_of_Pumpgirl_Filling_the_Tank_at_MTC_20071203. Accessed April 22, 2010.

Lyric Theatre. "Mission Statement." http://www.lyrictheatre.co.uk/about.

Mac, Taylor. "Artist Statement." Taylor Mac.net. [n.d.] Accessed July 20, 2016.

———. "I Believe: A Theater Manifesto by Taylor Mac." Taylor Mac.net. January 10, 2013. http://www.taylormac.org/i-believe/. Accessed July 20, 2016.

Maguire, Tom. *Making Theatre in Northern Ireland: Through and Beyond the Troubles*. Exeter, England: Univ. of Exeter Press, 2006.

Mannion, Elizabeth. *Urban Plays of the Abbey Theatre: Beyond O'Casey*. Syracuse, NY: Syracuse Univ. Press, 2014.

Martin, Carol. "Charabanc Theatre Company: 'Quare' Women 'Sleggin' and 'Geggin' the Standards of Northern Ireland by 'Tappin' the People." *The Drama Review* 31, no. 2 (1987): 88–99.

McCready, Sam. *Baptism by Fire: My Life with Mary O'Malley*. Belfast: Lagan Press, 2007.

McDonnell, Bill. *Theatres of the Troubles: Theatre, Resistance and Liberation in Ireland*. Exeter, England: Univ. of Exeter Press, 2009.

McDowell, Sara. "Commemorating Dead 'Men': Gendering the Past and Present in Post-Conflict Northern Ireland." *Gender, Place, and Culture* 15, no. 4 (2008): 335–54.

McGee, Lucy. *Girls and Dolls*. London: Nick Hern Books, 2006.

McKeown, Michael. "Spreadsheet of Deaths Associated with Violence in Northern Ireland, 1969–2001" (2009, version 1.1, revised February 4, 2013). Conflict Archive on the Internet (CAIN), http://cain.ulst.ac.uk/victims/mckeown/index.html. Accessed March 3, 2013.

McKittrick, David, and David McVea. *Making Sense of the Troubles: The Story of Conflict in Northern Ireland*. Chicago, IL: New Amsterdam Books, 2002.

McNulty, Eugene. *Ulster Literary Theatre and Northern Revival*. Cork, Ireland: Cork Univ. Press, 2008.

McWilliams, Monica. "Violence against Women and Political Conflict: The Northern Ireland Experience." *Critical Criminology* 8, no. 8 (1997): 78–92.

Melaugh, Martin. "Internment—Summary of Main Events." Conflict Archive on the Internet (CAIN), http://cain.ulst.ac.uk/events/intern/sum.htm. Accessed March 19, 2013.

Miles, Tim. "Fighting the Peace: Counter-Narrative, Violence, and the Work of Gary Mitchell." In *Performing Violence in Contemporary Ireland*, edited by Lisa Fitzpatrick, 65–84. Dublin: Carysfort Press, 2010.

Moore, Brian. "Black Taxis Play Program." *DubbelJoint Theatre Company*. 2003. LHL.

Morash, Christopher. *A History of Irish Theatre, 1601–2000*. Cambridge: Cambridge Univ. Press, 2004.

Morris, Catherine. *Alice Milligan and the Irish Cultural Revival*. Dublin: National Library of Ireland, 2010.

———. "Becoming Irish: Alice Milligan and the Revival." *Irish University Review* 33, no. 1 (2003): 79–98.

Morrow, Duncan. "Forgiveness and Reconciliation." *Democratic Dialogue*. Conflict Archive on the Internet (CAIN), http://cain.ulst.ac.uk/dd/report13/report13a.htm. Accessed March 14, 2013.

Mulholland, Marc. *Northern Ireland—A Very Short Introduction*. Oxford: Oxford Univ. Press, 2002.

Munro, Rona. *Bold Girls*. New York: Samuel French, 1991.

Murray, Christopher. *Twentieth-Century Irish Drama: Mirror up to Nation*. Syracuse, NY: Syracuse Univ. Press, 1997.

Nawaz, Joe. "Outburst Queer Arts Festival 2011." *Culture Northern Ireland*, November 3, 2011. http://www.culturenorthernireland.org/article.aspx ?art_id=4545. Accessed March 19, 2013.

Northern Ireland Executive. *Building a Prosperous and United Community: One Year On*. www.northernireland.gov.uk, July 2, 2014. http://www .northernireland.gov.uk/building-a-prosperous-united-community-one -year-on.pdf. Accessed April 20, 2016.

———. *Together: Building a United Community*. Conflict Archive on the Internet (CAIN), May 23, 2013. http://cain.ulst.ac.uk/issues/community /sharedfuture/2013-05-23_ofmdfm.pdf. Accessed April 20, 2016.

Northern Ireland Office. "Police (Northern Ireland) Act 2000—Review of Temporary Recruitment Provisions." www.gov.uk, November 2010. https://www.gov.uk/government/uploads/system/uploads/attach ment_data/file/136382/50_50_consultation.pdf. Accessed April 20, 2016.

Northern Ireland Tourist Board. "Perceptions of Derry/Londonderry UK City of Culture 2013." Tourism Northern Ireland, 2013. http://www .nitb.com/Portals/2/SharePointDocs/2644/UK%20City%20of%20 Culture%202013%20research%20feedback.pdf. Accessed April 4, 2016.

O'Brien, Cormac. "Following in Caryl Churchill's Footsteps: Rosemary Jenkinson's Spaces of Masculine Interrogation in *Bonefire*." *Hungarian Journal of English and American Studies* 19, no. 2 (2013): 395–414.

Ó Broin, Eoin. "A Clear Case of Political Censorship." *Fortnight Magazine*, September 1999.

O'Connor, Patricia. "Choosing Teaching as a Career." *Lagan* 2 (1944): 92–96.

———. *The Farmer Wants a Wife*. Belfast: Quota Press, 1955.

———. *Highly Efficient*. Belfast: Quota Press, 1943.

———. *Master Adams*. Belfast: Quota Press, 1949.

———. *Select Vestry*. Belfast: Quota Press, 1945.

O'Doherty, Malachi. "A Bit of Nuisance." In Carruthers, Douds, and Loone, *Re-imagining Belfast*, 74–81.

———. "Double Trouble." *Fortnight Magazine*, September 1999, 21–22.

O'Malley, Mary. *Irish Theatre Letter*. Amherst: Massachusetts Review, 1965.

———. *Never Shake Hands with the Devil*. Dublin: Elo Publications, 1990.

Paget, Derek. "Verbatim Theatre: Oral History and Documentary Techniques." *New Theatre Quarterly* 3 no. 2 (1987): 317–36.

Phelan, Mark. "Beyond the Pale: Neglected Northern Irish Women Playwrights, Alice Milligan, Helen Wadell, Patricia O'Connor." In Sihra, *Women in Irish Drama*, 109–29.

———. "The Critical 'Gap of the North': Nationalism, National Theatre and the North." *Modern Drama* 47, no. 4 (2004): 594–606.

Pilkington, Lionel. *Theatre and the State in Twentieth-Century Ireland: Cultivating the People*. New York: Routledge, 2001.

Police Service of Northern Ireland. "Workforce Composition Figures." January 11, 2014. http://www.psni.police.uk/updates_workforce_composition_figures. Accessed April 12, 2016.

Regan, Morna. *The Housekeeper*. London: Nick Hern Books, 2012.

———. *Midden*. London: Nick Hern Books, 2001.

Reid, Christina. *Plays: One*. London: Methuen Drama, 1997.

Roche, Anthony. *Contemporary Irish Drama*. New York: Palgrave Macmillan, 2009.

Rooney, Elish. "Women's Equality in Northern Ireland's Transition: Intersectionality in Theory and Place." *Feminist Legal Studies* 14 (Spring 2006): 353–75.

Sales, Rosemary. *Women Divided: Gender, Religion, Politics in Northern Ireland*. London: Routledge, 1997.

Sihra, Melissa. "Changing the Landscape of Irish Theatre Studies." *Theatre Research International* 36, no. 3 (2011): 269–71.

———, ed. *Women in Irish Drama: A Century of Authorship and Representation*. Hampshire: Palgrave MacMillan, 2007.

Smyth, Damian. "Shots in the Arts." *Fortnight Magazine*, November 1999.

Spallen, Abbie. *Pumpgirl*. London: Faber & Faber, 2006.

———. *Strandline*. London: Faber & Faber, 2009.

Spivak, Gayatri. "Can the Subaltern Speak?" In *Marxism and the Interpretation of Culture*, edited by Cary Nelson and Larry Grossberg, 271–316. Champagne: Univ. of Illinois Press, 1988.

Sullivan, Meagan. *Women in Northern Ireland: Cultural Studies and Material Conditions*. Miami: Univ. of Florida Press, 1999.

Tinderbox. *Convictions*. Belfast: Tinderbox Theatre Company, 2000.

Trotter, Mary. *Modern Irish Theatre*. Cambridge, MA: Polity Press, 2008.

Urban, Eva. *Community Politics and the Peace Process in Contemporary Northern Irish Drama*. Oxford: Peter Lang, 2011.

Valiulis, Maryann. "Neither Feminist nor Flapper." In *Chattel, Servant or Citizen? Women's Status in Church, State and Society*, edited by Mary O'Dowd and Sabine Wichert, 168–78. Belfast: Institute on Irish Studies, Queens University, 1995.

Wallace, Arminta. "From the North Country." *Irish Times Magazine*, December 15, 2007.

Watt, Stephen, Eileen Morgan, and Shakir Mustafa, eds. *A Century of Irish Drama: Widening the Stage*. Bloomington: Indiana Univ. Press, 2000.

Whyte, Pádraic. "Review of *Over the Bridge*." *Irish Theatre Magazine*, April 2, 2010. http://www.irishtheatremagazine.ie/Reviews/Current/Over-the-Bridge. Accessed March 7, 2013.

Wilmer, Steve. "Women's Theatre in Ireland." *New Theatre Quarterly* 7, no. 28 (1991): 353–60.

Winter, Brenda. "That's Not Theatre, Love!: The *Lay Up Your Ends* Experience." In *Lay Up Your Ends: A 25th Anniversary Edition*, edited by Richard Palmer, 17–39. Belfast: Lagan Press, 2008.

Yee, Shannon. "Gay & Troubled Synopsis." Shannon Yee Blog. *Wordpress*, July 22, 2011. http:shannonyee.wordpress.com. Accessed April 12, 2016.

———. "Interview with Marie-Louise Muir about 'Hatch' and the Belfast Fringe Festival." *BBC Arts Extra*. Audio file. October 2011. http://soundcloud.com/shAnneonyee/hatch-on-bbc-arts-extra-oct/s-mcgzZ. Accessed March 19, 2013.

Interviews

Ashe, Fidelma. Belfast, Northern Ireland. May 30, 2012.

Cafolla, Vittoria. Belfast, Northern Ireland. June 4, 2012.

Caldwell, Lucy. Dublin, Ireland. June 7, 2012.

Downey, Patricia. Belfast, Northern Ireland. June 1, 2012.

Gregg, Stacey. Belfast, Northern Ireland. May 27, 2012.

Howard, Aideen. Lecture given at the O'Connell House for the University of Notre Dame Irish Seminar, Dublin, Ireland. June 20, 2012.

Jenkinson, Rosemary. Phone interview. May 31, 2012.

McCarrick, Jaki. Dublin, Ireland. June 22, 2012.

McFetridge, Paula. Phone interview. September 21, 2012.

McGill, Bernie. Belfast, Northern Ireland. May 30, 2012.

Methven, Eleanor. Dublin, Ireland. June 27, 2012.

Moore, Carol. E-mail correspondence. November 6, 2012.

Parker, Lynn. Dublin, Ireland. June 21, 2012.

Seaton, Zoe. Derry/Londonderry, Northern Ireland. June 8, 2012.

Slattne, Hanna. Belfast, Northern Ireland. May 29, 2012.

Spallen, Abbie. Phone interview. May 22, 2012.

———. E-mail correspondence. September 10, 2012.

Yee, Shannon. Belfast, Northern Ireland. June 1, 2012.

Index

FIONA COLEMAN COFFEY holds a BA from Stanford University, an M.Phil. from Trinity College, Dublin, and a PhD from Tufts University. She has been published in *The Contemporary Irish Detective Novel* (Palgrave Macmillan), *Radical Contemporary Theatre Practices by Women in Ireland* (Carysfort Press), *The Theatre of Marie Jones* (Carysfort Press), and *Changes in Contemporary Ireland: Texts and Contexts* (Cambridge Scholars). Her research focuses on women in Irish drama and theatrical responses to the sectarian conflict in Northern Ireland. She teaches theatre history and Irish cultural studies.